Luminos is the Open Access monograph publishing program from UC Press. Luminos provides a framework for preserving and reinvigorating monograph publishing for the future and increases the reach and visibility of important scholarly work. Titles published in the UC Press Luminos model are published with the same high standards for selection, peer review, production, and marketing as those in our traditional program. www.luminosoa.org

The publication of this book was made possible by generous subventions, awards, and grants from the Institute of Scholarship in the Liberal Arts in Notre Dame's College of Arts and Letters; the University of California Press; and the AMS 75 PAYS Endowment of the American Musicological Society, funded in part by the National Endowment for the Humanities and the Andrew W. Mellon Foundation.

Middlebrow Modernism

CALIFORNIA STUDIES IN 20TH-CENTURY MUSIC

Richard Taruskin, General Editor

Middlebrow Modernism

Britten's Operas and the Great Divide

———

Christopher Chowrimootoo

UNIVERSITY OF CALIFORNIA PRESS

University of California Press, one of the most distinguished university presses in the United States, enriches lives around the world by advancing scholarship in the humanities, social sciences, and natural sciences. Its activities are supported by the UC Press Foundation and by philanthropic contributions from individuals and institutions. For more information, visit www.ucpress.edu.

University of California Press
Oakland, California

Suggested citation: Chowrimootoo, C. *Middlebrow Modernism: Britten's Operas and the Great Divide*. Oakland: University of California Press, 2018. DOI: https://doi.org/10.1525/luminos.57

Chapter 3 was originally published as "The Timely Traditions of *Albert Herring*" in *Opera Quarterly* 27, no. 4 (2011). Chapter 6 appeared as "Bourgeois Opera: *Death in Venice* and the Aesthetics of Sublimation" in *Cambridge Opera Journal* 22, no. 2 (2010). Both articles are reproduced here with kind permission of the publishers.

Library of Congress Cataloging-in-Publication Data

Names: Chowrimootoo, Christopher, 1985- author.
Title: Middlebrow modernism : Britten's operas and the great divide / Christopher Chowrimootoo.
Description: Oakland, California : University of California Press, [2019] | Includes bibliographical references and index. | Chowrimootoo, Christopher 2019 This work is licensed under a Creative Commons CC BY license. To view a copy of the license, visit http://creativecommons.org/licenses. |
Identifiers: LCCN 2018021983 (print) | LCCN 2018025344 (ebook) | ISBN 9780520970700 (ebook) | ISBN 9780520298651 (pbk. : alk. paper)
Subjects: LCSH: Britten, Benjamin, 1913–1976. Operas. | Opera—20th century. | Modernism (Music)—History—20th century. | Music—20th century—Philosophy and esthetics.
Classification: LCC ML410.B853 (ebook) | LCC ML410.B853 C47 2019 (print) | DDC 782.1092—dc23
LC record available at https://lccn.loc.gov/2018021983

28 27 26 25 24 23 22 21 20 19
10 9 8 7 6 5 4 3 2 1

CONTENTS

ILLUSTRATIONS

FIGURES

MUSIC EXAMPLES

ACKNOWLEDGMENTS

Those who know me well know that beneath my austere, modernist exterior resides a sentimentality as sickly as anything in *Peter Grimes*. If gushing acknowledgments threaten to overwrite a grueling process with a rose-tinted vision, as if this manuscript were penned in the midst of a cocktail party, this might not necessarily be a bad thing. After all, it was the conversations in between times—over coffee, lunch, dinner, at conferences and on holidays—that sustained me through the most difficult moments of writing. Even those teachers, colleagues, friends, and family who have little interest in its contents have helped to bring the book about in many different ways. It is a pleasure to thank some of them here.

Although I am generally skeptical of origin stories, this project has a specific one: a trip to Aldeburgh with Alastair Nichol, my school music teacher, fifteen years ago. I am grateful to Alastair for setting me on an unlikely career path and introducing me to the Britten myths against which I would productively recoil. Another East Anglian, Nicholas Mathew, helped this process along when I arrived in Oxford. Tutorials with Nick in the King's Arms—on *Albert Herring* and the *Philosophy of New Music*—are among the fondest memories of my undergraduate days. He has remained my methodological guru, consistently encouraging me to push my conclusions to their farthest points. Thanks are also due to Peter Franklin and Emanuele Senici for the kind of thought-provoking courses that set up a young scholar for life, and for supervising my undergraduate and master's theses respectively. Suzanne Aspden was another Oxford mentor who helped to set me on my musicological way. She taught me to bust binaries, so that I could eventually put them back together again. I would also like to thank Michael Burden for his early support, and for formal hall and afternoon tea; Roger Moseley for the distinction between history and criticism, and other Taruskinian debates; Jonathan Cross and Julian Johnson for putting the modernist side across with nuance and depth; Ben Winters for Blackwell's and G & Ds; Jo Hicks for fun musicological discussions during the MSt.

It was at Harvard that the seeds planted in Oxford began to bear fruit as a dissertation project. I am grateful to my fellow G1s, Will Cheng and Elizabeth Craft, for being there with experimental cooking, election parties in simpler times, and care-oriented musicology before it was a thing. Rowland Moseley made the transition to America much easier than it would have otherwise been, as did Toby Ottersen and Gavin Williams. Suzie Clark, another Mertonian at Harvard, was always on hand to offer moral support in the department lounge. Andrea Bohlman, Louis Epstein, Glenda Goodman, and Frank Lehman were model G2s, generous and challenging in equal measure. Matt Mugmon was an honorary middlebrow modernist. As dissertation adviser, Alex Rehding gave me the freedom to follow my own nose, but was always there for transatlantic Skype conversations when I needed him. Carolyn Abbate was a deep and careful reader, graciously continuing her involvement even as she moved away from Harvard and back again. The late and brilliant Dan Albright inspired me with his interdisciplinary virtuosity, offering incisive feedback on every chapter with superhuman speed. Martin Puchner afforded another model of interdisciplinary modernism, leaving a mark on the final chapter especially. Dana Gooley, Chris Hasty, Carol Oja, Sindhu Revuluri, and Anne Shreffler were also generous interlocutors, each leaving a palpable mark on my thinking, writing, and overall Harvard experience.

A grant from the Harvard Center for European Studies made a research year in London possible. I am grateful to Roger Parker for welcoming me into his KCL fold during this time and for serving as my new historicist superego. Although I resisted with characteristic stubbornness, the book has been strengthened by his early advocacy on behalf of thick history. At the same time, Roger's skepticism about composer-centered monographs spurred me on to write a Britten book that wore its broader implications on its sleeve. Danielle Ward-Griffin, a fellow non-Britten Brittenite, shared in the experience of being an American PhD student in London; Harriet Boyd-Bennett was always up for pizza and wine, along with ever-stimulating musicological debate. The fourth chapter of my dissertation was written while an Early Career Fellow in Opera Studies at Oxford Brookes, where Barbara Eichner and Alex Wilson were generous colleagues and supportive friends.

The journey from dissertation to book has been an arduous and circuitous one, but supportive institutions, colleagues, and friends have buoyed me along. Raina Polivka has been a patient acquisitions editor and Francisco Reinking has handled the production side with just as much care. Editorial assistants Zuha Khan and Elena Bellaart have provided much reassurance with their prompt responses to my many clueless emails. Kevin Vaughn expertly typeset the almost-impossible musical examples. Robert Demke copyedited the manuscript with meticulousness. Josh

Rutner was every bit the sharp and penetrating indexer that he was rumored to be. Debbie Kabzinski and Janet Rudasics have provided invaluable administrative support. Nicholas Clark and other staff at the Britten-Pears Library have answered queries and supported my work for over a decade now. Without this wonderful archive, this book would not have been possible. Benjamin Kolhmann has been my fount of literary knowledge, answering email questions thoughtfully and generously. Joe Auner and Joy Calico provided helpful leads on Schoenbergian matters. Brigid Cohen and Emily Dolan shared their book proposals and publishing advice, along with model monographs. Paul Kildea generously made unpublished material available even though he must have sensed differences of opinion and approach. Thanks are also due to Phil Rupprecht for late-night debates about British musical modernism and for all his encouragement and support. Arman Schwartz's work has been a model for my own for many years now. His friendship, enthusiasm, and penchant for scholarly gossip have made musicology more fun.

At Notre Dame, my colleagues and students in the Program of Liberal Studies have kept me on my intellectual toes, encouraging me to think about the broader stakes and communicate beyond the world of musicology. Nell Cloutier, Jenny Martin, Andy Radde-Gallwitz, Denis Robichaud, and Joseph Rosenberg deserve particular thanks for solidarity in junior faculty stress. Gretchen Reydams-Schils and Tom Stapleford have been sturdy chairs on which I have often leaned. Pierpaolo Polzonetti has been the world's best colleague, providing career and life advice, along with musicological discussions at Evil Czech. Margot Fassler's infectious enthusiasm and warmth have helped me to feel at home at Notre Dame. Tarek Dika's tragic disposition has, paradoxically, had the same effect. Peter Smith welcomed me into the music department and took an interest in my work. The Cultural Transformations in Modern Europe (CTME) writing group, sponsored by the Nanovic Institute, came along at just the right time. This group gave my work an interdisciplinary airing and a final polish as the project neared its end.

Richard Taruskin was the imagined reader long before he became involved in this book. His towering vantage on twentieth-century music history and historiography helped me to stake out my vista, albeit somewhat lower down. In transitioning from scholarly role model to series editor, he has weeded all-too-many of my stock phrases to count and watched (im)patiently as new ones sprung up in their place. Heather Wiebe has improved this book immeasurably, offering just the right mixture of skepticism and encouragement, along with incisive feedback at every turn. She has shown great forbearance in answering my "quick" Skype questions—about aestheticism, sentimentality, realism, and other minor topics—and has been a wonderfully supportive friend. Kate Guthrie, my middlebrow partner in crime, has been my most generous interlocutor and has come to know the stakes better than anyone else. She has answered email queries, talked through difficult passages, and edited every line too many times to count with boundless patience and care. Her steadfast support and enthusiasm have carried me over the finish line.

To my friends and family outside academia, there will never be enough words of thanks—for the unfailing love, support, and forbearance in the face of what can only be described as pathological obsession. My aunt Michele took an early interest in the project and talked through half-baked ideas as they emerged. Katherine, Liam, and now Lucy have been there with mind-boggling constancy to provide fun, laughter, and holidays in the rain. I am particularly grateful to Liam for reminding me of the plight of university administrators, without whom none of this indulgent research would have materialized. My parents-in-law, Jonathan and Deborah, have taken great interest in my work. In recent years, they have spent their summers in South Bend, providing childcare and weekend getaways—both of which helped me to finish this book. My own parents made everything happen, standing quietly in the background with unconditional financial and emotional support, along with sage advice. I owe them more than I could possibly enumerate here. My wife Christina has lived with this project longer than anyone else, journeying across the ocean with it multiple times. Along with my wonderful sons, Elliot and Oliver, she has shared the burden of days, weeks, months, and years at the writing desk. Without the love, patience, and ready distraction of my family, this book would never have seen the light of day. Thank you doesn't seem quite enough, but I'll say it anyway. This book is dedicated to them.

Notre Dame, June 2018

Middlebrow Modernism

But what, you may ask, is a middlebrow? And that, to tell the truth, is no easy question to answer. They are neither one thing nor the other. They are not highbrows, whose brows are high; nor lowbrows, whose brows are low. Their brows are betwixt and between . . . The middlebrow is the man, woman, of middlebred intelligence who ambles and saunters now on this side of the hedge, now on that, in pursuit of no single object, neither art itself nor life itself, but both mixed indistinguishably, and rather nastily, with money, fame, power, or prestige. The middlebrow curries favor with both sides equally.

—VIRGINIA WOOLF, "MIDDLEBROW," 1932[1]

On May 5, 1941, in Columbia University's Brander Matthews Hall Theater, Benjamin Britten's operatic career got off to an unpromising start. The occasion was the premiere of *Paul Bunyan*, an opera-cum-musical written in collaboration with his friend and fellow expatriate, the poet W. H. Auden. Their setting of the American legend of the giant lumberjack, who sets up a logging camp and guides his workers toward prosperity, left most commentators confused. One critic cast the operetta as the most "bewildering and irritating treatment of the outsize lumberman [that] any two Englishmen could have possibly devised," while Virgil Thomson dubbed it a "Musico-Theatrical Flop."[2] In hindsight, these reactions were no surprise, for Britten and Auden were driven by putatively contradictory aims. Writing self-consciously in the wake of early-twentieth-century modernism, they were on the one hand anxious to preserve their own creative autonomy and integrity—to make an original and challenging contribution to the history of musical theater. On the other hand, they sought to honor long-standing political and educational commitments, even as they hoped to enjoy the fame and fortune of Broadway.

If creating the opera was something of a balancing act, so was its plot. Britten and Auden structured the action around a series of symbolic compromises in America's progress from untouched frontier to industrial modernity: between revolution and conservation, iconoclasm and conformism, idealism and materialism. Within this context, the eponymous lumberman serves less as an independent protagonist than as a mediator between extremes, as Auden explained before the premiere.[3] Meanwhile Hel Helson, Bunyan's Swedish foreman, and Johnny Inkslinger, an artist-turned-bookkeeper, seem to represent Virginia Woolf's polar opposition of brows. The former is a "man of brawn but no brains."[4] When goaded into challenging Paul to a duel, Hel learns the hard way the importance of intelligence and compromise. As the highbrow foil, Johnny undergoes a complementary journey from the other side of the cultural divide. When we first encounter him, his pious devotion to art has him spurning the material world, refusing to earn a living. Hunger ultimately forces him to give up his artistic dreams and work as Paul's accountant: "And I dreamed of writing a novel / With which Tolstoy couldn't compete / And of how all the critics would grovel: / But I guess that a guy gotta eat."[5] This lesson in pragmatism prepares the way for an eventual move to Hollywood, where Johnny is able to strike a balance between artistic impulses and material needs. In casting this character as the opera's "real" protagonist, Auden marked his journey as a central theme, raising questions about the creators' own aesthetic positions and trajectories.[6]

This message of social and aesthetic moderation failed to convince the critics, who understood *Bunyan*'s stylistic eclecticism less as compromise between high and low than as canny duplicity—an attempt to have it both ways. While one commentator balked at the disjuncture between Auden's "literary" voices and the "folksy" subject, others noted that the style of the libretto itself shuttled uncomfortably between modernist allegory and vulgar slapstick, with almost nothing in between. "A little of symbolism and uplift, a bit of socialism and of modern satire, and gags and jokes of a Hollywood sort, or of rather cheap musical comedy," was the verdict of Olin Downes.[7] Eugene Bonner likewise complained that "it refuses to be categorically defined."[8] "High-flown allegory," he wrote, "gives way to flat-footed realism with disconcerting suddenness, diatonic writing to chromatic, large chunks of Gilbert and Sullivan being thrown in for good measure while folksy ballads jostle operatic arias."

At a time when ideals of aesthetic purity reigned, eclecticism and inconsistency were serious charges. Downes complained that text and music "wander[ed] from one to another idea, without conviction or cohesion," and railed at an "ingenuity" that failed only when "faced with the necessity of saying something genuine."[9] More damning yet was the suspicion of crass calculation, as if Britten and Auden were planning their stylistic mixtures with an eye on the audience. One commentator accused Auden of selling out modernist symbolism to the highest bidder, his "allegories brush[ing] each other aside in their mad rush for the spotlight."[10] After describing the opera as a "poor sort of bid for success," Downes laid the blame at the composer's feet instead: "Britten," he sniffed, "is a very clever young man, who can provide something [in] any style or taste desired by the patron."[11] Thomson sniffed even louder, accusing Britten of a distinctly bureaucratic kind of duplicity: "[*Bunyan's*] particular blend of melodic 'appeal' with irresponsible counterpoint and semi-aciduous instrumentation is easily recognizable as that considered by the British Broadcasting Corporation to be at once modernistic and safe."[12] Like the other modernist "eclectics" with whose work *Bunyan* was compared—Hindemith, Weill, Copland, Shostakovich—Britten was charged with playing both sides of the fence, drawing superficially on modernist prestige while simultaneously pandering to vulgarians in the gallery.[13]

. . .

In *Middlebrow Modernism*, I examine the nature of this aesthetic duplicity and excavate its stakes, using operas spanning Britten's entire career as case studies: *Peter Grimes* (1945), *Albert Herring* (1947), *The Turn of the Screw* (1954), *The Burning Fiery Furnace* (1966), and *Death in Venice* (1973). Where duplicity had led to *Paul Bunyan's* downfall, it proved altogether more successful in subsequent works. Rather than taking the operas' aesthetic ambivalence—their uneasy position between high and low, modernism and mass culture—as a problem to be resolved, I use it to explain their broad appeal. Drawing on discussions of cultural hierarchy from Britten's own time, I demonstrate that his success lay in allowing contemporary audiences to have their modernist cake and eat it: to revel in the pleasures of tonality, melody, sentimentality, melodrama, and spectacle, even while enjoying the prestige that comes from rejecting them. Ultimately, however, this is not a mere study of compositional prowess but a wider investigation of the everyday processes through which cultural boundaries are negotiated. For, as will become clear, the difference between *Bunyan's* catastrophic failure and subsequent successes depended not simply on Britten's developing creativity and subtlety but also on his critics, who dissembled and sublimated as resourcefully as he ever composed.

In charting Britten's rise to operatic acclaim, then, this book recounts a much broader story about aesthetic value in the long shadow of early-twentieth-century modernism. It tells a tale of composers, critics, and audiences torn between seemingly conflicting commitments—on the one hand to uncompromising originality and radical autonomy, and on the other to musical pleasure and communication with a new mass audience. It is a study of aesthetic and cultural ambivalence, and the creatively defensive postures that arose in response. It explores the friction between the mid-century critical impulse to categorize and stratify culture, and the ease with which these hierarchies broke down. In teasing out these historical stresses, *Middlebrow Modernism* ultimately invites us to take heed of our own guilty pleasures and ambivalence—as scholars, critics, and audiences—along with our strategies for assuaging this guilt. This means interrogating the conflicts, between what we think we "ought to like" and what we actually like, between aesthetic ideals and the messy realities of artistic taste.

HIGHBROWS, LOWBROWS, AND THE "GREAT DIVIDE"

While scholars have tended to put *Bunyan*'s failure down to its clumsy negotiation of national divides, it was due as well to anxieties about cultural hierarchy. After all, the twentieth century's early decades witnessed a series of culture wars in which artistic taste was increasingly polarized. The popularity of the terms "highbrow" and "lowbrow" was both testimony to this trend and one of its catalysts. Already by 1915, the American literary critic and historian Van Wyck Brooks complained of a gulf between the lofty highbrow aesthetes, incapable of dealing with ordinary life, and the "catchpenny" lowbrows, thinking of nothing but instant profit and cheap thrills: "between academic pedantry and pavement slang, there is no community, no genial middle ground."[14] "They are both undesirable," Brooks wrote, "but they divide American life between them."[15] By 1953, the terms of discussion had changed slightly, but the categorical division remained the same: "For about a century," the cultural critic Dwight Macdonald explained, "Western culture has really been two cultures: the traditional kind—let us call it 'High Culture'—that is chronicled in the textbooks, and a 'Mass Culture' manufactured wholesale for the market."[16]

The situation was no less polarized on the other side of the Atlantic, where Britten and Auden had come of age. Britain had seen antagonisms escalate in the 1930s into a full-scale "battle of the brows." The tipping point appears to have been a BBC radio debate between the novelist and playwright J. B. Priestley and Harold Nicolson, politician, biographer, and husband to the prominent author Vita Sackville-West. This debate spilled over into the local press and national newspapers.[17] In "To a High-Brow," Priestley's initial broadcast, the imaginary interlocutor was charged with an affected interest in works geared exclusively toward a social elite.[18] Nicolson's rebuttal, symmetrically titled "To a Lowbrow"—as if there could only be two sides—complained of philistinism, conformism, and intolerance, and warned that such reverse snobbery would "produc[e] a race which, like the wasps, have no ideas at all."[19]

In predicting imminent cultural apocalypse, Nicolson was tapping into a wider sense that once-incidental antagonisms were becoming ever more central even as they resisted mediation. Perhaps unsurprisingly, many saw the problem epitomized in modernism's supposed rejection of its potential audience, as though the movement had elevated highbrow snobbery into an aesthetic principle. For modernism's defenders, however, it was the public's philistine hostility that begat modernism's highbrow esotericism, not the other way around. F. R. Leavis insisted, "it would be as true to say that the attitude implicit in [the] 'high-brow' [slur] causes this [esoteric] use of talent as the converse."[20] Like most card-carrying highbrows, Leavis blamed mass-produced fiction, newspapers, and film, charging them with lowering public expectations and posing an existential threat to genuine art. Given the stakes, Q. D. Leavis explained, the only recourse was "conscious and directed effort[,] resistance by an armed and conscious minority."[21] Writers could either submit to commercial dictates for conventionality, sentimentality, and immediacy or martyr themselves for the modernist cause; unlike previous generations, from Shakespeare to Dickens, they could not have both popularity and prestige.[22] Even when modernists imagined themselves responding to purely "aesthetic" rather than social considerations, this very commitment landed them back at the center of the "brow" debate: as the epitome of elite resistance to mass-mediated culture.

These divisions impacted musical culture too, with Schoenberg and his Second Viennese School proving more polarizing than literature's "men of 1914."[23] In music, atonality provided a shibboleth, a boundary with which to sort "genuine" modernists from the rest. Schoenberg himself lashed out at those "who nibble at dissonances, and therefore want to rank as modern, but are too cautious to draw the consequences from it."[24] "Those who compose," he elsewhere complained, "because they want to please others, and have audiences in mind, are not real artists . . . the kind who are driven to say something whether or not there exists one person who likes it, even if they themselves dislike it."[25] Theodor Adorno elevated this uncompromising vision into an extended polemic in the *Philosophy of Modern Music*. According to Adorno, one could either follow Schoenberg's "progress" or pander to mass culture; there was no space for compromise or moderation. "The middle road"—as he began, quoting Schoenberg himself—is "the only one which does not lead to Rome."[26] This meant rejecting all aspects of musical convention—tonality, melody, representation, sentimentality, and so on—and courting isolation in order to preserve subjectivity in the face of state capitalism: "The shocks of the incomprehensible," he explained, "illuminate the meaningless world . . . its beauty lies in denying the illusion of beauty."[27] "Modern Music," Adorno concluded, "sacrifices itself to this effort, [dying] away unheard, without even an echo." Adorno outdid the Leavisite prognosis in gloom: "Modern music sees absolute oblivion as its goal. It is the surviving message of despair from the shipwrecked."

Far from limited to a modernist coterie, these images of polarization circulated widely in newspapers and periodicals. The Anglophone press lost no time casting Schoenberg as the *ne plus ultra* of a highbrow modernism, whose uncompromising radicalism and autonomy had thrown down a gauntlet. He was celebrated and denigrated for his "solitariness and inaccessibility," shunning popularity through artistic devotion and achieving notoriety despite himself.[28] In musical terms too, he was often said to have taken imperatives of autonomy and originality to their ultimate, asocial conclusion with his rejection of tonality, consolidated by the development of serialism. "With the publication of Schönberg's 'Klavierstücke,' Op. 11," one critic attested in 1933, "any dealings with the old language became acts of inexcusable cowardice."[29] Likewise for Constant Lambert, Schoenberg's "bomb-throwing" and "guillotining" had had a divisive effect: "Sophisticated composers are either becoming more sophisticated, like Alban Berg, or they are turning their sophistication to deliberately popular account, like Kurt Weill."[30] "Anything between the two," he elaborated, "is a *terrain vague*—a deserted kitchen garden littered with rusty rakes and empty birdcages." Where Adorno saw the great divide as necessary, Lambert understood it as a foolhardy failure to compromise: "Most of the great figures of the past," he reflected nostalgically, "have been content to leave their personal imprint on the *materia musica* of the day without remodeling it entirely . . . [A composer] cannot demand collaboration from his audience while deliberately turning his back on them."[31]

AFTER THE NEW MODERNIST STUDIES

It was this apparent antagonism between modernism and mass culture that the literary and cultural critic Andreas Huyssen sought to capture in 1986 when he famously theorized a "great divide": "modernism," as he argued, "constituted itself through a conscious strategy of exclusion, an anxiety of contamination by its other: an increasingly consuming and engulfing mass culture."[32] Drawing on the criticism of Adorno and Clement Greenberg, among others, Huyssen fore-grounded modernism's ideological commitment to difficulty and autonomy, shunning definitions based on style; in doing so, he sought to unsettle the lingering hold of these values on the academy by exposing their origins in esoteric cultural politics. At around this time, these same premises and objectives began to make a mark on musicology. While Susan McClary was denouncing the great divide as the root of the discipline's problems—esotericism, formalism, misogyny—Peter Franklin was identifying its pernicious shadow on twentieth-century musical historiography.[33] The problem, Franklin explained, was that standard narratives of the period had started life as propaganda for the Second Viennese School, dividing their histories between a select group of elite modernists and an unholy rabble of reactionaries and populists. In this "mythic picture," as Franklin described it, modernism was no neutral category but an aesthetic and ethical imperative, a standard of progress and autonomy against which most music was judged and found wanting.

Now that we have all learnt to be suspicious of binaries, few would openly endorse such a black-and-white account. Nevertheless, old habits die hard, and modernism's divisive legacy lives on in sometimes subtle, sometimes not-so-subtle ways. The most obvious examples come from those scholars who have sought to revive modernist notions of difficulty and autonomy in order to insist on the categorical distinction between high art and popular culture.[34] Less flagrant examples can be drawn from those musicological "expansionists" who have responded to Franklin's critique by redeeming putatively conservative or populist composers as "modernists."[35] In British music studies, this strategy has been charged with national imperatives, as if asserting the relevance of British composers to the history of twentieth-century music more broadly necessarily meant stressing their modernism.[36] While such revisionism offers useful rejoinders to long-standing denigrations of Vaughan Williams, Elgar, and Walton—to name but a few—it continues to invoke modernism as an honorific. More importantly, it keeps faith with the conviction that twentieth-century music can usefully be sorted into modernism vs. everything else. Nor has this dualistic vision been dislodged by the steady invective of anti-modernists who have echoed new musicological critiques of the great divide in recent years.[37] Indeed, in continuing to pour scorn over modernist values, modernism's staunchest opponents have helped to reinforce its terms, perhaps even making them seem more unassailable than they actually were. This has also had the unfortunate effect of impeding new perspectives on early- and mid-twentieth-century music. In those instances when modernism's defenders have fought back, musicology has risked restaging a latter-day "battle of the brows" of its own.[38]

Meanwhile, literary scholars have tended to go the opposite way, denying that the great divide ever existed. In the years since Huyssen's study, a range of "new modernist studies" have set out to prove him wrong, demonstrating that "modernism" was never as monolithic or esoteric as he implied.[39] Some have excavated modernisms that threw their lot in with popular forms.[40] Others have argued that even the highest of modernists were more ambivalent than critics have imagined.[41] Still others—including Huyssen himself—have demonstrated the extent to which modernism's idealistic self-image was undermined in practice: "Much valuable recent work," as Huyssen has recently complained, "misconstrued my earlier definition of a static binary of high modernism vs. the market. My argument was rather that there had been . . . a powerful imaginary insisting on the divide while time and again violating the categorical separation in practice."[42] In fact, as a number of "materialist" studies of modernist editing, marketing, and distribution have shown, opposition to the mass market was often an effective strategy for entering it.[43] Where musicological expansionism has generally sought to add select figures to modernism's hallowed canon, the "new modernists" have attempted to distance modernism from associations with canonicity and exclusivity: "Modernism," as Miriam Hansen insisted, "encompasses a whole range of cultural and artistic practices that register, respond to, and reflect upon processes of modernization and modernity."[44] Aside from striving to resist the kind of prejudices that permeate modernist studies in musicology, such broad definitions have opened the way up for an ever-growing list of putative modernisms: popular, vernacular, slapstick, domestic, global modernisms—to name a few—are now routinely invoked with little sense of contradiction or irony. Drawing on the work of Hansen and others, the musicologist Brigid Cohen has even gone so far as to define modernism *itself* as a kind of cultural ambivalence, which undermines the very oppositions—between autonomous and mass-mediated, high and low—it was previously imagined to have upheld.[45]

While such a redefinition offers an attractive alternative to the old dualisms and hierarchies, it carries with it a number of risks, as Cohen herself admits. The first is that the category of modernism will become so broad as to become meaningless.

After all, what twentieth-century cultural and artistic practices did *not* register, respond to, and reflect upon processes of modernization and the experience of modernity? The second problem is that of whitewashing history: a history of modernism without ideas of autonomy, difficulty, and hierarchy—one might argue—is like an action movie without violence. It risks, in other words, recasting modernist history in our own pluralistic image.[46] As Cohen concedes, many of the associations that she and other "new modernists" have been keen to shake off "inflected many modernists' own interpretations of themselves and their projects."[47] Yet, as we have already seen, it was not just modernist self-conceptions that were colored by these ideological prejudices; it was also their immediate reception, and the reception of contemporary culture more broadly. If Huyssen's great divide was too crude to capture modernist intention and practice in all their complexity, this was precisely its appeal, for it encapsulated polarized understandings of early- and mid-twentieth-century culture. The notion may not have been true but it was real, insofar as it defined how writers, critics, and audiences understood contemporary cultural battle lines.

The historiographical problem facing scholars is thus also a historical one, which we risk obscuring if we dispense altogether with cultural hierarchies. Acknowledging the centrality of rigid boundaries to historical conceptions of modernism, however, need not imply endorsing their implications or reinforcing their hegemony. This study takes up this challenge of striking a balance between erasing the historiography of the great divide on the one hand, and buttressing it on the other. It aims to revisit the issue of cultural hierarchy not through theoretical critique or defense, but by tracing its contours throughout history, surveying its impact on the everyday practice of mid-century composition, mediation, and criticism. Following on the efforts of scholars like Huyssen, Franklin, and Taruskin to historicize the great divide, I want to go further and sketch out a historical alternative. While acknowledging its historical power, in other words, I also want to look beyond—or, perhaps more accurately, *through*—the great divide.

It is here that the mid-century category of the "middlebrow" offers a powerful stimulus to the study of twentieth-century culture—the chance to deconstruct modernism from the "inside." Coined as a casual insult in the 1920s, it became the target of extended critique by modernist critics and polemicists for the decades that followed: from Virginia Woolf and Q. D. Leavis in interwar Britain to Clement Greenberg and Dwight Macdonald in the postwar United States. As the epigraph from Woolf makes clear, it was often invoked to shore up the great divide by discrediting those who fell "in between." Yet, evidently, it also had the opposite effect, calling attention to those institutions, artists, critics, and audiences that—more or less consciously—sought to mediate its supposedly irreconcilable oppositions. As cultural hierarchies began to lose force in the last third of the century, the term dropped out of common parlance. And given its imbrication in now-unfashionable modernist prejudices, one might be tempted to proclaim good riddance and leave the condescending category to the trash-heap of history. To do so, however, would be to overlook the historical practices, values, and tensions to which it pointed, along with the useful challenges that it poses to modernist historiography.

LOCATING THE MIDDLEBROW

In one of the earliest documented uses of "middlebrow," in 1925, the term christened a new type of aspirational cultural consumer: "The B.B.C. claim to have a discovered a new type, the 'middlebrow,'" *Punch* magazine reported: "It consists of people who are hoping that some day they will get used to stuff they ought to like."[48] Aside from the implications of conformism, which ran throughout critiques, the epithet carried seemingly paradoxical charges of philistinism and pretentiousness: "The highbrow sees as his real enemy the middlebrow," Russell Lynes—editor of *Harper's Magazine*—pointed out, "whom he regards as a pretentious and frivolous man or woman who uses culture to satisfy social or business ambitions."[49] If the "battle of the brows" threatened to implicate even the loftiest modernists in a vulgar form of social snobbery, the middlebrows provided convenient scapegoats: "we highbrows," Woolf insisted, "may be smart or we may be shabby but we never have the right thing to wear . . . [or] the right book to praise."[50] Where Woolf emphasized the desire to be au courant, others saw middlebrows in terms of stolid mediocrity: the "men and women, fairly civilized, fairly literate," as Margaret Widdemer put it, "who support the critics and lecturers and publishers by purchasing their wares."[51]

In regarding middlebrow consumers as symbiotic with those who mediated their cultural access, Widdemer echoed wider opinion. When Lynes published his pseudo-anthopological "brow" survey in 1949, this reciprocity was so central that he sub-divided the middlebrow in order to account for it: the upper middlebrows were the cultural mediators—the publishers, radio programmers, film producers, educators, and newspaper critics—who balanced artistic concerns with courting wide appeal; the lower middlebrows were their consumers—the course-takers, book-club members, record collectors, and newspaper readers—"hell bent on improving their minds as well as their fortunes."[52] Q. D. Leavis even went so far as to cast "middlebrow" as a synonym for "middlemen," those pesky bureaucrats who intervened in the relationship between artist and audience.[53] Her frustration was unsurprising, for the interwar period witnessed the birth of powerful new institutions charged with overcoming cultural divisions using mass media technology. Perhaps the most famous example on her side of the Atlantic was the BBC, dubbed the "Betwixt and Between Company" by Woolf.[54] As John Reith, its first director general, explained: "our responsibility is to carry into the greatest possible number of homes everything that is best in every department of human knowledge, endeavour and achievement."[55] By making high culture more accessible, these intermediaries sought to elevate the average person's tastes: "It is of necessity a slow process as for years the man in the street has been content to be pleased with music which is easily and quickly assimilated, and therefore not always the best—the sort which can be heard at night and whistled in the morning."[56]

For detractors, however, the effect of such initiatives was less to raise audiences up than to drag high culture down, simplifying it beyond recognition and reducing it to the status of commodity: "The differences in the reception of official 'classical' music and light music no longer have any real significance," Adorno complained.[57] Where Reith advocated mixing edifying and entertaining works, Adorno regarded this as eroding a crucial distinction: "the climaxes of Beethoven's Seventh Symphony are placed on the same level as the unspeakable horn melody from Tchaikovsky's Fifth. Melody comes to mean eight-beat symmetrical treble melody . . . which one thinks he can put in his pocket and take home."[58] Even Lambert, on the lookout for a cultural middle ground, insisted that mass mediation was not the solution. "The more people use the wireless, the less they listen to it," he lamented: "Classical music is vulgarized and diffused through every highway and by-way, and both highbrow and lowbrow are the losers."[59] Before comparing mass-mediated music to a cheap prostitute, readily available on every street corner, Lambert complained: "you can rarely escape from a B.B.C. gramophone hour by going to the next public house because they are bound to be presenting the same entertainment."[60]

The problem, evidently, was not just one of debasement but also of conformism imposed from above: "the whole of London," Lambert complained, "is made to listen to the choice of a privileged few or even a privileged one."[61] These "middlemen" were not limited to the most obvious pedagogical or commercial initiatives, but were apparently taking over the entire cultural domain. This meant controlling not just the art people accessed but also how they received it, framing it with a wealth of explanatory paratexts. For Q. D. Leavis, this dubious honor was often held by the contemporary journalist whose "power as middleman in forming popular taste," she complained, "c[ould] hardly be overestimated."[62] According to her, in other words, critics were the middlebrow mediators par excellence, able to determine the success or failure of individual works with their ill-informed and hasty judgments. This was an assessment with which Lambert concurred, invoking the term to describe the stultifying consensus pervading music criticism: "one felt the awful weight of middlebrow opinion against the whole thing," Lambert explained about the ballet *Apparitions* (1936) even before it was unveiled.[63]

Although this close relationship between cultural mediator and public risked nudging the contemporary writer or artist out, an even greater threat came from him or her being drawn in to these calculations. While most commentators agreed that the middlebrow had its origins in the social sphere, they took for granted its spread to the aesthetic realm, in ways that eroded this very distinction. In the term's early history, commentators slipped between modes of mediation, reception, and creation, as if to heighten the nature of the threat. Woolf evidently enjoyed mocking consumers most of all, but she also complained that middlebrow novels, lectures, and reviews were replicating their anxieties and prejudices, in ways that even threatened to corrupt the lowbrows. Q. D. Leavis went further, tracing concrete connections between middlebrow institutions, critics, audiences, and the novels themselves.[64] By the time Greenberg and Macdonald penned their postwar "mid-cult" critiques, the dissolution of these boundaries between art and its mediation had become a prominent—even definitive—feature of the middlebrow epidemic.

COMPROMISE AND SYNTHESIS

While detractors insisted that middlebrow values were infecting all areas of cultural life, there remained little agreement as to what they were. Perhaps the most obvious marker was a commitment to compromise—bridging the great divide by avoiding extremes. For defenders, this was less a mark of mediocrity than a means of restoring moderation to a divided cultural field. For instance, although Reith took seriously his Arnoldian mission to bring the "best" culture to everyone, he recognized that this required compromise. In programming, he urged balance between entertaining and edifying works before championing a happy medium instead: "While admitting the desirability or even necessity of catering for extreme tastes, the endeavour has been to transmit as much music as possible which, while perfectly good, should also be quite popular, easily understood and assimilated."[65] J. B. Priestley was reportedly even more enthusiastic, embracing this middle ground as his natural home: "Between the raucous lowbrows and the lisping highbrows is a fine gap, meant for the middle or broadbrows . . . We can be cosy together in it. We can talk about bilberry pie."[66]

If Reith saw this as the common ground that could gradually broaden the public's cultural horizons, detractors insisted it had the opposite effect, snuffing out aspiration and squeezing everything into a narrow, unadventurous middle: "even the dance music . . . has a quality of sickening and genteel refinement," Lambert complained; "we are fast losing even the minor stimulus of genuine healthy vulgarity."[67] Just as anxieties about the great divide persisted into the postwar era, so too did concerns about the middlebrow: "Hollywood movies aren't as terrible as they once were," Dwight Macdonald conceded in 1960, "but they aren't as good either."[68] "The question," he elaborated, "is whether all this is merely growing pains . . . an expression of social mobility. The danger is that the values of Midcult, instead of being transitional—'the price of progress'—may now become themselves a debased, permanent standard." For Macdonald, this standard was not just one of mediocrity but one of a sentimental nostalgia that excluded anything genuinely new. Woolf similarly insisted that middlebrow mediocrity and fetishization of antiques were intertwined: "Queen Anne furniture (faked, but none the less expensive); first editions of dead writers, always the worst, . . . houses in what is called 'the Georgian style'—but never anything new, never a picture by a living painter, or a chair by a living carpenter, or books by living writers, for to buy living art requires living taste."[69]

In music, this nostalgia was said to have taken hold with particular force, solidifying the concert repertory around a narrow set of nineteenth-century stalwarts. Adorno, for example, complained of "a pantheon of bestsellers," built on familiarity instead of quality.[70] But perhaps even more disturbing to detractors than this veneration of dusty "masterworks" was the worship of new works in old styles, as though such a compromise were still aesthetically viable. One particularly divisive figure in this respect was Jean Sibelius, whose symphonies became lightning rods for debates about the relationship between musical modernism and middlebrow culture. Thomson saw their popularity as a testament to the stodgy self-indulgence, provincialism, and nostalgia of the Anglo-American middlebrow.[71] Adorno was even more insistent: "That it is possible to compose in a way that is fundamentally old-fashioned, yet completely new: this is the triumph that conformism, looking to Sibelius, begins to celebrate."[72] "His success," he concluded, "is equivalent to longing for the world to be healed of its sufferings and contradictions, for a 'renewal' that lets us keep what we possess."

In a sense, Adorno was—from his perspective—right to fret, for defenders often championed Sibelius's music as a way out of the great divide: a middlebrow synthesis of originality and progress, high and low, dissolving the extremism that modernism had engendered. By 1916, Ernest Newman was already contrasting Schoenberg's self-defeating radicalism unfavorably with Sibelius's more moderate approach.[73] Gray and Lambert each elevated this idea into book-length theses, with their popular modern music surveys culminating with the Finnish symphonist. After championing Sibelius as Beethoven's twentieth-century heir, capable of combining formal concentration with musical immediacy, Gray explained: "if the value of Bartok's best works consists in the extent to which it seems to reveal old and familiar beauty in the novel procedures . . . that of Sibelius, on the contrary, seems rather to reveal a fresh and unsuspected beauty in the old, a wholly new mode of thought and expression embodied in the idioms of the past."[74] "Sibelius," as Gray went on to insist, "has conclusively shown, what most people had legitimately begun to doubt, that it is still just as possible as it ever was to say something absolutely new, vital, and original, without having to invent a new syntax, a new vocabulary, a new language."[75] Lambert was just as emphatic, casting Sibelius as the deus ex machina to salvage the "disappearing middlebrow," a beacon of compromise lighting a way out of modernism's dead end: "those who sit in the middle of a joy wheel may seem to move slowly but their permanence is more assured than those who for the sake of momentary exhilaration try to pin themselves to its periphery."[76] "The music of the future," he explained, "must inevitably be directed towards a new angle of vision rather than to the exploitation of a new vocabulary."[77]

As literary and film scholars have sought to revive the middlebrow category in recent years, these visions of a socially driven commitment to compromise or synthesis have offered a powerful means of marking its boundaries. While Joan Rubin's groundbreaking *Making of Middlebrow Culture* contrasted the middlebrow mediator's genteel roots with twentieth-century literary experimentalism, Janice Radway has imagined book-club readers' penchant for uplifting plots and sympathetic characters as a self-conscious reaction against modernist alienation, cynicism, and despair.[78] For more recent scholars, conceiving of the category in aesthetic terms, these principles have remained central: "middlebrow novels," as Tom Perrin has explained, "reject [modernist radicalism], opting to adapt the conventions of realism in order to represent modernity."[79] Nicola Humble has even cast the middlebrow novel as a solid middle ground, "offering narrative excitement without guilt, and intellectual stimulation without undue effort."[80]

Such visions of a kind of confident and stable center, with clearly defined boundaries, values, and goals, have helped to illuminate important facets of the middlebrow and redeem it as a coherent—even positive—category in its own right. However, limiting it to these attributes risks whitewashing its history, obscuring its contested and always-ambivalent status. The middlebrow was, after all, something of a moving target, charged with undermining hierarchies in contradictory ways. More problematic still, such scholarly defenses and apologetics have risked reifying a category marked above all by its ontological slipperiness. The middlebrow was not conceived in simple opposition to another category, as high was to low. It was a relational category that struggled to reconcile contradictory ideals, always looking in opposite directions. From this vantage, it would appear problematic to theorize it as a stable movement in and of itself. Anxiety and ambivalence were among its fundamental premises, making it inseparable from the aesthetic oppositions on which it depended. It is perhaps telling that even its advocates—including Priestley and Lambert, as we will see—wavered in their definitions and support, foregrounding the difficulty of occupying the "space between" in an age of conceptual extremes. For every commentator who lauded the middlebrow as a noble and sure-footed compromise, there were several who denigrated it as an altogether contingent terrain.

AMBIVALENCE AND DUPLICITY

Alongside historical accusations of "compromise," modernists often worried that middlebrows were mediating the great divide in less-than-forthright ways. Their detractors accused middlebrows of duplicity, of paying lip service to modernist ideals while undermining them in practice. This sense that middlebrows wavered between genuine and feigned tastes was already implicit in the early *Punch* definition. In Woolf's account, they had graduated to full-scale fraudsters, "curr[ying] favor with both sides."[81] This apparently meant saying one thing and doing the opposite, indulging base desires while laying claim to aesthetic purity. It also meant professing mutually exclusive positions without shame or irony. By the time Greenberg and Macdonald launched their polemics, the term was even more closely associated with a counterfeit vanguard, consuming modernism in ways that silently violated its core principles.

This dubious behavior was supposedly rifest in the mediation process through which modernist works were packaged for middlebrow consumption. Despite Reith's avowed rejection of the extremes, the BBC often stoked the flames of middlebrow anxiety, encouraging audiences to "get used to stuff they ought to like." This involved incorporating the latest and most challenging voices—especially Schoenberg's—into its radio broadcasts and print media.[82] One correspondent to the *Musical Times* took issue with listeners being "treated like naughty children," expected to swallow whatever the BBC's "Extremist [music] Department" shoved down their throats.[83] For Lambert, however, the problem was less the public's opposition than its passivity. "One might have thought," he sighed, "that the sturdy British working man . . . would have requested the [pub] proprietor to 'put a sock in it'—but he just sits there, drinking his synthetic bitter to sounds of synthetic sweetness, not caring whether the speaker is tuned to jazz, a talk on wildflowers, or a Schoenberg opera."[84] Meanwhile, magazines like *Vanity Fair* and the *New Yorker* were apparently setting middlebrow duplicity in even sharper relief, sometimes disavowing their modernist credentials, sometimes touting them as an aggressive form of marketing.[85] What is more, they were tacitly diluting hard modernism by setting work by Pablo Picasso, T. S. Eliot, and James Joyce alongside more palatable styles.[86]

Those sympathetic to the middlebrow naturally imagined this eclecticism as open-mindedness and even cosmopolitanism. After deflecting charges of herd mentality onto both high and low, Priestley suggested rebranding the middlebrow as "broadbrow" in order to emphasize this strength: "[The broadbrows are those who] do not give a fig whether it is popular or unpopular, born in Blackburn or Baku, who do not denounce a piece of art because it belongs to a certain category."[87] Looking beyond the provincial world of bilberry pie, he explained: "If you can carry . . . your critical faculty [with you] to Russian dramas, variety shows, football matches, epic poems, grand opera [and so on] . . . [then] you are the salt of the earth, and, of course, one of us."[88] According to detractors, however, the kind of middlebrow eclecticism associated with the BBC and smart magazines was motivated less by open-mindedness than the fraudulent desire to have it both ways, as though its modernist costume were covering up baser instincts, interests, and desires. In the minds of die-hard modernists, this was an aberration; for modernism was not the latest "style" or fashion but, rather, an aesthetic imperative that transcended fashion: "A magazine like *The New Yorker*," Greenberg explained, "is fundamentally high-class Kitsch for the luxury trade[: it] converts and waters down a great deal of avant-garde material for its own uses."[89]

According to detractors, this eclectic appropriation quickly became an aesthetic problem too, as writers and artists began to reproduce the fashionable variety of middlebrow broadcasts and magazines on the level of technique. As if retracting his positive invocation of the category—as indicative of Sibelian synthesis and compromise—Lambert gave the middlebrow an altogether negative spin when it came to Hindemith: "Paul Hindemith is the journalist of modern music, the supreme middlebrow of our times," "reflect[ing] the tempo and colour of modern life in the brisk unpolished manner of a newspaper reporter."[90] For Lambert, this meant reducing modern music to a set of "styles." After diagnosing *Life* magazine's "vulgarized modern art derived from impressionism and its immediate aftermath," Greenberg went even further, accusing middlebrows of transmuting the already-transmuted modernist "style" into mere subject matter.[91] He cited the complaint of the conductor, record producer, and music critic Kurt List to show that the same was true of music.[92] List had decried the use of Schoenbergian "mannerisms" to lend "contemporaneity" to an otherwise regressive jumble of musical styles—an assessment with which Adorno agreed.[93] Indeed, while the *Philosophy of Modern Music* opposes Stravinskian reaction to Schoenbergian progress, Adorno's real villains were the postwar eclectics—Britten, Shostakovich, Copland, among others—who wanted it both ways: "feigning unabashed pretensions of 'modernity' and 'seriousness'—[they have] adjusted to mass culture by means of calculated feeble-mindedness"[94]

For various reasons, these commentators saw this middlebrow version of modernism as the direst of all threats. It undermined modernist investments in aesthetic hierarchy and purity even as it stole audiences from modernism proper: "It has many levels," Greenberg complained, "and some of them are high enough to be dangerous to the naive seeker of true light."[95] Even the fiercest detractors admitted that these eclectic forgeries required considerable skill. After commending their capacity to reduce the most avant-garde works into middlebrow forgeries, Macdonald grumbled that "midcult is a more dangerous opponent since it incorporates so much of the avant-garde . . . [It is the product] of lapsed avant-gardists who know how to use the modern idiom in the service of the banal."[96] The overall effect, as Greenberg explained, made it almost impossible to distinguish the genuine article from the fake: "the demand now is that the distinctions be blurred if not entirely obliterated [and] the vulgarization be more subtle and more general."[97]

Perhaps the most serious challenge, however, was to aesthetic autonomy. Indeed, for many, the problem was less eclecticism per se than the duplicity it seemed to invite, as though creator, critic, and audience were involved in a conspiracy. By now, most scholars accept that artistic value and meaning are produced by these complex social relations. Yet even Pierre Bourdieu—one of aesthetic autonomy's most effective critics—resorted to conspiracy theorizing in the case of the middlebrow: "The imposture it presupposes would necessarily fail if it could not rely on the complicity of the consumers."[98] "This complicity," he explained, "is guaranteed in advance since, in culture as elsewhere, the consumption of 'imitations' is an

unconscious bluff which chiefly deceives the bluffer, who has most interest in taking the copy for the original, like the purchaser of 'seconds,' 'rejects,' cut-price or
second-hand goods, who need to convince themselves that 'it's cheaper and creates
the same effect.'" While Greenberg saw middlebrow duplicity inscribed within the
artwork, Bourdieu imagined it as an implicit pact between composer, critic, and
audience, all of whom stood to gain from the aesthetic counterfeits: "The producers and consumers of middlebrow culture share the same fundamental relationship to legitimate culture and to its exclusive possessors, so that their interests are
attuned to each other as if by a pre-established harmony."

It is these aspects of "middlebrow" ambivalence, duplicity, and complicity—the
characteristics that mid-century modernists most loved to hate—that *Middlebrow
Modernism* sets out to illuminate. My aim in so doing is not to reinforce modernist oppositions and prejudices, but rather to lay bare the processes through which
they were undermined. By excavating those aspects of middlebrow culture that
more defensive studies have overlooked, I want to sketch a fuller picture of the
challenges that they posed to the modernist critical tradition. In order to delve into
the strategies that allowed middlebrows to "curry favor with both sides," I focus
not only on Britten's music but also on the mainstream press, who demonstrated
a matchless aesthetic duplicity, in ways that responded to and fed Britten's compositional practice. In adding historical flesh to mid-century complaints about the
complicity between middlebrow artists, critics, and audiences, I attempt to steer
my own middle course within a methodological divide that has, ironically, opened
up within middlebrow scholarship—between studies of mediation and reception
on the one hand, and those of creation on the other, as if the category need necessarily be confined to either domain. By examining dialectically the relationship
between criticism and Britten's musical style, I demonstrate that the "problem"
of middlebrow culture lay not just in its ability to mediate between high and low,
modernism and mass culture, but also in the distinctive challenges it posed to
modernist fantasies of aesthetic autonomy.

BRITTEN AND THE MIDDLEBROW

Britten offers an ideal case study for exploring this ambivalence and duplicity,
for he was nothing if not a paradoxical figure, staking out space on both sides of
the great divide simultaneously. Born in 1913 into a "very ordinary middle class
family," he was one of the earliest products of the interwar middlebrow. His professional career stretched across its mid-century heyday. In his childhood home,
music was apparently one of the ways that the Brittens sought to maintain and
elevate their social standing.[99] His musical education benefited from relatively
easy access not only to the newly formed BBC Symphony Orchestra, but also to
a wireless, a gramophone, and music magazines, from *The Radio Times* and *The*

Listener to *Gramophone*.[100] Like many in the aspirational audience, he had the BBC to thank for his expansive knowledge of musical repertoire. His enthusiasm for radio, in particular, broadened his horizons beyond the largely romantic tastes of his childhood to include the latest and most challenging examples of continental modernism. If he had "half-decided on Schoenberg" by 1929, a wireless concert the following year elicited a more unequivocal response: "I go to a marvelous Schoenberg concert on the Billison's wireless . . . I liked [*Pierrot Lunaire*] the most."[101] Elsewhere he responded with the feelings of ambivalence and inadequacy that were the middlebrow stock-in-trade: "Listen to the Wireless—especially to a concert of contemporary music—Schoenberg—Heaven only knows!! I enjoyed his Bach 'St. Anne'; & quite liked his 'Peace on earth' for Chorus—but his 'Erwartung'—! I could not make head or tail of it—even less than the 'Peace on earth.'"[102] In good middlebrow fashion, however, Britten resolved to get used to the stuff he ought to like: "I am getting very fond of Schoenberg, especially with study," he reported after yet another contemporary music program.[103] By the time of Schoenberg's death, Britten was apparently confident—doubtless owing much to these early broadcasts—that "[e]very serious composer today has felt the effect of his courage, single-mindedness and determination."[104]

Given Britten's own experience as a consumer of middlebrow goods, he was predictably adept at catering to this market. As Paul Kildea has documented, Britten's correspondence with publishers, broadcasters, and recording companies demonstrated extreme sensitivity to the modern music industry.[105] The effects of canny behind-the-scenes negotiations were amplified by a powerful public presence, not only as an establishment composer—recipient of major national commissions, prizes, and honors—but also as performer, pedagogue, recording artist, festival organizer, and arts advocate, among other things. He was the subject of articles in such fashionable publications as *Vogue* and *The Saturday Review*.[106] And while the Metropolitan Opera premiere of *Grimes* in 1948 did not earn him a feature in his beloved *New Yorker*, his *Time* cover spot rehearsed all the usual middlebrow duplicities and ironies.[107] Even as the magazine sought to amplify Britten's celebrity, the accompanying photo represented him—as Paul Kildea has noted—"earnestly gazing into the distance, his mind on Higher Things."[108] By the following year, even some BBC administrators were worried about overplaying Britten's operas.[109] His unrivaled exposure generated resentment among contemporaries. Reporting that one elderly composer had complained that "Britten has only to blow his nose and they record it," Stephen Williams remarked contemptuously: "He is indubitably the Golden Boy of contemporary music, immensely successful and immensely fashionable."[110] Whether in the spirit of defiance or defense, Britten elevated this reputation into an aesthetic principle: "I want my music to be of use to people, to please them, to 'enhance their lives' . . . I do not write for posterity."[111] He went on to offer even more pointedly defensive jabs at modernist esotericism: "it is insulting to address someone in a language which they do not understand."[112]

These public repudiations of modernist difficulty and autonomy notwithstanding, Britten remained ambivalent. Immediately after outlining his utilitarian aesthetic, his Schoenbergian superego reared its head in a critique of mass-technological "popularization."[113] Earlier, he had denounced the BBC for not trying hard enough to get the public to engage with modernism's challenges, while simultaneously criticizing American programmers for trying too hard: incorporating it piecemeal into their eclectic programs.[114] After lauding the latter's success, he let out a positively Greenbergian appraisal of this middlebrow fashion: "How much this interest in [modern] music is founded on genuine taste and knowledge, and how much on the desire to be *au courant*, to hear the latest thing, is hard to say."[115] "One of the most serious dangers," he explained, "lies in the crop of interpreters, commentators, explainers and synthesizers, who make such comfortable livings telling the public that music is really very simple and easy to understand."[116] This snobbery affected his taste in music too: on one occasion he declared himself "sickened" by the "cheapness," "obviousness," and "emptiness" of Puccini's square tunes.[117] In more revealing moments, Britten even turned his esotericism and anxiety on himself. "I am a bit worried about my local success at the moment," he wrote to Elizabeth Mayer in 1943: "It is all a little embarrassing, & I hope it doesn't mean that there's too much superficial charm about my pieces."[118] "Perhaps I'd be a better composer," he worried elsewhere, "if I were more avant-garde."[119] Like the middlebrow audiences that modernists loved to mock, Britten was evidently divided against himself, at once craving popularity and embarrassed by it.

This ambivalence made its presence felt in Britten's music, which shuttled toward and away from a distinctly modernist musical voice, both between works and at different phases of his career. There was no Straussian volte-face, but a consistent inconstancy—shuttling back and forth between the Schoenbergian *Sinfonietta* (1933) and the populist *Simple Symphony* (1934), with most music falling somewhere in between. Attempting to make sense of Britten's stylistic "contradictions," critics appealed to classic middlebrow tropes. Sometimes this meant reaching for the Sibelian model of synthesis, often appropriated as a marker of Englishness: "Is it beyond the bounds of possibility," one commentator pondered in 1933, "that composers will sooner or later try to discover what modern skill and resources can do with the fundamentals of music?"[120] Having praised Vaughan Williams for using common chords in a "new-old" way, the same writer nominated a successor: "See for example what Benjamin Britten does with the chord of C major in his *Te Deum*, and with a modern use of primitive devices and material in 'A Boy [was] Born.'" Like the defenses of Sibelius at roughly the same time, Britten was lauded for renovating traditional musical language instead of inventing it anew. At the time of his death, these images were still going strong, with

Robin Holloway lauding Britten's music for its "power to connect the avant-garde with the lost paradise of tonality": "it shows how old usages can be refreshed and remade, and how the new can be saved from mere rootlessness, etiolation, lack of connexion and communication."[121]

From the beginning, however, these images of synthesis rubbed up against the identification of fracture: disparate styles pitted against one another in ways that heightened their incompatibility. Just as with Priestley's "broadbrow" defense, some gave this a positive spin. Charles Stuart championed Britten's omnivorous tastes over Schoenbergian "subjectivism," while Massimo Mila lauded him as an "encyclopedic" model for the "civilized," a "man of culture": "Purcell and Monteverdi, Verdi and Wagner, Mahler and Alban Berg, Stravinsky and Schönberg—these and others were the springs from which the musician drank with eager impartiality."[122] For Denis ApIvor, Britten's eclecticism was both fruit and seed of middlebrow attempts to educate the British public in the latest musical styles, and required an audience as "cosmopolitan" as Britten himself to appreciate it.[123] For most commentators, however, such eclecticism signaled superficial and passive skill—a virtuosic ability to mimic the language of others without saying anything new. Lambert predictably criticized Britten for emphasizing texture over content, style over substance—the opposite of his beloved Sibelius—just as he had done with Hindemith's middlebrow journalism.[124] William Glock's complaints were even more telling, associating Britten's eclectic assimilation of disparate musical styles with the literal passivity of middlebrow consumers at large: "We should ask whether English music (of which Britten is not the sole phenomenon) is so defunct that we must continue to be a nation of consumers, or to be placed in that state by business men to whom concert-going is an industry and nothing more."[125] Many years later, Elizabeth Lutyens returned to Lambert's metaphor, impugning Britten as "a brilliant journalist able to produce an instant effect at first hearing, understandable to all."[126] "Each repeated hearing," she went on to explain—as if imagining the tabloids—"yields less—or so I find."

MIDDLEBROW MUSIC AND CRITICISM

These critical strictures assigned Britten's music firmly to the middlebrow orbit. Yet, if modernists associated his eclecticism with fraudulence and forgery, this open discussion of it also bespoke failure to keep the middlebrow mask in place. The stories recounted throughout this book are, on the surface, accounts of more positive reception. Explicit accusations of cleverness, insincerity, superficiality, and even eclecticism are rare. However, far from representing a move away from middlebrow ambivalence and duplicity, they exemplify a more successful form of it, almost as if critics were in on the act. While Britten scholars have tended to play up negative critical reactions to Britten's cleverness and eclecticism, ostensibly in order to confirm his "outsider" image, we will see that a more common response among mid-century reviewers was to defend and prevaricate. They praised the works on terms they thought most respectable, while ignoring, erasing, or sublimating aesthetic elephants in the room: sentimentality, romanticism, tonality, lyricism, spectacle, and the list goes on. Middlebrow ambivalence and duplicity are, in other words, a constant "absent presence" in the chapters that follow, rarely admitted but easily detected in critical exaggerations, defenses, obfuscations, subtractions, and apologies.

These creative critical strategies are as much the subject of this book as Britten's music. In taking journalistic criticism seriously enough to read between its lines, *Middlebrow Modernism* aims to challenge modernist modes of analysis even as it complicates modernist historiographical models. For, as Richard Taruskin has pointed out, traditional musicological indifference to matters of mediation and reception has often been bound up with the cultural politics of modernism—that is, with the very divide that this study sets out to complicate.[127] In recent years, this oversight has been remedied by a wave of reception histories, many of which have sought to demonstrate the contingency and mutability of musical meaning.[128] But while press responses serve as starting points for the chapters that follow, this is not a *Rezeptionsgeschichte* in the traditional sense. It treats reception not as a separate activity, as if to grant it the same autonomy traditionally accorded musical works. Rather, it seeks to understand criticism as an inextricable part both of the creative history of Britten's operas and of the landscape from which they hailed— the hinge upon which the mid-century middlebrow turned.

Despite modernist attempts to distance journalists from the "ordinary" public, critics endeavored to mediate between artists and the audience. This meant charging themselves with gauging and representing public opinion, even relaying it back to artists in a kind of feedback loop: "The 'essay in dissonance' by Arnold Schoenberg," one critic reported, "moved [the public] beyond to laughter, hisses, and applause."[129] But when it came to modernism, critics were often just as confused as the audience they were supposed to guide. After recounting Schoenberg's fiasco the commentator complained of the "new problem" facing the press: "Past generations of critics unhesitatingly condemned the new and strange and unintelligible, and are now held up to pity and ridicule." "If we pour scorn on our 'Futurist' school," he asked anxiously, "are we preparing the same fate for ourselves? On the other hand, the movement may be ephemeral and its supporters become known as victims of a passing craze." Critics, in other words, were not just enforcers of middlebrow anxiety about what people ought to like, but also subject to it. This often meant tropes passing quickly from previewers to reviewers, as if to demonstrate the conformist force of opinion. Indeed, it is noteworthy that, despite the notorious hermeneutic and stylistic ambiguity of Britten's operas, there was often relative consensus among critics even across traditional cultural, aesthetic, and political divides.

These critical orthodoxies were not confined to a narrow circle of critical elites. While scholars have rightly been cautious about conflating journalistic responses with those of contemporary audiences, the middlebrow music press often had the will and the power to frame the terms of discussion and shape contemporary experience. Many of the reviews that appear in this study—from local newspapers to specialist music periodicals—combined analytical detail and specificity with a didactic style. Some were even put out before the premieres in order to maximize their power and reach. Indeed, Britten was apparently worried enough about the power of critics to complain of "the people who *won't* judge for themselves," casting Leavisite aspersions of his own: "I heard recently, of a woman who learned a certain critic's phrases off by heart in order to appear knowledgeable and witty herself."[130] Elsewhere, he was even more explicit, anxiously denying the influence of critics except on "those dreary middlebrows who don't know what to think until they read the *New Statesman!*"[131]

In turning his nose up at those who took criticism seriously, Britten was as disingenuous as the next middlebrow. For someone who claimed never to read press reviews—reportedly on doctor's orders—he was often painfully aware of what had been written about each of his works.[132] His letters and diaries reveal extreme sensitivity to criticism and he was bothered enough to hit back publicly, not just at individual critics but also at the profession of criticism itself.[133] Like Q. D. Leavis, Britten was annoyed by the rashness and incompetence of these parasitic meddlers, coupled with their enormous power: "We are admittedly not quite as far gone as New York where, I gather, bad notices can kill a play or opera stone dead; here they can at least wriggle a little," he sighed morbidly.[134] It is perhaps for this reason that, as Paul Kildea has shown, Britten occasionally took to currying favor with particular critics, twisting their arms behind the scenes.[135] Indeed, despite his complaints about negative treatment, most composers were envious of his relationship with the press, not excepting Stravinsky, who insisted that the adulatory reception accorded the *War Requiem* "was a phenomenon as remarkable as the music itself."[136] Elsewhere, Stravinsky shook off the tepid reception of his own *Abraham and Isaac* with a jealous shrug: "Well, what can you do, it's not for everybody to have Benjamin Britten's success with the critics."[137]

Although Stravinsky emphasized the critical creativity involved in sublimating Britten's works, he also implied that the music—with its fake counterpoint, cinematic grandeur, and counterfeit modernism—invited the press dissimilation it eventually received. Nor is this surprising, for Britten's self-consciousness about his critical reception underpinned his anxious play between disparate "styles." After warning young composers of journalists trying "to find the correct pigeon-hole definition," he explained: "These people are dangerous . . . because they make the composer, especially the young composer, self-conscious, and instead of writing his own music, music which springs naturally from his gift and personality, he may be frightened into writing pretentious nonsense or deliberate obscurity."[138] As with most of Britten's warnings, it is hard not to read this as a confession. This makes him a compelling case study not just of complicity between composition, criticism, and consumption, but of broader historical fears about the erosion of these very distinctions. In denouncing music by the likes of Hindemith and Britten as a form of middlebrow "journalism," in other words, critics may have been shrewder than they imagined. For Britten's music not only worked in tandem with criticism but—insofar as it attempted to guide its own reception—was a form of criticism itself: at once a part of and commentator upon the latest musical fashions. If criticism involved a creative shaping of music into stylistic categories, the process could just as easily work the other way around, with music serving as a quasi-journalistic chronicle of styles. Indeed, it is doubtless telling that Britten's image of music critics as parasites—living off the musical creativity of others, digesting it, and spewing it out into easily recognizable "styles"—is one that, ironically, attached itself to his music.

REHEARING BRITTEN

Just as this reciprocity between Britten's music and its criticism can help to flesh out hitherto unexplored facets of the middlebrow, so making space for this precarious category promises fresh perspectives on the composer. Britten scholars have often sought defensively to minimize the composer's ambivalence.[139] On a biographical level, this has meant touting Britten's rejection of modernist esotericism and painting him as an unashamed populist, despite his lifelong anxieties about pandering.[140] Yet this tendency has gone hand in hand with the opposite approach to the music, with many of the same scholars focusing on and exaggerating aspects that accord with modernist aesthetics: attenuated or extended tonality; motivic unity and coherence; transgressive plots or themes. By 1953, Peter Tranchell was already complaining about the canny selectiveness of Britten studies as an emerging field, citing a volume that would go on to set the defensive tone for subsequent scholarship.[141] Even one as recent as Kildea, whose painstaking research has illuminated Britten's shrewd market calculations, has striven to insulate the major works from these processes, as if to protect their originality and autonomy.[142] In most scholarly accounts, then, Britten still emerges somehow as both a man of the masses and an uncompromising modernist, with very little acknowledgment of the contradictions involved.

In those instances where these paradoxes have been addressed, it has only served the better to defuse them. Negative critical reactions have been adduced in implicit defense, a way of associating Britten with modernist alterity despite himself.[143] Another common tactic has been to invoke Britten's supposedly countercultural politics—whether pacifism, socialism, or queerness—as a counterweight to his success: "For anyone inclined to explore beyond [the] deceptively 'conservative' and desperately 'inviting' surface [of Britten's music]," Philip Brett explained, "it offers not only a rigorous critique of the past but also a vision of a differently organized future."[144] Brett's interpretations of course broke new ground in queer musicology, opening up the way for a wave of scholarship exploring the relationship between Britten's operas and his homosexuality—a topic that up until that point had been actively suppressed.[145] Perhaps unsurprisingly, this outpouring has—with a few notable exceptions—tended to focus on reading between lines, in ways that draw on a much older, value-laden differentiation between a superficial level of perception and a deeper one.[146] In this respect, Brett exemplified the continuing legacy of modernism in even ostensibly postmodern interpretations of Britten's operas. After all, it was this same metaphor of surface and depth that had allowed Keller to explain away Britten's popularity as a mass misunderstanding: "[Britten's] music is approachable on various levels . . . so that the superficial listener, moving on the most superficial level, may yet be strongly impressed and may think he knows all about what he hears."[147] This strategy has also been deployed by more recent scholars from Claire Seymour to Paul Kildea, who pay lip service to the notorious "ambiguity" of Britten's textual and musical surface only to resolve it by excavating the "real" meaning buried below.[148]

These critical strategies have evidently outlasted their roots in the mid-century middlebrow. Indeed, one of this book's central arguments is that Britten's operas invite the selective reception they have enjoyed, in ways that still encourage listeners to defend and to dissimilate. Yet scholarship can and should try to see through the terms that the works themselves appear to propose. This is particularly important in the case of Britten. For in papering over the cracks in his operatic aesthetic, scholars have masked key aspects of his musical language. More importantly, they have evaded the broader challenges that he poses to modernist aesthetics. As a corrective, this study seeks to recover the more compromising features of Britten's operas, which have lain hidden so long in plain sight, overlooked by scholarship and criticism that value depth, difficulty, and complexity above all else.[149] In this respect, it adopts a musical version of "surface reading," a term coined by recent literary scholars to advance alternatives to the deep reading practices that have hitherto dominated literary and cultural criticism.[150] Rather than merely reversing black and white by turning Britten into an unashamed populist, however, I will show how conventional features were combined with and set against explicitly modernist traits. Instead of attempting to defuse ambivalence, my aim is to take it seriously as an aesthetic stance in its own right, central to middlebrow negotiations of the great divide.

OPERA AND THE MIDDLEBROW

If Britten offers a vivid portrait of these tensions, so too does the operatic medium through which he made his name. As one of the most expensive, elaborate, and spectacular of artistic genres, it naturally drew the most critical comment, both in relation to individual works and within broader discussions of cultural policy. For some, it was a symbol of high culture at its most extravagant. According to modernists like Pierre Boulez, it was this high cultural performativity that made opera a lightning rod for middlebrow duplicity, those "who go to the opera because one must go to the opera, because that is what society likes to see, because it is a cultural duty."[151] It was for this reason that the opera house was—for Boulez—a hotbed of middlebrow conservatism, a "musty old wardrobe," a "relic, a well-cared for museum . . . full of dust and crap."[152]

It was not just social and institutional factors but also aesthetic considerations that marked opera as irredeemably middlebrow. Indeed, at a time when composers like Boulez were imagining musical formalism as the apogee of modernist autonomy, opera's concrete scenarios and dramatic spectacles struck them as all too compromising, making musical artworks superficially accessible.[153] According to Adorno, this tension was compounded by opera's investment in duplicity, mirroring its middlebrow audience even more acutely: "that aura of disguise, of miming, which attracts the child to the theater—not because the child wants to see a work of art, but because it wants to confirm its own pleasure in dissimilation."[154] "The closer opera gets to a parody of itself," Adorno elaborated, "the closer it gets to its own particular element."[155] In the case of "modern" opera—viewed by both Adorno and Boulez as a contradiction in terms—attempts to resist the genre's illusionism compounded, rather than remedied, operatic duplicity: "Opera has reached the state of crisis because the genre cannot dispense with illusion without surrendering itself, and yet it must want to do so."[156] After describing a swan-less *Lohengrin* or *Freischütz* without the Wolf's Glen, Adorno complained: "Demystified opera inevitably threatens to degenerate into an arts and crafts affair, where stylization threatens to substitute for disintegrating style. Modernity, which does not really intervene in the matter, becomes mere packaging, becomes modernism."[157]

Britten's operas provide a revealing lens through which to explore the kind of middlebrow tensions that mid-century modernists associated with the genre. Britten was, after all, both an advocate for and a beneficiary of postwar attempts to promote opera to a wider audience.[158] Yet, if his operas were conceived with this end in mind, they did not always wear their compromises proudly on their sleeves, especially when compared with overtly pedagogical pieces like *The Young Person's Guide to the Orchestra* (1945) and *Noye's Fludde* (1958).[159] At the same time, Britten was uncomfortably aware of opera's troublesome reputation among modernists, describing the modern opera composer—himself especially—as an "anachronism."[160] This self-consciousness manifested itself in the operas themselves and their reception, in ways that aggravated his already ambivalent musical style in distinctly operatic ways. Indeed, throughout this study, we will see the kind of struggles that Boulez and Adorno identified: between theatrical illusionism and abstract symbolism, extravagant spectacle and modernist austerity. Yet, we will also see that these tensions were not limited to the visual sphere, as anti-operatic detractors tended to imply. For one thing, Britten's librettos often drew self-consciously on the allegorical mode—as we have already seen in *Paul Bunyan*—marked as it was by a similar disjuncture between real world referents and "higher" significance.[161] Perhaps even more provocative, however, was Britten's musical eclecticism, which combined the putatively "cheap" and immediate conventions of nineteenth-century opera with the formalist markers of contemporary modernism. In doing so, Britten's operas not only raised questions about modernism's aesthetic oppositions but also threatened to knock music itself off its pedestal of autonomy.

· · ·

The eclectic variety of Britten's operas was such that each work offers an opportunity to explore a different middlebrow challenge to modernist critical categories. Chapter 2 examines how *Peter Grimes* (1945) undermined oppositions between realism and difficulty on the one hand, and "easy" sentimentality on the other. After describing attempts of early critics to stylize *Grimes* as an authentic modernist opera that shocked audiences, I uncover the more sentimental charms that commentators struggled to erase: its idealized vision of love, its melodrama, its manipulation of sympathy, and its compelling musical lyricism. Beyond pointing out previous omissions, I seek to explain how Britten's opera encouraged the subtractive reactions it received. I argue that by pitting "romantic" tropes against "modernist" ones, sumptuous lyricism against its erasure, *Grimes* was able to stage its own difficulty, translating modernism's supposed rejection of nineteenth-century sentimentality into a rhetorical style for easy consumption. As sketched here, the story offers two challenges to modernist criticism. It suggests that modernism's aesthetic of difficulty was actually quite fashionable among middlebrow critics and audiences. More provocatively, it raises the possibility that the infamous difficulty of modernism was itself like that of *Grimes:* a stylistic affectation that depended on the very sentimentality it seemed to reject.

This idea of modernism as a performative style or rhetorical mode is explored further in the third chapter, on *Albert Herring* (1947). If *Grimes* muddied the waters between difficulty and sentimentality, *Herring* caused trouble for the equally strict opposition between tradition and innovation. After detailing the ways in which the text and music of Britten's operatic comedy of manners simultaneously undermine and embrace tradition, I discuss the various strategies that early commentators used to finesse this ambivalence. Critical selection and subtraction will come in for some analysis, along with journalistic appeals to modernist irony, in an effort to unsettle long-standing assumptions about musical modernism's relationship with the past. The reception of *Albert Herring* demonstrates that modernist voices were indeed heard in even the most eclectic patchwork of past traditions, and that this was necessarily the case. Drawing on middlebrow criticism from Priestley to Lambert, I argue that modernist oppositions are most profitably understood in dialectical terms, according to which old and new, tradition and innovation, depend on one another for definition.

Ever since its premiere in 1954, commentators have tried to steer *The Turn of the Screw* away from the traditions of gothic melodrama. Fearing that it might be dismissed as a "cheap" ghost story, commentators maintained that Britten's opera was a paradigm of modernist restraint: an up-to-date ghost story, whose phantoms were supposedly more psychological than real. In chapter 4, I discuss the ways in which Britten's operatic adaptation of Henry James's novella, published in 1898, simultaneously summons and confounds such defenses. I draw attention to willfully ignored gothicisms in the libretto, stage designs, and music, revealing the influence of popular literature, radio, and film. I also trace the critical anxiety and reticence about these elements to early- and mid-century rejections of the gothic tradition. Rather than attempting to resolve the interpretive question that has preoccupied critics and scholars—whether the opera's ghosts are real or imaginary—my chapter excavates its stakes. In mediating between gothic melodrama and modernist psychodrama, Britten's *Screw* showed how much these alleged aesthetic opposites had in common.

In the fifth chapter, I consider *The Burning Fiery Furnace* (1966), the second of Britten's parables for church performance. After setting the work against the backdrop of modernist repudiations of religious kitsch and the reception of Britten's own *War Requiem* (1962) and *Curlew River* (1964) more specifically, I discuss the fine line it trod amid contemporary critical oppositions: between sacred asceticism and aestheticism, mystical transcendence and authoritarian sublime. I explore how the *Furnace*'s appeal to musical exoticism and minimalism freed its sublimity from associations with High Anglican demagoguery, fashioning a spirituality more compatible with the modernity, rationalism, and secularism of the mid-century middlebrow. I also suggest that the work managed to smuggle back religious registers of a more explicitly sensuous and monumental nature, often in association with Babylonian rituals. Ultimately, however, I argue that the trouble critics had separating religious aestheticism and asceticism—or even deciding which they found more compelling—raises much broader boundary questions about twentieth-century sacred music.

My sixth and final chapter considers the ways in which *Death in Venice* (1973) responded to the fraught discourse surrounding opera in the second half of the twentieth century. If the genre as a whole often threatened to fall on the wrong side of contemporaneous oppositions—between abstraction and immediacy, intellectual and visceral—the opera's early critics still tended to cast its visual spectacles and musical rhetoric into rarefied terms. As an opera that is essentially "about" translating base pleasures into abstract intellectual reflection, *Death in Venice* offers an opportunity to explore middlebrow critical apologetics in detail. After identifying an "aesthetic of sublimation" in contemporaneous criticism, I explore how Britten's operatic swansong resists the suppressions that it incites. Drawing on

Adorno's ambivalent diatribe about opera from 1955, I argue that *Death in Venice* may be fruitfully regarded as a "bourgeois opera," a postwar operatic version of the middlebrow. In simultaneously staging and confounding oppositions at the heart of anti-operatic discourse, the work illuminates the wider ways in which composers, directors, critics, and audiences sought to overcome twentieth-century opera's supposedly terminal illness.

MODERNISM BETWEEN THEORY AND PRACTICE

Ultimately, this study attempts to recapture the heated contention in which Britten's operas were unveiled. At the same time, it holds back from issuing value judgments of its own. My aim is neither to champion the middlebrow as a grand synthesis nor to denigrate it as a duplicitous compromise, the way its mid-century defenders or detractors did. One of the main pitfalls in scholarly accounts of modernism especially has been a tendency to continue the mudslinging of twentieth-century polemicists. Rather than replacing a modernist canon of works or values with a middlebrow one—as literary scholars have often attempted to do—I want to formulate an "archaeology" of value in the Foucauldian sense.[162] This means demonstrating how the everyday practice of music composition and criticism implicated broader debates about the relationship between modernism and middlebrow culture. More importantly, it means excavating the underlying stakes. For, as will become clear, the anxieties and strategies detailed throughout this study were about much more than Britten's operas or even a discrete set of "middlebrow" products or practices. Rather they spoke to much broader concerns about the relationship between aesthetic ideals and the everyday exigencies of market society.

The point at issue was, after all, the middlebrow's notorious inconsistency. Middlebrow stylistic eclecticism was viewed as a proxy for vacillations with respect to audiences, not to mention the audience's own inconsistencies and ambivalence. This flew in the face of modernist commitments to purity and autonomy—to following aesthetic ideals through to the bitter end. For all their denigration, in other words, commentators like Adorno and Stravinsky were not wrong to bring out the duplicity and ambivalence of Britten and his devotees. The operatic case studies that follow are steeped in contradictory aims and objectives. Creators said one thing and did another. There was a pervasive mismatch between works and their critical reception and manifest contradictions within criticism itself. The middlebrow, then, becomes a useful category for unsettling modernist expectations of consistency, carving out space for examining the mechanics—even aesthetics— of duplicity. In foregrounding these aspects, my perspective approaches that of the theater scholar David Savran, who understands the category in terms of an underhanded selling out of its own principles.[163] Yet while Savran replicates the snobbery he rails against—denouncing middlebrow inauthenticity and imagining a more "authentic" form—my account avoids such utopian fantasies of aesthetic purity. In reality, "middlebrow" calculations were never the aberrant conspiracies that modernist commentators made them out to be. They were, rather, the routine processes by which aesthetic, political, and social ideals were negotiated in everyday practice. Britten and other middlebrows, in other words, were not special cases but pressure points. They typified the broader paradoxes of twentieth-century art, torn between originality and autonomy, and the desire to communicate with mass audiences.

This expansiveness was for good or ill fundamental to historical conceptions of the category. Where modernism was seen as an investment in rigid boundaries and hierarchies, not to mention purity, the middlebrow was marked by a capacity to overstep its bounds, drawing everything up into its orbit: "Unlike [mass culture], which has its social limits marked out for it," Greenberg complained, "middlebrow culture attacks distinctions as such and insinuates itself everywhere . . . Insidiousness of its essence, and in recent years its avenues of penetration have become increasingly difficult to detect and block."[164] In part, these fears were inspired by the popularization of modernism in middlebrow media, which recent scholars like Daniel Tracey and Lise Jalliant have begun to explore.[165] Modernists regarded the middlebrow as even more pernicious than mass culture because it threatened to turn the great divide into a slippery slope, on which they might lose their footing. On a deeper level, though, the middlebrow aroused fears that modernists had already slipped, serving less as an outside threat than as a mirror and scapegoat for modernism's own duplicity: "we are all of us becoming guilty in one way or another," Greenberg sighed.[166] It is this sense of modernist abjection that underlies many of the tensions detailed throughout the present study, making it as much a story of modernism as of its middlebrow other.

At roughly the same time that Woolf was voicing her rejection of those "betwixt and between," she was working on some middlebrow projects of her own.[167] As Joseph Auner has shown, Schoenberg was likewise rejecting "concessions" to audiences and performers even as he worked to make his work more accessible.[168] Much like Britten, he simultaneously courted public attention and was repulsed by it.[169] Schoenberg's relationship to critics was equally paradoxical.[170] According to Lambert, Schoenberg relied upon—even colluded with—critics to advertise his fabled radicalism and autonomy, masking an ambivalence plainly audible on the musical surface: "the spiritual conflict in his works is obvious, even though he may cry 'A la lanterne' with more fervor than the most bloodthirsty of sans-culottes."[171] "Behind his most revolutionary passages," Lambert observed, "lurks the highly respectable shade of Mendelssohn"—a music torn between abstract formalism and a much older romanticism.[172] Similarly, even as Adorno championed Schoenberg's categorical radicalism over the halfhearted innovations of Britten, Shostakovich, and others, he admitted that even Schoenberg's position fell short of his hopes. At the end of his meditation on "progress," Adorno conceded—echoing Lambert, Priestley, and other card-carrying middlebrows—that any attempt to eradicate convention led into an infinite regress. If the only way to avoid compromise was to fall silent, it followed that even Schoenberg was implicated in middlebrow duplicity and ambivalence.

Perhaps the problem with Britten's "middlebrow" operas, then, was not that they reconciled irreconcilable binaries so much as that they undermined them, suggesting that modernism itself was irredeemably middlebrow. In theorizing the deliberately paradoxical concept of "middlebrow modernism," this study seeks to harness the concept's deconstructive potential. When seen through this lens, twentieth-century music may begin to resemble the visions sketched by the new modernist studies: a space in which ambivalence and variety reign, and boundaries disappear—adding yet another modernism to the growing list. Indeed, this study even seems to support definitions of modernism itself as a kind of ambivalence, destabilizing the oppositions it was imagined to uphold. And yet the stories recounted throughout this book also support the opposite conclusion: that the great divide ran deeper than even Huyssen supposed. It shows that its mythical oppositions were not limited to polemics but left an impression on the everyday practice of composition, mediation, and reception even when they were not explicitly invoked. It was, after all, the contours of the great divide that made for the musical and critical strategies to be traced herein, even if these strategies ended up undermining the great divide in turn.

If the new modernist studies have risked broadening out modernism into a flat, limitless terrain, with values and hierarchies erased, my study seeks to recover the aesthetic prejudices and battles that were fundamental to early- and mid-twentieth-century conceptions. Hierarchical categories like high, middle, and low were real enough to have social and aesthetic consequences and thus retain their historical significance, subject to ideological critique. Replicating middlebrow doubleness on the level of historiographical technique, this study shows how even the crudest oppositions and hierarchies affected the everyday practice of composition, mediation, and reception, while simultaneously laying bare the process through which they were undermined. Ultimately it was this tension between theory and practice, aesthetic ideals and their everyday articulation, that made the mid-century debate such a fraught one. By focusing on this agonistic tension, my study permits a new understanding of musical modernism without losing a sense of its narrowness. It seeks to challenge modernist historiography without writing over its history. Rather than replacing modernism's unequivocal ideals with its messy, ambivalent practice, *Middlebrow Modernism* foregrounds the tension—between the erection and erosion of hierarchy, mythic rhetoric and pragmatic realities—as a central, even definitive, part of the story of twentieth-century musical culture.

Sentimentality under Erasure in *Peter Grimes*

An admiral with three rows of medal ribbon was standing up at Sadler's Wells the other night. A good many other people were standing, too; but it is something when an admiral has to stand to hear an opera. And the opera was not one of your popular, hum-the-tune-on-the-way-home, Italian pieces of Verdi or Puccini. It was Benjamin Britten's new Peter Grimes . . . At the end the audience cheered [the composer] as if he scored for Chelsea. Well might he smile; Peter Grimes is spreading like measles.

—PHILIP WHITAKER, "THE ADMIRAL HAD TO STAND," 1946[1]

On the evening of June 7, 1945, before even a note of Britten's new opera was sounded, emotions were running high: "The return of the Sadler's Wells Company," one critic speculated, "would have been welcome enough in any case, even if the occasion had been celebrated by nothing fresher than *Madam Butterfly*. But the Wells have done the thing in style."[2] This unveiling of a new British opera—rare enough at the best of times—came less than a month after VE Day, serving simultaneously as a celebration of victory, a symbol of peace, and the re-opening of a beloved theater after the war. "Not since 1934," another commentator gushed, "had London heard a new English opera [Lawrence Collingwood's *Macbeth*]. Not since the war had a new opera been heard in any of the world's capitals. Not since the night of September 7, 1940, . . . had music echoed through world-famed Sadler's Wells."[3] As the first postwar premiere in any major capital, it was touted with triumphalist overtones, as if Lady Britannia had added "pen, harp, and buskin" to her shield and trident.[4] Beverly Baxter, a Conservative MP and *Evening Standard* critic, went even further: "It may be," he conceded, "that the political domination of London is to be challenged by Moscow or Washington . . . but there is compensation in the thought that London will become the artistic centre of the world."[5]

Edmund Wilson, by contrast, located the work's significance in the immediate past: "This opera could have been written in no other age, and it is one of the very few works of art that have seemed to me, so far, to have spoken for the blind anguish, the hateful rancors and the will to destruction of these horrible years."[6] In wartime, the Sadler's Wells Theatre had sheltered displaced locals while the principals toured the war-weary provinces, thereby reinforcing the strong associations between the so-called "people's company" and "people's war."[7] After recounting his tale of an admiral standing in the gallery, Whitaker reinforced this vision, stressing that the work's enthusiastic reception straddled traditional class lines.[8] Another critic suggested that the mania had even spread outside the auditorium:

> A friend boarded a 38 bus at Green Park, asked the conductor whether he went past Sadler's Wells. "Yes, I should say I do," he replied. "I wish I could go inside instead. That will be threepence for *Peter Grimes*" . . . as he left the bus he heard the conductor shouting at the top of a loud voice: "Sadler's Wells! Any more for *Peter Grimes*, the sadistic fisherman!"[9]

With these images of rich and poor, admirals and bus conductors, coming together to cheer Britten's opera enthusiastically, *Grimes* appeared to bring wartime images of national unity and solidarity into a postwar future. Indeed, to judge from several accounts, it was almost as if this single event made good on the cultural democracy that the war had promised to inaugurate.[10]

In leading with these hyperbolic discussions and vignettes, commentators were seeking both to do justice to and to justify their emotive responses. Yet even the most enthusiastic critics were anxious about the propriety of these responses. At a time when fears about cultural commodification were high, the bus conductor's treatment of an opera as a tourist attraction threatened the boundaries between art and commerce. Whitaker's ambivalence was even harder to miss. While the image of an admiral standing in the gallery played into utopian representations of Sadler's Wells as a place where class took a back seat to culture, the transformation of a traditionally austere opera audience into a crowd of football zealots revealed the darker side of the same coin. In going on to compare *Grimes*'s success to the spread of measles, Whitaker laid bare its pathological implications.

For this reason, several commentators attempted to distance Britten's opera from its own reception, as though it were something of an innocent host in the spread of this cultural epidemic. One critic raised the possibility of journalistic exaggeration, while another admitted difficulty in maintaining critical distance: "Our emotions were too strongly stimulated with memories of the past and this plunge into the future gave us no time to collect our thoughts."[11] In stressing Britten's rejection of the popular Italian mold, Whitaker went even further to imply that the opera had garnered popularity despite itself: "Peter Grimes," he reported defensively, had "never a melody to stick in the memory, no glamorous, erring heroine, no exotic foreign setting—and not a single singer over 12 stone or so."[12] Not confined to early critics, this defensiveness has taken root in scholarship too. While some have emphasized the plot's existential realism, others have fashioned a *Grimes* that was emphatically more Schoenberg than Puccini.[13] Donald

Mitchell, for instance, has recounted tales of jeering critics and a resigning cast in order to stress the shock and indignation of mid-century audiences: "It may be difficult, certainly, to re-imagine the first, sharp shock that was part of the early experience of *Grimes*, not only a shock in musical terms but also a *culture* shock: it was a work that appeared . . . radically to overturn the expectations and conventions that the image of opera summoned up."[14] For all this, however, *Grimes* was never as shocking as Mitchell and others would have us believe. In fact, in anxiously stressing the opera's uncompromising realism and difficulty, Mitchell was not returning us to some original state of indignation so much as picking up the early reception's defensive thread. For even the earliest critics reacted in similarly apologetic ways, apparently worrying that *Grimes* was neither realistic nor difficult enough.

In this chapter, I want to return to June 1945, the time of *Grimes*'s now-mythic premiere. By tracing tropes of realism, difficulty, and transgression back to their mid-century roots, I will show that they were, from the very beginning, designed to obscure as much as they reveal. As I elaborate how early commentators sought to style *Grimes* as an emblem of modernist realism and difficulty, I will also uncover those "sentimental" aspects that they struggled to erase: its idealized image of love; its melodramatic staging of good and evil; its evocation of sympathy; and its musical lyricism. Ultimately, my intention is not to rebuke past commentators for their subtractive reactions but to ask what it was that encouraged their selectiveness.

OPERA AND SENTIMENTALITY

In a context in which popularity was regarded as a mark against an artwork's integrity, it is hardly surprising that commentators responded nervously to *Grimes*'s success. However, in reporting a reception that was not merely enthusiastic but flagrantly emotive, critics gestured toward a more specific problem than popularity. After all, images of audiences "possessed" by the opera and cheering uncontrollably at the end stood as classic symptoms of sentimentality, an affliction that had been diagnosed by I. A. Richards, one of the torchbearers of modernist criticism.[15] According to Richards, sentimentality implied, first and foremost, a form of quantitative excess: "a response is sentimental," he explained, "if it is too great for the occasion."[16] It also had a qualitative dimension, implying a crudeness of emotion quite separate from its intensity.[17] The third and final definition stressed a certain narrowness of vision, as if viewing art and the world through rose-tinted spectacles.[18] The common thread was that sentimentality substituted an easy and unrealistic response for the kind of intellectually challenging engagement that modernist critics were eager to promote.

In elaborating a theory of sentimentality, Richards was primarily concerned with a mode of reception, with the kinds of poetic "misreadings" he came across in criticism. At the same time, he suggested that certain poems—particularly those of the Victorian and Georgian writers—invited sentimentality more than others.[19] These poems apparently deployed hackneyed ideas and situations in order to elicit common emotional responses: "such stock poems are frequently very popular; they come home to a majority of readers with a minimum of trouble, for no outlook, no new direction of feeling is required."[20] By the time Q. D. Leavis published *Fiction and the Reading Public* in 1932, antipathy toward sentimentality had blossomed into a full-blown thesis about the great divide: that the difference between highbrow novels and best-selling fiction was tantamount to the distinction between realism and sentimentality. The best sellers of her day, she argued, had guaranteed their popularity by regurgitating the most artificial and emotive story lines of the nineteenth century, affording readers maximum emotional stimulation with a minimum of effort.[21]

Against this backdrop, *Grimes*'s ambivalent reception begins to make sense. Often, the concept of sentimentality was invoked explicitly, usually as an example of what the opera was not. One critic lauded *Grimes* as a "tale without romance, sentiment or glamour."[22] Another insisted: "There is no facile emotionalism, no obvious operatic thrill or Mediterranean grand passion."[23] As we have seen, Whitaker's denials of Italian opera were even more specific.[24] Opera criticism clearly had its own sentimental benchmark: while the novels of Dickens and Trollope drew literary insults, "Mediterranean Opera"—the operas of Massenet, Gounod, Verdi, and, above all, Puccini—bore the brunt of musical anxiety. In their *Key to Opera*, published in 1943, Frank Howes and Philip Hope-Wallace cast Puccini's operas as "too sentimental for most English stomachs," belying assertions that they evinced "refinement of taste."[25] Even Mosco Carner, a staunch Puccinian, conceded:

> For a variety of causes we may feel out of sympathy with the world of Puccini's operas. There is his all-pervasive eroticism and sentimentality; he deliberately aims at our tearducts: two of his three most celebrated operas are "tear-jerkers" *in excelsis*. There is a streak of vulgarity—inevitable in fullblooded artists' instinct with animal vitality . . . Puccini does not set his sights high.[26]

In striving to identify what many found so unsettling about Puccini's operas, Carner came close to articulating a theory of operatic sentimentality: a calculated effort to manipulate the emotions of one's audience and a tendency to pander to the vulgarians. While the models of musical sentimentality differed, the implications remained the same as in literature: French and Italian Romantic opera was charged with tugging gratuitously at heartstrings, via story lines that were at once far-fetched and conventional.

DOWN AND OUT IN ALDEBURGH AND LONDON

One of the principal ways critics sought to distance *Grimes* from the fantastical aspects of operatic sentimentality was by invoking "realism"—a concept even more slippery than sentimentality. While one commentator insisted that the opera "is, and is meant to be, life in the raw," another contrasted its "real" and "English" subject matter with opera's traditionally "fantastic" and "far-fetched" plots.[27] If sentimentality was associated with rose-tinted representation, realism was the antidote. By the time Britten's opera was premiered, commentators could draw considerable critical support for oppositions between realism and sentimentality. F. R. Leavis would soon hold up the "great tradition" of realism against lowbrow sentimentality, while leftist critics were investing "new realism" with ethical and political imperatives.[28] "A good book," Edward Upward insisted in 1937, "is one that is true to life . . . [I]f its emotional generalisations about life are able to help us live rather than to beguile us or dope us, [it] must view the world realistically."[29] Montagu Slater, the opera's librettist, was even more emphatic: "To describe things as they are is a revolutionary act in itself."[30]

Perhaps the most obvious symptom of the period's realist concerns was in the exponential rise of the documentary film. As John Grierson explained, documentaries attempted to reflect "real life" accurately—in terms of both style and subject matter—at a time when cinema was attracted to sentimentality and artifice. "Its origins," he went so far as to suggest, "lay in sociological rather than aesthetic aims."[31] Such aspirations were taken even further by the Mass Observation movement, which conducted interviews and surveys with "ordinary" people all over the country.[32] Yet this urge to establish connection with working life, free from the conventions and exaggerations of bourgeois sentimentality, also left its mark on more established genres. While Barbara Nixon framed the Left Theatre plays as an antidote to "worthless, sentimental and romantic plays" and "grandiose melodramas," others held up Auden for bringing poetry into contact with "real life."[33]

Britten and Slater had both cut their teeth on social realism, collaborating with Grierson, Auden, Isherwood, and others on left-wing documentaries and theater throughout the 1930s.[34] While *Grimes* seemed to mark a turn from these preoccupations toward a genre that—by Britten's own admission—was ill suited to realism, it carried over some of the same aesthetic features and aspirations.[35] Adapted from George Crabbe's poem *The Borough,* published in 1810, the opera is set in Aldeburgh, the provincial home of a poverty-stricken fishing community. In a *Listener* article from 1941, which originally piqued Britten's interest, E. M. Forster cast Crabbe as a documentarist avant la lettre: "We are looking at an actual English tideway," he insisted, "and not at some vague vast imaginary waterfall, which crashes from nowhere to nowhere."[36] After the premiere, Peter Pears confirmed that it was Crabbe's "amazing powers of observation" that ultimately made Britten settle on *The Borough* as a source text.

It is perhaps unsurprising, then, that the creators chose to emphasize its realistic credentials when introducing the opera to the public. In the publicity materials distributed at the Wigmore Hall's Concert-Introduction, the producer Eric Crozier pitted both the source poem and the opera alike against the sentimental conventions of their respective genres:

FIG. 1. Original Set Design for the Borough Street Scene (June 1945). Photographer: Angus McBean. © Harvard Theatre Collection, Harvard University. Image reproduced courtesy of the Britten-Pears Library.

> *Crabbe* was a realist. At a time when poetic fashion shunned "low" subjects, [Crabbe] set out to describe daily life . . . in all its meanness and familiarity. In basing their opera on his poem, the composer and librettist have broken away from the romantic scenes and heroic situations of operatic fashion, setting their action and their people in a homelier native background.[37]

On the whole, early critics picked up this trope. Desmond Shawe-Taylor lauded Crabbe's "minute and realistic picture" as "neither flattering nor romantic," while others saved their biggest cheers for the opera itself. In a review titled "Opera for Tomorrow," Harold Sear applauded *Grimes's* brave new world of operatic realism, predicting new audiences would be attracted to the once-stylized and forbidding genre:

> It has often been said that the subject matter of opera is so fantastic, so far fetched that honest John Bull can hardly be expected to endure even the warblings of triple-starred angels in so poor a cause. Well, here we are on entirely new ground. Crabbe's folk are real enough and English enough in all conscience.[38]

According to many, the most sustained realism could be found in the mise-en-scène. As Crozier later explained, the aim "was to evoke those ordinary streets, the curiously distinctive shapes and textures and juxtapositions of Aldeburgh buildings and the particular quality of light that bathes them."[39] Modeled on designer Kenneth Green's native Southwold and Aldeburgh, the sets included a level of historical detail not usually encountered at Sadler's Wells. While the three-dimensional backdrops (see Fig. 1) made every roof tile and flint-stone visible to audiences, the forestage (see Fig. 2) was littered with workaday fishing props and objects (from boats and nets to ropes and pulleys).[40] Such fastidiousness was also evident in the costumes, which—being modeled on actual early nineteenth-century examples— departed from the company's usual practice of recycling costumes and sets. After praising the "detailed, realistic setting," one audience member added: "Kenneth Green's excellent scenery and costumes . . . have all the fascinations of a series of old prints."[41] Another commentator was even more explicit: "Kenneth Green's sets and costumes are more than beautiful: they are right."[42]

Such visual markers were echoed by the opera's text, which occasionally ges- tured toward a similar kind of naturalistic authenticity. Spread thinly throughout Slater's libretto are colloquial words and phrases, suggesting a documentarist's desire to capture local workers' idioms. Our first encounter with Balstrode in Act I sees him chasing off local boys with a string of maritime metaphors and clichés—"Shoo, you little barnacles! Up your anchors, hoist your sails"—while the second scene's choral round presents a more sustained encounter with fishermen's-speak:

> ALL
> Old Joe has gone fishing and
> Young Joe has gone fishing and
> You Know has gone fishing and
> Found them a shoal.
> Pull them in in handfuls,
> And in canfuls,
> And in panfuls
> Bring them in sweetly,
> Gut them completely,
> Pack them up neatly,
> Sell them discreetly,
> Oh, haul a-way . . .[43]

While such colloquialisms are few and far between, commentators seized upon them as signs of a broader linguistic naturalism. One winced at the parts that "come a trifle too near photography and everyday talk," while another was more positive: "the words of the libretto," he snapped defensively, "shift sometimes into the imagery of poetry but never depart far from the colloquial."[44] Yet another brought Britten's text setting into his realistic defense: "The greater part of the stage action is carried on in a sort of song-speech that keeps as faithfully as pos- sible to the accents and the rise and fall and easy flow of ordinary speech."[45]

If the dilapidated huts and Suffolk dialect convinced some of an authen- tic encounter with working-class life, this was bolstered by the actual setting of the first production in a theater in the heart of one of London's poorest districts.

FIG. 2. Ellen Orford and the Apprentice (June 1945). Photographer: Angus McBean. © Harvard Theatre Collection, Harvard University. Image reproduced courtesy of the Britten-Pears Library.

The Sadler's Wells Company was often championed in mythical terms for bringing opera into contact with "real life," accomplishing on an institutional level what *Grimes* was said to have achieved aesthetically.[46] Edward Dent's history of Sadler's Wells, published in 1945, even arranged photographs of the work's first production against illustrations of the wartime stage—when it functioned as a shelter for displaced locals—in ways that drew none-too-subtle connections between the opera's humble scenes and its staging in the "theatre for everybody."[47]

For all the attention devoted to accuracy and authenticity, however, there was more to "realism" than met the eyes and ears. Nixon insisted, "realism is concerned with the essence of a character, situation or problem, not only its apparent characteristics."[48] Grierson likewise stressed the importance of distinguishing "between a method which describes only the surface values of a subject, and the method which more explosively reveals the reality of it."[49] Drawing on modernism's value-laden metaphors of surface and depth, these writers stressed a commitment to capturing the underlying experience of working-class life, exposing difficulties, hardships, and injustices without flinching or sugarcoating. This was an objective to which the opera's creators apparently subscribed. Crozier spoke of a "selective realism," devoted as much to the inner experience of a particular place and its people as to the "outer" photographic representations.[50] In Britten's preface, he professed a similar faith in the representation of difficulty: "I wanted to express my awareness of the perpetual struggle of men and women whose livelihood depends on the sea."[51]

The realization of this concern was hardly subtle. *Grimes* not only is set against the background of working life but is "about" it in a more thematic sense. At the heart of the narrative is an overworked fisherman, persecuted by the local community after his apprentices' mysterious deaths-at-sea. While full explanation of the deaths is ultimately withheld, long hours and harsh working conditions are crucial to the tragedy. In Peter's account of the first death, unforgiving working conditions take center stage:

> PETER
> Picture what that day was like
> That evil day.
> We strained into the wind
> Heavily laden.
> We plunged into the wave's shuddering challenge
> Then the sea rose to a storm
> Over the gunwales,
> And the boy's silent reproach
> Turned to illness.
> Then home
> Among fishing nets
> Alone, alone, alone
> With a childish death![52]

In drawing connections between labor conditions, death, and alienation, this scene might appear more at home in leftist theater than in the opera house. While one critic commended its depictions as a "sober record of the life of the common people in a place where life was won hardly," another insisted that they "present a view of Regency life seen rarely on stage. We are away from the Quality Streets and gay pavilions."[53]

Occasionally, the opera included even more pointed jabs at capitalism, as several critics pointed out.[54] In the first scene, the lecherous preacher decries the reduction of workhouse children to commodities, while Grimes's downfall is elsewhere put down to his bourgeois aspirations:

PETER
They listen to money
These Borough gossips
I have my visions
Fiery visions.
They call me dreamer
They scoff at my dreams
And my ambition.
But I know a way
To answer the Borough
I'll win them over.

BALSTRODE
With the new prentice?

PETER
We'll sail together,
These Borough gossips
Listen to money
Only to money:
I'll fish the sea dry,
Sell the good catches—
That wealthy merchant
Grimes will set up
Household and shop
You will all see it!
I'll marry Ellen![55]

These dreams ultimately prove illusory. The protagonist's attempts to redeem himself through hard work are marked as increasingly futile as the narrative progresses. Already by the opening scene of the second act, Ellen Orford comes to a prescient realization:

ELLEN
This unrelenting work,
This grey, unresting industry,
What aim, what future, what peace
Will your hard profits buy?

. . .

You cannot buy your peace
You'll never stop the gossips' talk
With all the fish from out the sea
We were mistaken to have dreamed . . .
Peter! We've failed! We've failed!
[He cries out as if in agony. Then he strikes her. The basket falls][56]

From this moment onward, the protagonist proceeds through a downward spiral, culminating in his suicide: "The story," as one critic pointed out, "is the grim tale of an ambitious visionary Suffolk fisherman who, in reaching for the stars, causes the death of two apprentices and eventually, helpless against public feeling, commits suicide."[57] Given this trajectory, it is unsurprising that commentators reacted as they did, with one dubbing the opera a "realistic picture of grim life," and another concluding: "The tale is fierce, its development tragic."[58]

In championing the opera's realism, in other words, critics were alluding not just to its narrative of struggle but also its apparent pessimism. Nor is it difficult to see why: as Ben Singer has suggested, happy endings were strongly associated with sentimental melodramas, especially in the wake of modernism's infamous apocalypticism.[59] In fact, some cast Britten's opera not merely as a commentary on the "difficulty" of life—in the manner of *Traviata* or *Bohème*—but as a bleaker, even nihilistic, rejection of life itself.[60] One reporter mused on the opera's Kafkaesque trajectory, while another imagined it surpassing even *Elektra*, *Wozzeck*, and *Lady Macbeth of the Mtsensk District* in its harrowing cynicism:

> [T]his is about the last literary subject in the world which can be imagined in the form of an opera. It is gloomy, harrowing and depressing in the extreme, whereas the fundamental fact about opera is, historically and in the matter of its general practice, that it is festive—and to this even such grim specimens such as "Elektra," "Wozzeck," and "A Lady Macbeth" are not altogether exceptions.[61]

Invoking images of darkness and "gloom," commentators were writing literally as well as metaphorically. One of the ways that Crozier and Green advertised the work's pessimism was by plunging the stage into progressive darkness. While one commentator pleaded for "a little more light . . . at the beginning and end of the main action," another sighed: "the décor was on the whole most effective, though I felt the lighting (or rather the lack of it) was rather overdone."[62] For all the complaints, though, this staple of modernist realism—apparently common in Slater's own plays—succeeded in making the point.[63] After adding to the protests, one commentator ran with the symbolism anyway. "At times, the gloom is too profound: when night falls on the Borough, it is dark indeed, without glimmer of moon or star."[64]

SENTIMENTAL REALISM

In foregrounding the opera's literal and metaphorical darkness, its violent images of poverty and suffering, commentators were fashioning a realism compatible with modernism.[65] Just as important: they were advertising the opera's categorical rejection of sentimentality. In wielding realism against sentimentality in this way, however, critics were on shaky ground. While many mid-century commentators pitted the two modes against each other in ways that line up with the opera's reception, others threatened to wash away these precariously drawn lines in the sand. In an essay from 1940, George Orwell argued that Dickensian "realism" was actually a form of "middle-class sentimentality": "[Dickens] sees the world as a middle-class world . . . He is vaguely on the side of the working class—has a sort of generalized sympathy with them because they are oppressed—but he does not in reality know much about them."[66] Nor was Orwell's own generation immune to this problem. Where Virginia Woolf accused Auden, Isherwood, and other "leaning tower" poets of ambivalence and insincerity, Orwell turned the documentary lens on his own *nostalgie de la boue*:

> When I thought of poverty . . . my mind turned immediately towards extreme cases, the social outcasts: tramps, beggars, criminals, prostitutes. These were "the lowest of the low," and they were the people with whom I wanted to get in contact.[67]

In going on to describe class boundaries as a "plate-glass pane of an aquarium," Orwell implied that genuine contact was as undesirable as it was impossible. Just as no one would actually want to live among the fishes, so realism's appeal lay in a kind of voyeuristic spectacle, in which middle-class readers could experience the *illusion* of working-class contact without the water gushing in—that is, without compromising their own privileged positions and traditions.[68]

These discussions implicate *Grimes* on multiple levels. In the year of its premiere, Dent cast Orwellian aspersions on the opera's institutional setting. Taking issue with the idea of Sadler's Wells as a "theatre for everybody," which he otherwise helped to promote, he implied that the opera house thrived instead on a form of middle-class voyeurism:

> [Lilian] Baylis may honestly have believed that in both regions there was a culture-starved proletariat hungry for Shakespeare and Mozart, but in reality both theatres were kept going by middle-class audience that came from all parts of London and the suburbs . . . [F]or certain plays and operas, especially if any sort of star was performing, the audience was quite obviously a West End one.[69]

Beyond questions of West End audiences slumming in London's East End, this accusation cast shadows on the opera itself. As a handful of critics implied, *Grimes* could be said to offer a similar experience on the level of style and subject matter—that is, not an authentic engagement with working life but a stylized and sentimental vision for middle-class consumption.

Some of the most obvious strictures were leveled at the libretto. While one commended Slater's text as a masterpiece of "everyday speech" and another insisted that "little of the text is cast in set forms," an even greater number argued the opposite.[70] After lauding the opera's "sincerity and integrity as a whole," Dent complained of the text's "hackneyed . . . tricks of effect": "I have come to the conclusion," he explained, "that it is a mistake to try to write highly 'poetical' and 'literary' librettos. The poet ought to concentrate entirely on drama and absolute truth to human nature."[71] A large part of the problem was Slater's heightened poetic style. While the prosaic prologue came the closest to everyday speech, the greater part of the libretto was cast in four-beat lines with half rhymes. Slater spun the pattern as "appropriate for the quick conversational style of the recitatives," but its effect seems more like a compromise between realistic prose or free verse on the one hand, and the grandiloquent five-stress line form on the other.[72] When it came to more static operatic numbers, Slater was unapologetically "poetical." As the curtain rises on Act I, the chorus of fishermen and women borrows heroic couplets from Crabbe's original, singing of life's difficulties in iambic pentameter:

CHORUS OF FISHERMEN AND WOMEN

CHORUS
Oh hang at open doors the net, the cork,
While squalid sea-dames at their mending work.
Welcome the hour when fishing through the tide.
The weary husband throws his freight aside.

FISHERMEN
O cold and wet and driven by the tide,
Beat your tired arms against your tarry side.
Find rest in public bars where fiery gin
Will aid the warmth that languishes within.[73]

In casting aspersions on such passages, commentators were responding not just to poetic eloquence but also to philosophical abstraction.[74] In "What Harbour Shelters Peace?" (Act I, Scene 1), Grimes extends the storm metaphor in order to describe his own suffering. His subsequent aria invokes astrology to reflect upon the nature of fate:

PETER
Now the great Bear and Pleiades
where earth moves
Are drawing up the clouds
of human grief
Breathing solemnity in the deep night.

Who can decipher
In storm or starlight
The written character
of a friendly fate—
As the sky turns, the world for us to change?

But if the horoscope's
Bewildering
Like a flashing turmoil
of a shoal of herring
Who can turn skies back and begin again?[75]

In response to such scenes, some raised concerns about abstraction—noting that "it strains my sense of the appropriate when . . . Grimes starts philosophizing in this fashion"—and added elevated vocabulary to Slater's list of sins.[76] Ernest Newman complained of "bookish diction," while Dent implored the librettist to "use the very simplest words which everybody can understand."[77] These concerns were exacerbated by the context of Grimes's starry-eyed soliloquy, coming as it did directly before the aforementioned sea shanty: "I could wish," Newman explained, "that some of the dialogue had been less colloquial and some of the more highly strung passages less 'literary.'"[78] Tyrone Guthrie was even more emphatic on this point: "Britten is not consistent: snatches of verismo are interpolated with the boldly abstract expression of atmosphere and emotion."[79]

Such concerns were not limited to the critical reception, but were a source of tension in planning, as Crozier and Britten apparently fought with Slater to eliminate his "purple patches."[80] They also spoke to wider debates within the literary world. If Woolf often complained of eclectic passages just like *Grimes's* pub scene—"cracked in the middle" between beauty and reality—she elsewhere cast aspersions on the broader paradox of "realistic" poetry: "[Poetry] has never been used for the common purpose of life . . . Her accent is too marked; her manner too emphatic. She gives us instead lovely lyric cries of passion."[81] As a prose writer who felt excluded from poetry on the grounds of gender instead of class, Woolf had her own reasons for railing against realistic poetry. Yet she also captured wider concerns. Much like *Grimes's* critics, Woolf jeered at the gap between poetry's exalted register and the "real life" it strove to represent. At the same time, she clarified that the problem was not simply one of stylistic propriety. Poetry's pattern of iambs and dactyls, its metaphors and abstractions—she insisted— risked redeeming an otherwise bleak existence, sentimentalizing its supposedly unromantic meaning.

Where some critics echoed Woolf, identifying stylistic tension between realism and sentimentality, others implied that the subject matter pulled in contradictory directions too. While the difficulties of working life are often center stage, they occasionally recede, as backdrops—or even foils—to explicitly sentimental tropes. The most obvious is the love story, which had commentators writhing in their seats. After conceding that "one woman stands out from the crowd, the gentle schoolmistress, whom Peter loves," one critic hedged: "But as love does not affect his actions its value as a dramatic theme is not important."[82] Others opted for outright denial: in this "somber tale of an ill-adjusted fisherman, there is no love interest."[83] Titling an entire subsection "Love Is Abolished," another commentator explained:

> Mr. Slater was further commissioned to avoid the well-trodden paths of the librettist of opera. The great stand-by of composers and dramatists, the love passion, was to be avoided at all costs as it was felt, no doubt, that such feelings would be alien to a race described by Crabbe as fierce, intolerant of check and curb on its primitive instinct.[84]

Such assertions are curious not only because the love potential between Ellen and Grimes persists throughout, but also because it was added to Crabbe's poem, presumably to provide precisely the "conventional" intrigue that critics denied. Ellen is, as it were, Elisabeth to Grimes's Tannhaüser; as she strives to set him on the straight and narrow and restore his name, her love, compassion, and friendship promise redemption. After the noise and violence of the courtroom prologue, Ellen brings the protagonist back from the angry brink: "My voice out of the pain," she sings, "Is like a hand / That you can feel and know: / Here is a friend."[85] Elsewhere she is cast as a shelter from the storm:

> PETER
> What harbour shelters peace?
> Away from tidal waves, away from storm
> What harbour can embrace
> Terrors and tragedies?
> With her there'll be no quarrels
> With her the mood will stay,
> A habour evermore
> Where night is turned to day.[86]

Contrary to claims that Britten's opera was entirely without light, this aria seems to foreground the tension between day and night, love and suffering, as a central theme. Although commentators may have been right to cite the tragic conclusion as evidence that the opera was not just another heartwarming romance, the problem remained that—at several points—it comes perilously close.[87]

Although "love interest" was the sorest spot, it was not the only aspect that threatened a sentimental spin. As Newman pointed out, romantic love was part of the broader humanistic strain that Slater injected into Crabbe's original scenario. After praising the librettist for taking the poet's characters "from under the sometimes pitiless glass of the poet's microscope, and mak[ing] them breathe and move in company," he added Balstrode's "bluff, honest seafaring humanity" to the limited list of benevolent types.[88] If Ellen sides unequivocally with the persecuted Grimes, Balstrode extends compassion to whomever is in need. After protecting Auntie's "nieces" and their lecherous aggressor (Bob Boles), Balstrode implores everyone to get along:

> BALSTRODE
> Pub conversation should depend
> On this eternal moral;
> So long as satire don't descend to
> To fisticuff or quarrel.
> We live and let live, and look
> We keep our hands to ourselves.
>
> *And while Boles is being forced to his chair again, the bystanders comment:*

CHORUS
We live and let live, and look
We keep our hands to ourselves.

BALSTRODE
We sit and drink the evening through
Not deigning to devote a
Thought to the daily cud we chew
But buying drinks by rota.[89]

As the chorus takes up Balstrode's refrain to the lilting rhythms of an operatic drinking song, the Borough sounds less like the violent mob of Gissing's *Nether World* (1889) and more like the Plornishes from *Little Dorrit* (1855–57)—people who endure their suffering with fortitude and good humor. Much as in the opening chorus, the pub is imagined as a place of respite and solidarity, where human bonds are forged through a shared sense of stoicism—a common commitment to enjoying life despite.

Even when Slater's libretto offered less redemptive visions, the sentimental specter loomed nevertheless. Although most critics saw darkness and pessimism as signs of modernist realism, Joseph Kerman took a different tack:

> The libretto is not only effective, it is positively slick, reading sometimes like a textbook of tried devices of verismo melodrama—the milling chorus, the tavern scene, the storm, the fight on-stage, the set song, the stage-band and all the rest. Local colour is spread on much too thick, with emphasis on the seamy side of village life; and though Britten makes good and legitimate use of it, the general effect would seem more appropriate to [*Porgy and Bess's*] Catfish Row.[90]

For Kerman, *Grimes's* bleakest moments were its most affected and sentimental. To his compilation of working-class clichés, we might add drunkenness, drug addiction, domestic violence, workhouse orphans, maltreatment of children, and prostitution. With these images in mind, it is hard not to think of Orwell's aestheticization of dirt—a voyeuristic spectacle of suffering staged less as a window into reality than as a stylized means of evoking cathartic sympathy.

SYMPATHY AND THE SENTIMENTALIST'S GRIMES

If the foregoing patterns, styles, and tropes suggested sentimentality, the issue of sympathy cut right to its heart. While Richards defined sentimentality primarily as a mode of reception, James Chandler has more recently associated it with contrivance about audience sympathy, as if the affective response were somehow inscribed within a sentimental text. Drawing on a visual metaphor to describe relationships between characters and the audience, he explained: "The spectator faces the virtual action of the printed text, but that action is itself often constituted by the interaction of virtual faces viewed by virtual eyes."[91] Chandler elaborated that this "orthogonal (or triangular) structure[—]the spectator who beholds what amounts to a mutual beholding on the part of two other parties [within the narrative]—becomes a hallmark of the sentimental mode and its way of making a world." If sentimental artworks are those that not only elicit emotional responses but also represent them in their narratives, *Peter Grimes* is no exception. Running alongside its themes of poverty, hardship, and suffering is an interrogation of the affective dilemmas that they pose. According to some critics, the opera was as much about responses to Grimes as about the title character himself, with the chorus often serving as a proxy for the audience's interpretive dilemmas and vacillations.[92]

From the moment the curtains rise on Grimes's inquest, self-consciousness about how to respond takes center stage. Sympathy had long been associated with moral judgment, with the trial scene functioning as a sentimental conceit—a way of staging oppositions between good and evil, sympathy and an absence thereof.[93] But while Dickensian readers are usually privy to information hidden from judge and jury, *Grimes*'s audience is left in the dark in yet another way: it lacks sufficient evidence to arbitrate between contradictory responses to the protagonist's testimony. The Borough gossips respond with passionate hostility, casting moral aspersions while refusing to feel sympathy. Swallow comes to a similar position via a different route, modeling a legalistic—even mechanical—detachment: "Peter Grimes," he declaims with stiff, staccato rhythms, "we are here to investigate the cause of / death of your apprentice William Spode, whose body / you brought ashore from your boat, 'The Boy Billy' on / the 26th ultimo. Do you wish to give evidence?"[94] At the other end of the spectrum is Ellen, who stands and feels with Grimes as though his suffering were her own. "I did what I could to help," she explains, inaugurating her role as the Borough's long-suffering teacher of sympathy.

According to several commentators, Britten's music was on her side. When Swallow instructs Grimes to take the stand with dry, brash, wind-punctuated patter, the protagonist's slow, pathetic string dominant sevenths and chant-like response invite an altogether more sympathetic hearing (Ex. 1). "The strings in the prologue," William Glock remarked, "express beyond a doubt the composer's tender attitude towards Grimes."[95] When the Borough chorus enters immediately afterward, the sinister whispers, noisy crescendo, and jagged vocal lines set the protagonist's "tender" accompaniment in even sharper relief.

This melodramatic opposition returns in Grimes's "Now the Great Bear and Pleiades" aria (Act I, Scene 1), where his aforementioned poetic eloquence and sensitivity are brought out by comparable musical signs. As the townsfolk guzzle ale and banter noisily, the protagonist bursts into the pub, looks to the sky, and sings of the stars with the same shimmering string halo and floating melody as in the prologue. After responding, "he's mad or drunk . . . his song alone would sour the beer," the chorus descends into a harsh, patter-filled round that swells into a harrowing mass of sound. This image is reinforced by the text, which moves quickly

EX. 1. *Peter Grimes* (Prologue)—"Take the Oath".

from the playful "Old Joe has gone fishing" refrain to altogether more sadistic imagery: "Gut them completely / Pack them up neatly / Sell them completely."[96] One commentator put it mildly, observing: "There is supposed to be something poetic and elemental about [Grimes] that sets him apart from the bickering and petty gossip of the township."[97] Others appealed to the music too, citing both the "beauty" of Grimes's vision and the musical "anger" directed at his Borough foes.[98]

Evidently touchy about such melodramatic gestures, some commentators were defensive: "[Grimes] is not presented as a worthy character (that would be too much)," one commentator explained, "but as an outcast: romantic, Byronic and misunderstood."[99] Others denounced the "romanticized hero" explicitly, lamenting that the "sadistic side of 'Peter Grimes's' complex nature [was] watered down as compared with Crabbe."[100] Robin Holloway, writing in 1964, went even further to complain of "artistic falsification":

> In Crabbe's poem the hero was a straightforward ruffian . . . a thoroughly anti-social person whom the crowd did right to persecute. But in Britten's intensely sentimental version Grimes has become the outcast from society, the lonely, sensitive-souled visionary (in itself a romantic cliché) and the crowd an aggressive, destructive force.[101]

This "struggle of the individual against the masses" was not just a romantic staple but also, by his own admission, "a subject very close to [Britten's] heart."[102] At *Grimes*'s premiere, however, it touched several nerves. Some commentators raised aesthetic objections, citing its status as operatic cliché, much as Holloway would later do. Others had moral reservations about what kinds of characters merit sympathy and to what effect: "Despite attempts to present this bully in a sympathetic light with the help of Ellen Orford," one critic proclaimed, "he remains a repellent character whose fate arouses little pity."[103] Shawe-Taylor was even more combative: "what neither composer nor librettist seems to realize is that, after all, the sympathetic schoolmarm was wrong . . . whereas poor Mrs. Sedley was dead right."[104] For some, in other words, the problem was evidently not sympathy per se but the unworthy character upon whom it was bestowed.

The majority, however, parting company with those who bemoaned Grimes's heroism, praised the "modern" opera for avoiding precisely this trope. "Determined to avoid anything smacking of conventional opera," one commentator explained, "the composer and his librettist . . . have given us an opera, which has [no] hero."[105] "Peter," the critic concluded enthusiastically, "does not and is not meant to engage very deeply our sympathies." Where some saw the chorus as purposefully dissolving sympathy for the protagonist, others thought him capable of doing that for himself. One reviewer gleefully invoked the "grim and, it must be said, unlikable figure of Peter Grimes" while others drew connections with infamous modernist miscreants. Comparing Britten's opera to Shostakovich's *Lady Macbeth*, one commentator enthused: "In both, we have an unromantic central figure, repelling rather than engaging sympathy."[106] Anti-heroism had recently become a benchmark in mid-century criticism, a way of sorting high from low.[107] As F. R. Leavis's "Diabolic Intellect and the Noble Hero" essay makes clear, defending a work from sentimentality in this period often—somewhat counterintuitively—involved debunking or even denouncing its protagonist.[108]

For those wanting to add Grimes to the expanding canon of anti-heroes, the disagreeable traits were there. "He is seen in the prologue," one commentator noted, "accused of causing the death of a first apprentice at sea; then we see him contriving the death of a second apprentice; he finally appears as a raving lunatic who goes to seek death by drowning in the raging sea."[109] As several critics pointed out, there were musical sides to *Grimes*'s sadism too. After concluding that "this hero remains curiously negative," one commentator offered musical evidence up to the prosecution's bench: "The music which presents Grimes himself—in the witness-box, in his fierce approaches to Ellen, in that half-drunken outburst which silences the brawling pub, above all in that curious scene of muttering self-communing . . . is music of an uncannily chilled and anguished sort."[110]

Yet this was only one side of the story, and those who asserted Grimes's antiheroism had also to explain away some heroic tropes, such as his aforementioned love for Ellen. Indeed, the very fact that critics were able to espouse such contradictory perspectives suggests that the protagonist was more ambivalent than either side cared to let on. While most of the opera has Grimes shuttling back and forth between saint and sinner, the Act III, Scene 2 "mad scene" sets this conflict in relief (see Figs. 49–51 in the published score). As the chorus chants his name, doubling as the voice of the approaching Borough and those in the protagonist's head, Grimes's mutterings mark him as the best and worst of all the cast: the violence of the Borough, Ellen's hope and compassion, not to mention his own moments of visionary eloquence. This tension is matched by a corresponding musical struggle: between the Borough's speech-like patter and Ellen's redemptive lyricism. From this extended rumination upon his name and identity, Grimes emerges as a patchwork of textual and musical quotations; his subjectivity less a stable substance than an ongoing reaction between disparate impulses and traits. "[T]he opera," as William McNaught pointed out enthusiastically, is "a study of a distempered character, at once the victim and maker of his evil fate."[111]

If a handful recognized this complexity, it did not make them more openminded about the question of sympathy. On the contrary, in the fight against sentimentality, these tensions and struggles became yet another line of defense. After all, such ambivalent visions were advanced by post-Freudian critics to confound the supposedly crude binaries of Victorian sympathy. Modernism's fragmented subjects—Eliot's Prufrock, Joyce's Bloom, Berg's Wozzeck—were seen as more psychologically "realistic."[112] Some of Grimes's defenders appealed to these notions, describing him as a "real man," "very far from the common operatic conventions," while Peter Pears proudly cast him as neither hero nor villain but "an ordinary weak person."[113] Hans Keller gave this an explicitly Freudian spin: "His pride, ambition, and urge for independence fight with the need for love; his self-love battles against his self-hate."[114]

For Q. D. Leavis, these warring psyches—typical of literary modernism—were more inimical to sympathy than straightforwardly anti-heroic ones, and Britten's critics apparently agreed. One, writing about the mad scene in particular, suggested that "the strokes by which the revelation was made" were neither cogent nor coherent enough to elicit sympathy: "We never really meet the man. His death breaks no heart. His suicide is a mere item of police court news."[115] For Keller, however—writing against the grain of contemporary criticism—these complexities and tensions were less a rejection of sympathy than an invitation to it: "in each of us there is something of a Grimes, though most of us have outgrown or at least outwitted him sufficiently not to recognize him too consciously."[116] "But we do identify him," he concluded, "and ourselves with him, unconsciously, which is one reason for the universal appeal of the work."[117] While most mid-century critics associated sympathy with black-and-white moralism, Keller instead insisted that it was the opposite: the struggles, tensions, and ambivalence that compelled sympathetic response instead. Nor is this all that surprising; as, from Dickens's Nancy, through Hardy's Tess, to Verdi's Violetta, moral struggle was a well-established romantic convention of evoking sympathy—indeed, one with a considerably longer heritage than even Keller's Freudian diction would suggest.[118] Only one critic suggested as much, insisting: "The poet's powerful study . . . would not have made, just as it stands, satisfactory material for opera, if only for the reason that brutality and final madness so unrelieved would have chilled the sympathies of the audience."[119] "Mr. Slater," he noted, "has wisely shown the self-haunted man as a complex of warring impulses, fatally prone to harshness but with a vein of poetic imagination running through him, a frustrated sensitive who breaks himself against the sharp angles of the world." Yet it was this same romantic convention of unconventionality that allowed critics to play up sentimentality's associations with morality, re-writing its nineteenth-century history as more moralistic than it was. In this, they had a pointed objective in mind; by doing so, they could distance Britten's opera from long-standing conventions of evoking sympathy even as it drew on them all the same.

MUSIC UNDER ERASURE

Discussions of Britten's score were just as fraught, matching the long list of literary denials—of poetry, love interest, redemption, sympathy—with a musical lineup just as elaborate. On the most general level, this meant disavowing connections with nineteenth-century opera, in its infamous artificiality, emotionalism, and excess. Whitaker, we might recall, insisted that *Grimes* resisted Italian opera's easy conventions and he was not the only one.[120] "[I]t will not do," another critic warned, "to listen to [the work] in the constant hope of something happening that will bring it into the category of standard opera."[121]

For most commentators, "operatic" meant lyrical: "There is little, on the whole, for the Butcher Boy to whistle on his rounds" enthused one critic, following a remarkably common trope.[122] As we have seen, lyricism was associated with sympathy, but there was more to it than that. In refusing to write "good singable tunes," the composer could bolster his modernist musical credentials: "With the courage of youth, Britten casts aside all convention. There is no love duet, no coquetting Musetta, or melodious Mimi, no Prize or Flower song."[123] For other commentators, realism was at stake: "Sombrely realistic," one critic insisted, "there are no catchy airs."[124]

These assertions were selective at best. If one critic could insist, with relatively clear conscience, that the action "rarely halts for purely 'operatic' purposes," this was arguably because musical numbers were written into the narrative: the workers' choruses and drinking rounds; the Church *scena*, based on an actual hymn; the tavern dance; and so on. These set pieces had a long history in nineteenth-century opera, but—as Arman Schwartz has explained—they took on heightened significance in the push for operatic realism.[125] Yet these "self-justifying performances"— to borrow Schwartz's phrase—were not the only extended numbers. Britten's own professed eschewal of Wagner's "'permanent melody'" in favor of "separate numbers that crystalize and hold the emotion of a dramatic situation" was evident throughout the score.[126] The Act II women's quartet bears a striking resemblance to Strauss's *Rosenkavalier* trio, and Ellen could indeed easily be described as the Borough's "melodious Mimi": every time she opens her mouth, we hear luscious strings, angelic harps, and sumptuous lyricism that seems to halt dramatic time.[127] When Ellen passes her lyricism on to Grimes at the end of the prologue (Ex. 2), we hear the stirrings of the kind of love duet that critics anxiously denied:

In this example, the jagged edges of Grimes's speech-like "agitato" collide with, then give way to, Ellen's soaring lyricism; before we move into the duet proper, the star-crossed lovers come together vocally and harmonically as Peter gives up his somber F minor and joins Ellen on a sustained high E (m. 18). As we move into this short duet, in which they declare their friendship in almost matrimonial unison with swooping gestures and sequential thirds, Puccini could easily be put in one's mind. It is not, however, just the melody that focuses attention on this moment of lyrical reconciliation; it is also the text, which is "about" the voice's redemptive power. Slater's metaphorical invocation is, in other words, actualized by Britten's setting: Peter and Ellen begin singing about singing to each other, and about melody's capacity to elicit sympathy out of pain.

In erasing these passages, critics were rehearsing their concerns about what we might call redemption through melody; yet their anxieties were not without grounds in the score. After all, the text itself proves rather anti-climactic, culminating less in a passionate declaration of love than in an agape-driven promise of friendship. These tensions were present in the music too. Even at its most mellifluous, Britten's music often undermines its own lyricism, as if to invite the defensive

EX. 2. *Peter Grimes* (Prologue)—Love Duet.

EX. 2 (continued).

reactions it received. While the love duet mimics the gestures of nineteenth-century Italian opera, it is riven by harmonic tensions and ambiguities. Admittedly Britten's note-spelling—putting a D♭ arbitrarily in place of C#—makes the melody look more awkward than it actually sounds. Nevertheless, the passage constantly shifts harmonic focus, passing quickly through 11 out of 12 notes in the chromatic scale. The lack of accompaniment compounds this meandering effect. And while the melody's swooping gesture smacks of Italianate lyricism, the minor ninth is quite difficult to sing, as if the result of an octave leap pushed too far. If this characteristic interval implies overstretching, Britten's dynamic markings suggest the opposite impulse: to pull away from lyricism at its most cathartic moments. Instead of swelling into the climactic notes on "voice" and "hand," the composer backs away, moving against the expansive lyricism of the opening.

Britten's "love duet" is neither the only nor even the most obvious instance in which lyricism is at first advanced and then retracted. When describing "that evil night" when his apprentice died, Grimes's melodies are interrupted and scrubbed out by contradictory material (Ex. 3). To the same rising minor ninth in a now more symmetrical vocal line, the orchestra responds with short, brash, and violently syncopated chromatic half-steps. Elsewhere, it is Peter himself that interrupts, "checking" himself—as one critic described it—"on the verge of simple melody."[128] In the opening of "What Harbour Shelters Peace", a variant of the same melody—now sporting a major ninth—is reined in by speech-like and tonally disruptive interjections (Ex. 4). In the continuation of this aria, where Grimes's lyricism is allowed to blossom into something resembling a climax (Ex. 5), the composer finds other means of undermining his sentimental melodies. Even as Grimes works his way up to his melodic peak—now bolstered by a dominant pedal

EX. 3. *Peter Grimes* (Act I, Scene 1)—"We Plunged into the Waves".

EX. 4. *Peter Grimes* (Act I, Scene 1)—"What Harbour Shelters Peace".

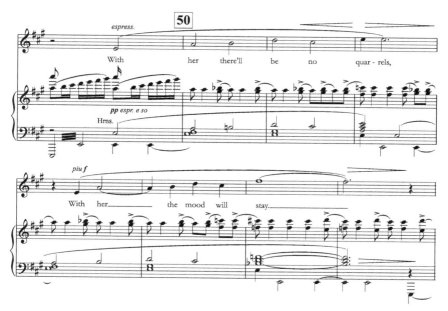

EX. 5. *Peter Grimes* (Act I, Scene 1)—"With Her There'll Be No Quarrels".

with doubling horns and cellos—we hear storms brewing in the syncopated string dissonances. The B♭/E juxtaposition on the word "stay" has a similarly destabilizing effect, poised uneasily between romantic coloration and dissonant irony.

This shuttling back and forth between melody and speech, lyricism and its erasure, made the sentimental melodies less conspicuous, allowing critics to disavow them. In following Grimes's lyrical harbor with the famously violent orchestral "storm" interlude, moreover, Britten matched these local-level gestures of erasure with larger, formal ones. For almost as common as denials of vocal lyricism was a tendency to overwrite it with moments of orchestral prowess. One commentator followed his quip about there being neither Prize nor Flower song with an instrumental substitute: "'My theme is mob and the sea' [Britten] seems to say 'and the orchestra tells their story.'"[129] Apart from the "rare" lyrical outpourings, another insisted: "the main burden . . . is laid on the orchestra in a number of interludes."[130] "[P]articularly impressive," he enthused, "are the prelude (and postlude) to the opera that defines the grey atmosphere of the hard-bitten little fishing town, the brooding night-piece that introduces Act III, and the superb passacaglia between the first and second scenes of Act II."[131] This praise was obviously bound up with the opera's much-vaunted realism. Where some found authenticity in the harrowing subject matter, detailed sets, or speech-like utterances, others evidently found it in the orchestral imagery: "Britten has written salt-water music of unequalled intensity—the sting and crash and the scream of great waters have never been caught and translated into music with such fidelity."[132]

In some respects, this response was unsurprising. Britten's preface trumpeted his own firsthand experience of the Suffolk seascape, and his time in the documentary film unit was nothing if not an apprenticeship in faithfully rendering "objective" sounds.[133] Much like the composer's melodies, however, his "realism" was conflicted. The fifth interlude harks back to the nineteenth-century tone poem, which would have been considered sentimental by "new" realists of Britten's own time.[134] With the exception of the sporadic chinks of "moonlight" in the flute, harp, and percussion, it represents its maritime subject matter only in the most general sense: the expansive phrases and swells evoke oceanic grandeur, but the emphasis seems to be on the solidly "musical" criteria of formal proportion and development. At the other end of the spectrum is the sixth interlude, which comes as close as possible to the documentary ideal of pure, unmediated sound: after the opening burst of white noise—including snare drum, rattle, and whip—the only consistent feature is the unrelenting drone of the horn chord. Against this musical fog, we hear snippets that, while based on prior motifs, invite hearing as evocative but elusive sound effects.

While these orchestral portraits demonstrate Britten's extremes, his now-famous "storm" interlude was more representative: at times, confounding oppositions between music and sound; at others, shuttling back and forth between them. Much like the fifth interlude, it begins with musical processes front and center: a mock fugue, itself based on the choral fugato from the previous scene ("Now the flood tide"). Yet even here, alterations to the once-lyrical melody—thematic fragmentation, oscillating patterns, and chromatic scales at breakneck speed—threaten to derail the counterpoint into noise. This is compounded by the "nonsensical" dissonance—as one critic described it—of the Phrygian seconds: "dissonance has been heard [before]," another commentator noted, "but Britten's music runs from perky jigs in the woodwind to forceful, dissonant barkings in the brass."[135] The threat of disintegration is realized in the interlude's "Molto animato" section at Fig. 58 (in the published score), where spiraling sequences erupt into a sonic picture evading "musical" sense: wave-like crashes of brass and percussion, fishlike flailing of woodwinds and contradictory rhythms. The fugal order reestablishes itself at Fig. 59, but it soon dissolves again into sound. In the run-up to Fig. 60, the gentle hum of the seascape sets the stage for an orchestral reprise of "What Harbour Shelters Peace." If this "aria" originally staged a tension between lyricism and speech, its re-appearance here—with its slow A-major string melody pitted against the staccato seaside effects—at Fig. 60 implicates a broader opposition between music and noise.

Critics naturally sought to diffuse this tension, whether by supplementing melodic denials with those of music generally; or by casting Britten's score as unmediated sound: "it is full of eerie sounds, of terrifying silences, of monotonous sea waves, and in one scene a recurrent fog horn."[136] These strategies had the advantage of speaking to popular images of musical modernism as "noise" while bolstering what Schwartz describes as the realist "fiction of authorial abdication."[137] But this rhetoric existed in tension with long-standing beliefs about music's deep-seated resistance to realism. Where Woolf saw poetry as capable of sentimentalizing the bleakest subjects, music was riskier still. Even Auden—the target of Woolf's critique—dubbed operatic realism a contradiction in terms, pitting the genre's subjectivism against the "impersonal necessity" and mechanical objectivity to which documentary aspired: "music is in essence dynamic, an expression of will and self-affirmation, and opera . . . is a virtuoso art."[138] "[A]n actor who sings," Auden concluded, "is an uncommon man, more a master of his fate . . . than an actor who speaks."

Given opera's image as the epitome of romanticism—"the last refuge," as Auden put it, "of the high style"—this position is not hard to understand.[139] Yet, as Schwartz has pointed out, verismo's sonic fantasies often performed the collapse of will and agency that Auden disallowed.[140] While scholars have tended to hear *Grimes*'s musical tensions through a psychological lens—extending the mad scene's struggles between good and evil—this context suggests something broader at stake. Indeed, it seems plausible that the shuttling back and forth between music and noise gestured less to fragmented subjectivity than to the erasure of subjectivity itself. Much like Schwartz's Tosca, Britten's protagonist often risks disappearing into the scenic void, "left by the lack of music."[141] Nor was this the first time that the composer used noise to evoke this dystopian idea. The threat of drowning out individual subjectivity by the machinery of modern industry, for instance, was an important theme in documentaries like *Coal Face* (1935), upon which both Britten and Slater worked. In this film about coal miners, the perspective veers between a "scientific" description of industrial systems, against which man is rendered insignificant, and a more "human" view where family relationships and friendships take center stage. As Philip Reed has argued, moreover, the composer and his collaborators often drew on precisely these dichotomies—between poetry and prose, singing and speech, music and noise—to draw this thematic tension out.[142]

In *Grimes,* it is the storm and seas that constantly threaten to erase subjectivity, giving the overwhelming force a potentially more romantic spin. From the working men's chorus beaten by the tide to the storm clouds gathering overhead, an indifferent nature threatens to wash away human life: "O Tide that waits for no man," the chorus pleads, "Spare our coasts!"[143] When the storm interlude finally hits, its tensions seem a reflection less of Grimes's psychological struggles than of the various vantage points—sympathetic or otherwise—from which they are viewed. This theme, introduced in the prologue, comes to a dramatic head in the final scene (Ex. 6). As Grimes stands reeling from his mad scene, we hear the "objective" sounds of the distant foghorn and Borough chorus while Ellen and Balstrode look on.[144] Echoing the prologue, Ellen interrupts the diegetic noise

EX. 6. *Peter Grimes* (Final Scene)—"Peter, We've Come to Take You Home".

by calling out with redemptive song. This time, however, Grimes appears not to notice, as she falls—flat and dejected—into reportorial speech (see Fig. 52). His reprise of "What harbour shelters peace," along with the chorus's softening from diegetic shouts to choral lament, suggests that subjective connection is not lost.[145] At the same time, the distant foghorn beckoning Grimes out to sea gives this lyrical outburst an ironic tinge, marking it less as a triumph of human agency and connection than as a tragic ode—as one critic described it—to "what might have been."[146]

Regardless, the cold, hard lens of documentary soon returns as Grimes's redemptive song of "night turned to day" ironically gives way to a harsh reality: the stage is plunged into darkness in response to Britten's musical cues. "[A]ll colour and sound drain out of the world," reported one critic enthusiastically, as the "only lines of spoken dialogue in the work" are uttered.[147] At the climactic moment of death, in other words, we fall out of music entirely into unadorned speech, accompanied by only stifled sobs and shingles crunching as Ellen and Balstrode retreat.[148] For those anxious about sentimentality, this might seem the perfect way to end. One commentator dubbed the silent death a "clever touch," while another highlighted abstemiousness: "Slater and Britten leave in the air by their fastidiousness" a point that "would have been driven home by Boito and Verdi with a touch of barnstorming."[149] Yet, as with most assertions of this kind, the opposite was equally true. If following Verdi meant his "broken hero singing to the last"—to borrow the words of Carolyn Abbate and Roger Parker—the collapse into silence and speech could have a similarly sentimental effect.[150] One need only recall the spoken endings of *Bohème* or *Traviata* to understand why some heard Grimes's conclusion as even more melodramatic than the full-throated ones it sought to avoid. After noting that "at the crucial moment . . . the spoken voice intrudes," one commentator concluded: "[Britten's] audacity succeeds everywhere but in the last scene of all."[151]

Despite the impression given by most critics, however, the opera does not end there. "After a long pause," one noted, "life returns: dawn breaks, the mist disperses, the music on the high strings which began Act I comes back again, the townsfolk begin to go about their daily business."[152] For hardcore pessimists, this signaled betrayal: "a hazardous passage from climax to anti-climax, from tragic night to common day," from coldly objective noise to music's restorative power.[153] Yet, in many respects, the episode seems not to resolve the opera's tension so much as it prolongs it. Even as the musical dawn suggests the optimism of a clean slate, it also implies a crushing indifference to the tragic events. When critics described the suicide as a "mere item of police court news," they meant it literally as well as metaphorically:

> SWALLOW
> There's a boat sinking out at sea,
> Coastguard reports.

FISHERMAN
Within reach?

SWALLOW
No.

FISHERMAN
Let's have a look through the glasses.
[Fishermen go with Swallow to the beach and look out. One of them has a glass.][154]

As the onstage spectators watch Grimes disappear into the sea, they offer no response, as if the cold objectivity of nature finally merges with the indifferent crowd. The return of the dawn music seems to reinforce this "realistic" reading with its phonographic sound: the rising tide evoked with an ethereal violin and flute melody, the waking birds with clarinet, harp and viola arpeggios, and the gentle warmth of the morning sun with a brass chorale. When the chorus comes in at Fig. 54 (in the published score), their words double down on this reading: "To those who pass the Borough sounds betray / The cold beginning of another day." Critics latched on to it: "the townsfolk begin to go about their daily business, we reach the 'cold beginning of another day.'"[155]

Yet, for all this, the ending was even more ambivalent still. Tucked away amid the final chorus's imagery of unpitying nature, the distant toll of mourning resounds: "O hollow sound from the passing bell / To some departing spirit bids farewell."[156] Nor is this without musical parallel: if the violin's grace notes can be heard as ornithological noise, they also suggest the sobbing of a human lament, which soon develops into pathos-laden flute melody. And while the chorus's words mostly thematize indifference, its hymn-like textures recall the opening solidarity—the sense of community that comes from being vulnerable to the same overwhelming forces of nature. As these gestures suggest the enduring possibility of sympathetic connection, the warm A major brass chorale and harp arpeggios confirm that the prospect of redemption is not altogether lost.

SENTIMENTAL MODERNISM

Surveying press responses soon after *Grimes*'s premiere, the critic William Glock found himself bemused. As one of the few to admit the opera's sentimental tropes, Glock railed against the modernist rhetoric of realism and difficulty that had already taken root: "During the last fortnight, I have heard and read several comments on *Peter Grimes* . . . which describe it as a fierce and challenging work. What spoiled babies we have become."[157] We have seen the sophisticated ways critics tipped the anti-sentimental scales, but Glock reminds us that some got straight to the modernist point. "'Peter Grimes' is no child's play," insisted Scott Goddard: "The tale is fierce, its development tragic, and the music fascinating."[158] Baxter described the opera in similar terms, stubbornly predicting that "'Peter Grimes' will shock the fashionable first-nighters" even after it was hailed a success: "The music is merciless, arrogant, tempestuous, and strangely moving, but it makes no concession to the ear which had been tuned to crooners and the jungle-wailing of the foxtrot."[159] Elsewhere, the same critic drew hyperbolic connections between Grimes's suffering and the experience of being in the opera's audience:

> The music is so harsh and relentless that the ear cries for mercy, but Britten's retort is: "Did the people show mercy to Peter Grimes?" In the whole of the long first act, there is hardly a touch of beauty in the score, and none at all of tenderness. The harmonies are modern and discordant, as if the composer were some kind of robot with a hatred of mankind. "There is no bodily pleasure in it" said a well-known operatic tenor to me as he went out for a breath of air.[160]

While such accounts appear to confirm the carefully crafted visions of *Grimes* as an archetype of modernist realism—which shocked and offended early audiences— we have seen that things were never this straightforward. For one thing, its modernism was invariably framed as a defense, not an accusation. That this difficulty was explained negatively—in terms of what the opera was not—allowed critics to identify its less "difficult" characteristics even as they denied them. Baxter's portrait of audience suffering was, after all, inseparable from the denials—of romance, sentiment, love duet, flower song, beauty—seen throughout this account. Although Glock put this down to simple prejudice, this chapter has uncovered something more sustained and reciprocal at work. For, in raising sentimentality in order to deny it, *Grimes*'s critics were arguably reenacting gestures written into the opera itself. In fact, there is a sense in which this sentimentality can *only* be read under erasure in the Derridean sense; in pitting love against pessimism, moralism against cynicism, lyricism against fragmentation, music against noise, it was as if composer and librettist put a line through the most sentimental features. But it was a line that not only left them legible, but highlighted them all the more.

This explains how audiences were able to enjoy sentimentality, realism, and difficulty at the same time, while revealing something more fundamental about the relationship between them. By pitting "romantic" tropes against "modernist" ones, sentimentality against its erasure, *Grimes* was able to stage its own difficulty, translating modernism's aesthetic challenges into a recognizable style.[161] This meant turning the rejection of sentimentality into a kind of literary and musical rhetoric, but also a more literal staging of difficulty in the narrative of struggle too. By interpreting the work's style and subject matter as a proxy for the aesthetic experience, Baxter—in other words—arguably laid bare a broader critical sleight of hand, one that penetrated far deeper into the heart of twentieth-century modernism than most commentators would be prepared to admit.

In its explicit blend of realism and modernism, Joyce's *Dubliners* (1914) offers an obvious example. However, we might ask similar questions about *Ulysses*—the *locus classicus* of literary modernism—too. For all its experimentalism, Joyce's novel from 1921 shared with sentimental realism all the paradoxes and tensions that Orwell outlined.[162] While the inclusion of defecation, urination, and prostitution took concerns with "ordinary" life to a transgressive extreme, it also gestures to the same aestheticization of dirt. Like Grimes, Bloom is something of a sympathetic outsider; despite his flaws, his ability to imagine a brighter future makes him feel the cold, sharp edges of modern life with peculiar force. While Clive Hart has described Bloom's vision of his dead child, Rudy, at the end of "Circe" as harking back to Dickensian sentimentality, we might see it looking forward to Grimes's "fiery visions" as well.[163] Like the latter, these glimpses of redemption are at once more sentimental and difficult for being offered and then denied. Where Robert Scholes has cast Joyce's difficulty as a "cloak" for inner sentimentality, we might suggest that they were two sides of the same coin.[164] It seems likely that—much as with Britten's opera—the novel's infamous "difficulty" had as much to do with the literal struggle and suffering of the Grimesian protagonist as with the formal experimentation and originality that critics have often prized.[165]

There were comparable examples in the musical world. To allow for what Suzanne Clark has called a "sentimental modernism"—that is, a sentimentality within and without modernism—is to recognize that even *Wozzeck* was never as cold and austere as *Grimes*'s critics supposed: here too we have the same anxious flitting back and forth between suffering and redemption, lyricism and speech, music and noise, set against the stylized grit of working-class life.[166] Though Berg's reputation as the soft touch of the Second Viennese School makes this unsurprising, his more hard-nosed colleagues were implicated too. At roughly the same time that critics were stopping their ears to *Grimes*'s melodies, some were doing the opposite to Anton Webern's works, struggling to hear lyricism in this proverbially difficult music.[167] That they were able to do so suggests that even Webern's music enacted similar gestures of erasure, whereby musical sentimentality was at first advanced and then retracted, offered and then denied. Indeed, the problem with works like *Grimes* was not simply that they performed their "difficulty," reducing modernism to the level of style. It was, rather, that in doing so they exposed the extent to which modernism's difficulty was always thus, a rhetorical performance that depended for its effect on the very sentimentality it rejected.

The Timely Traditions of *Albert Herring*

*Every summer, for seven summers now, Isa had heard the same words; about
the hammer and the nails; the pageant and the weather. Every year they said,
would it be wet or fine; and every year it was—one or the other. The same
chime followed the same chime, only this year beneath the chime she heard:
"The girl screamed and hit him about the face with a hammer."*

—VIRGINIA WOOLF, *BETWEEN THE ACTS* (1941)[1]

Set in the idyllic grounds of an English country house, Virginia Woolf's *Between the
Acts* tells of the preparation and performance of a village pageant on the eve of war.
As the spectacle journeys through literary history, the villagers respond with mixed
reactions that turn to frustration as they search in vain for a useful "message." By
setting the novel in the shadow of war, Woolf stages a collision between the pageant
and apocalyptic events. Yet it is not simply the play but also the manners and habits
associated with it that come to appear unacceptably trivial. While Lucy Swithin frets
about posters, rain, and the interval spread, Isa Oliver reads in the newspaper of
soldiers raping young girls. No longer capable of speaking to modern experiences,
cultural tradition becomes a mode of escape. It allows people to imagine community and continuity where there is division and destruction, to block their eyes and
ears to more pressing concerns. But far from simply dismissing the pageantry of
the past, Woolf's novel revels in it; its sporadic allusions to contemporary events
are overshadowed by an emphasis on historical continuity, its satirical send-ups are
suffused with affection, and the pageant's pastiche spills over into the novel proper.
For all the self-consciousness about nostalgia's pitfalls, in other words, *Between the
Acts* offered traditional images at a time when tradition was under threat. In doing
so, it implicates itself and its readers in the very myopia it diagnoses.

Premiered six years after the publication of *Between the Acts*, *Albert Herring*
(1947) presents many of the same critical problems. Set in the turn-of-the-century
Suffolk countryside, the opera tells the tale of a group of village busybodies who
revive the tradition of crowning a virtuous "May Queen." When no young lady
is deemed suitably virtuous, they crown Albert—a naïve greengrocer—as "May

King" instead. Spurred on by some rum-laced lemonade, Albert takes off for a night of drunken debauchery, rebelling against the social strictures for which he has become a mascot. When he returns home, he asserts his independence, teaching the village worthies a valuable lesson.[2] Much like Woolf's novel, *Herring* plays with themes of obsolescence, nostalgia, and irrelevance, sketching traditions that were bound to appear precious in the shadow of war.

It is perhaps unsurprising, then, that Britten's opera has provoked many of the same critical misgivings. As Michael Kennedy pointed out in his biography published in 1981, *Albert Herring* appears to represent a regrettable retreat from the cosmopolitanism and contemporaneity of Britten's previous forays into the operatic genre.[3] Like most other critics, however, Kennedy advanced this perspective as a pretext to deny it, defending the opera from the charges of conservatism that it would otherwise seem to invite. As recently as 2008, Paul Kildea drew on an identical strategy, insisting that "more contemporary concerns" were buried beneath the ostensibly nostalgic surface.[4] Although such defenses have often been couched as revelations, they depend on strategies that date back to the opera's premiere in 1947. By tracing these fraught responses back to their roots, I want to reframe *Albert Herring*'s apparently paradoxical position—at once serious and trivial, timely and traditional, original and obsolete—as another window into the mid-century mediation of the great divide.

STAGING TRADITION

In staging the tension between timeless traditions and mid-century concerns, Woolf's novelistic swansong grappled with a subject close to the heart of her generation. Since the early decades of the century, her contemporaries had characterized theirs as a period qualitatively different from those before, one that required radically new forms of art as a result. While Wyndham Lewis announced the end of history, Ezra Pound's injunction to "make it new" appeared to capture the general mood, with the effect that scholars have often nominated the desire to break radically with tradition as modernism's raison d'etre.[5] In recent years, scholars have worked to nuance modernist "myths of originality," yet—as we have seen—they nevertheless were important in shaping the way critics and artists understood their cultural battle lines.[6] In a series of essays from around 1920, Woolf herself dismissed late Victorian and Edwardian literature as irrelevant to her generation.[7] On the one hand, her frustration was the customary aesthetic one: that their idiosyncrasies had hardened into styles and conventions, working against the creativity and originality of younger writers. On the other hand, the obsolescence of past literature was said to reflect fundamental changes: "In or about December, 1910," Woolf famously wrote, "human character changed."[8] Edwardian materialism, she explained, with its obsession with buildings, possessions, and manners, could only appear unacceptably trivial in the perilous modern world.

Such consensus only grew louder as the century continued, and war and devastation once again loomed. By 1938, Woolf's accusations had widened to encompass not just Victorian and Edwardian fiction but all past literature: "We are not here to sing old songs or to fill in missing rhymes. We are here to consider facts. . . . So let us shut the New Testament; Shakespeare, Shelley, Tolstoy and the rest, and face the fact that stares us in the face at this moment of transition."[9] According to Jane de Gay, Woolf's writing from the late 1930s and early 1940s testifies to "an almost physical discomfort in trying to read literature at a time when more urgent issues command[ed] attention," a discomfort that spilled over into *Between the Acts* in the figure of Isa Oliver.[10] As one of the younger generation, Isa carries the weight of the modern world on her shoulders, plagued as she is by the violent stories she reads in the newspaper. Most others, by contrast, are so immersed in the past that they are oblivious to the present. When the village elders sporadically turn their attention to contemporary politics, for instance, they explain it away as part of the routine upheavals to which people have always been subject, as if to embody the myopia born of cultural tradition.[11]

For writers, one of the most obvious solutions was to eschew traditional plots and subjects in favor of themes that engaged the present. "The historian today," Woolf opined in 1936, "is writing not about Greece and Rome in the past, but about Germany and Spain in the present; the biographer is writing lives of Hitler and Mussolini, not of Henry the Eighth and Charles Lamb; the poet introduces communism and fascism into his lyrics; the novelist turns from the private lives of his characters to their social surroundings and their political opinions."[12] In the year Woolf worried about literature's irrelevance, Britten's friends and collaborators, W. H. Auden and Christopher Isherwood, were being championed for their "outspoken topicality," dealing "not only with dictators and war, but boldly and sincerely with the problems which dictatorship and war have set for every member of the audience."[13] By the early 1940s, it was not just the usual left-wing subjects that flew topicality's flag. While few would be surprised by George Orwell's assertion that "a novelist who simply disregards the major public events of the moment is generally either a footler or a plain idiot," even T. S. Eliot began to defend artistic timeliness.[14] In an essay from 1940, Woolf herself explained:

> To-day we hear the gunfire in the Channel. We turn on the wireless; we hear an airman telling us how this afternoon he shot down a raider; his machine caught fire; he plunged into the sea . . . Scott never saw the sailors drowning at Trafalgar; Jane Austen never heard the cannon roar at Waterloo. Neither of them heard Napoleon's voice as we hear Hitler's voice as we sit at home of an evening.[15]

Although Woolf was all too aware of the pitfalls of a culture that looked to the past instead of the present, she was willing neither to turn her back on literary tradition nor to embrace a narrow topicality. Even as she derided convention as "ruin" for the modern writer, she warned of going too far in severing links with the past.[16]

On the one hand, she defended conventions as the building blocks of communication, comparable to the common greetings exchanged "as a prelude to the more exciting intercourse of friendship."[17] On the other, she admitted deriving pleasure from familiar conventions in and of themselves: "I confess I cry out for the old decorums, and envy the indolence of my ancestors who, instead of spinning madly through mid-air, dreamt quietly in the shade with a book."[18] This desire for a lost innocence by no means subsided in her later writings as the urge to break with tradition took on new political imperatives. Even after diagnosing the complicity of English cultural tradition in Fascism, Woolf still found herself tempted "to listen not to the bark of the guns and the bray of the gramophones but to the voices of the poets, answering each other, assuring us of a unity that rubs out divisions as if they were chalk marks only."[19] Much like the village elders that she satirizes, she drew comfort and perspective from past literature, along with the sense of continuity offered by literary tradition.

Whether in the early reception of Britten's works or the most recent scholarship, commentators have shown themselves similarly preoccupied with matters of timeliness. Throughout the 1930s, Britten's collaborations with the likes of Auden and Isherwood yielded the kind of "topical" films and plays that Woolf lamented.[20] For those eager to uncover such a preoccupation with war, violence, and oppression in Britten's operas, his first two essays in the genre were veritable gifts. *Peter Grimes* appeared to wear its timely concerns on its sleeve with the persecution of its misunderstood protagonist symbolizing the modern "loss of innocence." First performed while Europe was clearing its rubble, it was partly this that endeared it to postwar audiences. As we saw in the previous chapter, Edmund Wilson praised the work's topicality, as much a matter of style as of subject matter.[21] With the exception of the Christian epilogue—to which critics, tellingly, objected—*The Rape of Lucretia* (1946) staged a similarly bleak trajectory, representing lost innocence graphically through the onstage rape of its chaste heroine.

After these two tragic operas, the composer advised readers of *Life* magazine that his third would "depart from somber themes and be a 'comedy of manners.'"[22] He told BBC listeners that the work's very raison d'être was to provide light relief from its "serious" and "gloomy" operatic siblings. At least one critical preview offered a similar warning, insisting that *Herring* "promises a lot of surprises . . . to any who may not imagine the composer of 'Peter Grimes' and 'Rape of Lucretia' as a humorist."[23] Although advocates have stressed affinities between *Albert Herring* and *Peter Grimes*, the former could just as easily be described as an inversion of the latter: while *Grimes* stages the undoing of its outsider protagonist, *Herring* depicted a much more positive rite of passage.[24] As the climax to the original synopsis made clear, Britten's comic opera is ostensibly a tale of triumph over adversity: "[Albert] has plunged into unforgivable excesses—but at least he has learnt the value of his own independence and can stand up for himself in the future."[25]

As Laura Mooneyham has pointed out, this kind of comic optimism was at odds with modernism's ascetic ideals and—at least in highbrow circles—came to seem virtually obsolete by the Second World War.[26] In a context in which art was supposed to have lost its innocence, critics were put off by comedy's triviality and naïveté. According to Jonathan Greenberg, satire—with its "double movement" between affirmation and destruction—fared much better than straightforward comedy, but some still declared its critical edge too subtle to survive.[27] "Satire," Auden explained in 1952, flourishes "in times of relative stability and contentment, for it cannot deal with serious evil and suffering."[28] "In an age like our own," he continued, "it cannot flourish except in private circles as an expression of private feuds; in public life, the serious evils are so serious that satire seems trivial and the only possible kind of attack is prophetic denunciation." No matter how pointed the satire, then, there was always the risk of getting caught up in the play with obsolete conventions and styles. Indeed, according to P. G. Wodehouse, it was not just the pessimism of the age but also the cult of originality that had rendered comedy—with its reliance on traditional plots, characters, and turns of phrase—an anachronism.[29] This conventionality is even more pronounced in the "comedy of manners," the subgenre to which *Albert Herring* belongs, which flaunts convention as both style and subject matter.

Britten's opera, no exception, is "about" tradition and suffused with it. It was based on Guy de Maupassant's "Le Rosier de Madame Husson" (1887), a short story about the endurance of customs in the rural French village of Gisors. In transplanting Maupassant's tale to the fictional Suffolk village of Loxford, Britten and Crozier retained this emphasis on tradition even as they introduced implications of lateness and obsolescence into their tale. Much as in *Between the Acts,* the characters divide sharply between the village elders, blindingly faithful to past traditions, and the younger generation, for whom these traditions are irrelevant and restrictive. From the moment the curtain rises, Lady Billows, the self-appointed guardian of custom, can be heard lamenting changes in village life: the new custom of putting poppies in the altar vases, the laxity of the choirboys' responses, and the immorality of the young make her blood boil. Soon after, she delivers an ode to tradition—"There's a lot of wisdom in these old / traditions"—before embarking on a nostalgic trip down memory lane:

> Competition to be May Queen
> When I was a girl was amazingly keen!
> Among the village girls, I mean.
>
> All dressed in white –
> Met on the Green
> At noon on May the First to parade
> Before the Squire.
> Squire picked the winner
> And sat beside her during dinner.

> Oh! You're too young to remember
> How these things were done![30]

For Lady Billows, traditional values are bound up with the pomp and ceremony of English cultural tradition. She is, of course, right to speculate that the younger generation neither knows nor cares "how these things were done"; Albert and his peers regard the May Day tradition as a nuisance, if not a downright embarrassment. Indeed, this indifference propels the plot, as the Loxford establishment struggles to "make virtue attractive, exciting, *desirable* for young people."[31] In this respect, *Herring* was responding to—even staging—contemporary critiques of tradition in much the same way as Woolf. Yet however much Maupassant's reverential treatment of tradition was tempered by self-conscious implications of obsolescence, the opera's subject matter still afforded a pretext to revel in all kinds of references to the past—from archaic settings and conventional themes to stock characters and stylized dialogue.

Perhaps the most obvious nod to the past was in the opera's "provincial" setting.[32] The story's rural village setting symbolized "provincial" historicism: a space where time appears to stand still. According to Britten and Crozier, one of the most important tasks in adapting the story was to transport it to a comparable English setting, settling on the fictional town of Loxford (adapted from Yoxford), around Ufford, Orford, Iken, and Snape. Mention of these towns and villages recurs throughout the opera and, even at a distance of fifty years, Nancy Evans recalled the audience's gleeful recognition of the quaint old English place names: "Every time we mentioned Iken and Snape, the Saxmundam Police are out—and that sort of thing—they just all sort of giggled and started stirring every time something local was mentioned . . . a terrific response to that."[33] In reveling in the details of its local setting, *Albert Herring* appears to have skated close to the edge of what Orwell called "the nostalgia of place names," a late Victorian and Edwardian tradition of using archaic-sounding places to evoke sentimental images of "buried villages, thatched roofs, and the jingle of smithies."[34]

The provincialism of the opera's subject matter was mirrored in the setting of its first production at Glyndebourne—a private estate deep in the East Sussex countryside. In staging the opening scene in a country house, its producers sharpened these reflections and offered a nod to English literary tradition. The country house was, after all, a bedrock of the national literary heritage: from *Northanger Abbey* to *Brideshead Revisited,* authors had drawn on it as a symbol of timeless historical continuity and a metaphor for cultural patrimony with all its privileges and problems. Although the composer and the librettist had supposedly pushed forward the date of Maupassant's tale by just over a decade—from 1887 to the turn of the twentieth century—critics speculated that John Piper's country house setting (Fig. 3) belonged firmly to the nineteenth century. One apparently even felt the need to apologize: "If the room belongs rather to 1880 than to 1900 (the date of

FIG. 3. Production Photograph of *Albert Herring*, Act I Scene 1, Lady Billows's Breakfast Room, June 1947. Photographer: Angus McBean. © Harvard Theatre Collection (MS Thr 581), Houghton Library, Harvard University.

'Albert Herring'), well, Mr. Britten's Lady Billows was old-fashioned in 1900."[35] While this commentator was reminded of Henry James's *The Spoils of Poynton* (1896)—a novel about a houseful of dusty antiques—others were content simply to bask in the old-fashioned details of Piper's handiwork: "If I cavil a little at the too farcical appearance of the police constable and the too fussy acting of Lady Billows's housekeeper, I have otherwise nothing but praise for the stylized late Victorian profusion of John Piper's designs (above all, those clothes!)."[36] Whether Piper's set designs were from the 1880s or the 1900s, he tapped into the long-standing symbolism of the setting, much as Woolf's description of Pointz Hall had done in *Between the Acts*. One of the few details that he included in his sketches was a series of ancestral portraits (see Fig. 4), hardly a subtle symbol of cultural heritage.

If the country-house setting was the most obvious bow to tradition, the stock characters drew the most criticism. In a radio interview and *Listener* article from 1937, Lord Elton pared "highbrow" antipathy to conventional characterization down to its quintessence: "We smile . . . at what appear to us to be the stilted and unnatural conventions in the Victorian novels our grandparents read."[37] Citing characters from Gilbert and Sullivan's *Trial by Jury* (1875), he elaborated: "The

FIG. 4. Production Photograph of *Albert Herring*, Act I Scene 1, Portraits on the Wall, June 1947. Photographer: Angus McBean. © Harvard Theatre Collection (MS Thr 581), Houghton Library, Harvard University.

blushing Angelina, the whiskered Edwin seem to us mere figures of pasteboard." For actual critics, the problem was naturally a little more complicated. Q. D. Leavis complained that novelists had traditionally substituted boldness and familiarity for the subtleties of reality, while Woolf lamented Edwardian neglect of the "inner" mind in favor of the "outer" signs—the stylized possessions, clothes, and interactions—of conventional characterization.[38]

In good modernist fashion, Crozier initially sought to inject the stock personages of Maupassant's story with "hints of an individual way of life."[39] By the time it came to penning the actual dialogue, however, complexity and originality had taken a back seat to theatrical economy: "I wanted to introduce Lady Billows *straightaway* as a beneficent local tyrant, actively concerned with good works, narrow in her views, and meddling in all the affairs of the town."[40] After revising early drafts and erasing inessential detail, he was left with a more "conventional" cast than in Maupassant's original. Although Crozier intended to represent Lady Billows as a "beneficent . . . tyrant," her "benevolence" is—unlike her French counterpart—quickly replaced with a more familiar moral conservatism. For one critic, this "Victorian matron" archetype was representative of the wider cast, who "with one exception are not human beings [but] well known comic types," drawn from the national literary heritage.[41] One commentator complained that the work "is not a comic opera, but a rendering in opera of the English comedy," while another listed the familiar characters:

> Lady Billows, an elderly autocrat, . . . her house-keeper, more rigid than her mistress, whose list also recorded the behavior of the village girls; Miss Wordsworth, prim head-teacher at the school; the dear Vicar; the pompous Mayor; the rustic Superintendent of Police; the local greengrocer and her son, Albert Herring; Sid from the butcher's; Nancy from the bakery, and three tiresome village children. Nothing could be more English.[42]

If Lady Billows was the most obvious relic of literary history—amalgamating the moral evangelism of *Middlemarch*'s Nicholas Bulstrode with the dogmatic conservatism of Galsworthy's Soames Forsyte—Superintendent Budd came a close second. In transforming Maupassant's proud Commandant Desbarres into a bumbling police superintendent, "heavy, slow-thinking and a good sort," Crozier was doffing his cap to the simple but warmhearted police officers of literary tradition. It was to such a character that Woolf had turned in *Between the Acts*, when she represented "The Nineteenth Century" with the "husky and rusty" police constable known as Budge.[43] In his devotion to Empire and lament for a policeman's lot, Superintendent Budd exhibited striking affinities with Budge, not to mention the Sergeant of Police from *The Pirates of Penzance* (1880).

Along with conventional characterization went stylized dialogue. For despite the creators' aspirations to drag opera's "creaky" texts into the modern age, *Herring* often sounds every bit as dated as the examples Britten and Crozier denigrated.[44] One reason for this was the "controlled verse" in which the libretto was cast, fitting oddly with pretensions to everyday, realistic dialogue. Perhaps even more significant was the verse's clichéd content, such as the "Good Morning" (Act I, Scene 1) ensemble's extended paean to the timeless English tradition of discussing the weather:

MAYOR
Wonderful weather for April, Mr Gedge!

SUPER
Wants oiling, I expect. Dust in the works . . .

MISS WORDSWORTH
Look! that hedge of rosemary is humming with
bumblebees!

VICAR
Quite perfect, Mr Mayor. Promises a splendid May and
June.

MAYOR
That it does—

SUPER
"In like a lion, out like a lamb!"—that was true of March
this year—

MAYOR
It was—!

MISS WORDSWORTH [RADIANT]
"And lo! the winter is past!—

VICAR [JOINING IN]
"The rain is over and gone. The flowers appear on the earth . . . "

VICAR [EXPLAINING]
Solomon's Song, you know!

MAYOR [IMPATIENTLY]
Well, since we're here . . .[45]

Stylized communication is imagined here as closer to ritual than to genuine inter-action, with verbal and literary commonplaces affording a mode of conversing without actually making contact. As Miss Wordsworth and the Vicar carry on about the weather, Superintendent Budd remains stuck in the previous conversa-tion, pondering—appropriately—the cause of his watch's tardiness.

Ultimately, however, it is an actual literary allusion—a half-baked memory of the Song of Solomon—that pushes the Vicar and Miss Wordsworth over the edge, so far into a different world that the Mayor is forced to pull them back with an impatient quip, "Well, since we're here." As he directs attention away from these "old songs" and "missing rhymes"—to borrow Woolf's words—toward the imme-diate item on their agenda, poetry becomes marked as an emblem of nostalgia, drowning out the concerns of the day. Nor is this the only—or even the most extreme—example of a shift from cliché to quotation, as Lady Billows's Act II speech makes clear:

Irreligion!
Patriotism is not enough!—Drink!
The HAVOC wrought by gin! Oh, never start
That dreadful habit, or you're lost forever!

King and Country! Cleanliness is next to—
God for England and Saint—Keep
Your powder dry and leave the rest to
Nature!—Britons! Rule the deep!
[Enthusiastic cries of Hooray!][46]

Such an outburst demonstrates how Crozier marks convention as a relic of the past that impedes engagement with the present. This pile-up of literary non-sequiturs epitomizes the extent to which old sentiments, sayings, and quotations abound, heightening the opera's cartoonish conventionality of style and subject matter.

SEARCHING FOR TIMELINESS

Where timeliness and tradition were widely supposed to be mutually exclusive, one might have expected *Albert Herring* to draw criticism for nostalgia and myopia. Sure enough, after observing that the "characters are largely conventional skits on figures of village life," Martin Cooper insisted that "it is *not enough* to create flat, cardboard figures of fun and proceed to laugh at them."[47] Complaints were also raised in connection with the provincial setting: one critic lamented that "a salacious French story of Maupassant [had been] translated by Eric Crozier into a rustic English comedy of the way a bumpkin kicks over the traces," while another criticized the turning of "one of Maupassant's most cuttingly ironic stories . . . into a comedy of Suffolk village life that leaves nothing but its indestructibly funny situations."[48] Other commentators noted the lack of a meaningful story line: "Albert's binge is expected. Nothing comes of it: and it has, of course, to be watered down, for polite English ears," Anderson complained.[49] Richard Capell, by contrast, dealt with this ambivalence by appealing to wishful thinking and imagining a more "modern" interpretation:

> Was not a really modern Cocteauesque version possible? Cocteau would have looked for something more interesting for the centre-piece of a libretto than the sight of a young greengrocer being drunk for the first time. He would have known that neurasthenia is not cured by rum. One pictures a Cocteauesque scene with the greengrocer undergoing some drastic sort of electric therapy ("E. C. T.") to rid him of his feeling of deference for his mother. Albert Drunk! One felt quite embarrassed by the naïveté of the young authors.[50]

Yet despite the many features seemingly calculated to make mid-century critics anxious, *Herring* was not widely written off. If, as Michael Seidel has argued, the satirical impulse always involved subverting the very conventions upon which it relied, it is easy to see how even seemingly affectionate examples of satire could be recuperated as a form of modernism.[51] Many reviewers did so, casting the opera as more serious and timely than it appeared. "I venture a prediction," Hans Keller wrote even before the premiere: "The serious musical aspect of this lyrical comedy will tend to be underestimated, or even neglected."[52] Keller was one of many who redirected charges of superficiality from Britten's opera to those who called it that.[53] After positing that "real humor is obvious . . . but cannot exist without an underlying seriousness," he identified deeper levels of meaning that inexperienced critics were apparently guaranteed to miss:

> There seem to be one or two parallels between *Albert Herring* and Britten's two previous operas, quite apart from formal principles, scoring *(Lucretia),* and setting (Suf-

folk: *Peter Grimes*). I am thinking of a number of psychological and sociological correspondences, e.g. the motif of sullied chastity (treated from the tragical point of view in *Lucretia*), or the theme—"opposition to (society's) tyranny," which plays such an important part in both *Grimes* and *Lucretia*. I thought this might be worth mentioning as there is bound to be much ado about "how different" *Albert Herring* is from anything previous.[54]

As Keller's exegesis makes clear, it was not just modernist rhetoric of surface and depth but also the comparison with *Grimes* and *Lucretia* that was wrested from would-be detractors. Although *Herring*'s broader trajectory appears a world away from its operatic siblings, Keller initiated a defensive trope that came to dominate the work's reception. Given the forcefulness of his rhetoric, it is not difficult to understand why: by denigrating the imaginary philistine who opts for the "obvious" interpretation, Keller virtually assured that commentators would pay lip service to such "psychological and sociological correspondences."[55] One critic focused on affinities between Albert and the eponymous hero of Britten's first opera: "In short, A. Herring (brilliantly created by Peter Pears) is a social misfit like Grimes."[56] After asking, "Why, then, did Britten choose such a subject?" another responded similarly: "because of the 'hero'—an odd character like Grimes, not an ordinary accepted member of society. Mr. Britten obviously sympathizes with such characters."[57] More emphatically, Lockspeiser argued that "some element of uncontrollable frustration appears in the heroes of each of Britten's operas—even more so in 'Albert Herring,' perhaps, than in either 'Peter Grimes' or 'The Rape of Lucretia.'"[58]

The episode on which a large part of the defense's case rested comes in Act II, Scene 2, when Albert returns home from his coronation banquet. As the inebriated protagonist reflects on his humiliating day, he sets off on an extended monologue, perhaps more at home in *Mrs. Dalloway* than *Carry On, Jeeves* Crozier temporarily gives the conventional village idiot a more sensitive soul. After overhearing Sid's condescending cliché—"heaven helps those who help themselves"—Albert lays his feelings bare, making it clear that his problems are not born of simple ignorance:

ALBERT
"Heaven helps those who help themselves."

"Help myself!" Oh go, go away
And leave me here alone
With doubts and terrors
You have never known . . . !

Enjoy your evening as you will!
Kiss and hug your fill! Embrace until
The stars spin round like Catherine-wheels
Against the rainbow-covered hills.

Then hurry home at dawn,
Proud of what you've done,
And smile to think I slept alone!

Nancy pities me—Sid laughs—others snigger
At my simplicity—offer me buns
To stay in my cage—parade
Me around as their Whiteheaded Boy—

Albert the Good! Albert who Should—!
Albert who Hasn't and Wouldn't if he Could!
Albert the Meek! Albert the Sheep!
Mrs Herring's Guinea Pig!
Mrs Herring's Tillypig!
Mrs Herring's—*Prig!*

But?—when?—
Shall I dare and dare again?
How shall I screw
My courage up to do
What must be done by everyone?
The tide will turn, the sun will set
While I stand here and hesitate . . .[59]

Unlike the moralistic proclamations of Lady Billows or Sid's fun-loving ditties, Albert's monologue moves rapidly between conflicting themes and sentiments. To the frustration, isolation, and oppression that critics touted in connection with *Grimes,* one may add self-pity, anxiety, fear, and impatience—all tempered by determination and even resolve. Such an outpouring would have surely reminded critics of the "mad scene" from Britten's first opera, which—as we have seen—was also associated with post-Freudian characterization. Like Septimus Smith, Leopold Bloom, and Peter Grimes, Albert is haunted by the voices of his mind. In drawing on modernist stream-of-consciousness, the librettist invited deep-rooted psychological speculation from audiences and critics who were only too happy to oblige. While Charles Stuart predicted that "opera-goers of a certain sort are sure to start grubbing frantically for bits of Freud between the lines," Capell confirmed: "in the interval at Glyndebourne, the word went round that Albert represented a psychological problem, and, that his revolt against a strong-willed mother . . . contained a meaning and a moral."[60] Much as with Keller, the underlying meaning of the rebellion was less important than its existence per se. For, with just a little squinting, they could frame it in modernist terms. Even commentators who did not directly invoke Freud could sense that Albert was cast from an entirely different mold than the other characters: "Albert Herring is after all no mere laughing stock, like the half-wit in Smetana's 'The Bartered Bride,' but a gentle and essentially sensitive being with a secret longing for love (witness his delicious song about Nancy in the second act)."[61]

Apart from injecting the opera with a frisson of literary modernism, this gesture to isolation and conflict encouraged critics to hear the serious concerns of the modern world after all. An even more common means of staking a claim for timeliness was by touting the opera's "tragic" elements over its comic ones. As Christopher Herbert has pointed out, even the most casual use of adjectives such as "serious," "tragic," and "realistic" as terms of praise stemmed from modernist aesthetics of timeliness and existentialism.[62] In the account of one critic, the impression that "'Herring' casts longing glances at the somber drama of 'Grimes'" served as a prelude to a sustained attempt to rescue the composer and his work: "one feels that, like Verdi, with whom he [Britten] has more in common than one might expect, he is inclined to look for drama and even tragedy in the most inconsequential and frivolous farces . . . and he will surprise you with almost tragic outbursts after scenes of immense gusto."[63] For another commentator, the opera redeemed itself only through these "moments of intense seriousness," "an expense of spirit in a waste of brittle giggling."[64] Besides Albert's aforementioned monologue, there was one other place to which these critics looked—the final-act threnody for the "deceased" protagonist. Quite apart from its general morbidity ("death awaits us one and all"), its grief-stricken sentiments struck a familiar postwar chord ("that one so young should die in vain"). While Lockspeiser commended the ensemble as "a very moving dirge with hardly a touch of comedy in it," Neville Cardus heard the "poignant threnody" as redeeming the work "from almost parodistic origin to significant life capable of revealing sore wounds and pitiable humanity."[65] For Shawe-Taylor, it was moments such as the "solemn threnody" that "make it a superficial judgment to write the work off as a farce or a charade."[66]

Commentators were under no illusions about the rarity of these "melancholy echoes." But while the extent to which these tragic moments tipped the interpretive scales in the opera's favor is striking, it is easy to understand why they kept commentators scratching their heads. In offering "tantalising glimpses" of a level of sentiment otherwise unplumbed, they exposed a hermeneutic void that audiences were eager to fill. The threnody, in other words, angles for the cryptographic attention it has received, marking itself as a beacon that illuminates the entire opera. For Clifford Hindley, both the monologue's pathologizing sense of Albert as "different" and the threnody's tragic seriousness spoke to the protagonist's homosexuality.[67] Still more recently, Paul Kildea has identified pacifist and socialist meanings bubbling up from exactly the same fissures.[68] But while the specifics of interpretation have changed, the sense of these passages as game changers has remained.[69] In violating the opera's unity and consistency, these passages arguably functioned as "unconsummated"—even unconsummatable—symbols, inviting interpretation while simultaneously evading definitive readings. In marking timeliness as an absence rather than a direct presence, they encouraged critics to justify their enthusiasm for the opera in terms of hidden depths, even as they heightened the playful superficiality of the rest of the work. By highlighting the opera's pressing omissions, it excuses them, allowing audiences simultaneously to revel in and disavow the opera's nostalgic myopia.

ALBERT'S MUSICAL REBELLION

Much as in the literary sphere, musical modernism was often associated with extreme antipathy to tradition, whether this was true in practice or not. Schoenberg became the poster boy for this radicalism, despite the nuances and complexities of his own position. Over a decade before Adorno's apocalyptic account of Schoenbergian "progress" in *The Philosophy of Modern Music* (1949), critics were already lamenting the extremism of what Constant Lambert irreverently dubbed the "Official Revolution."[70] If Adorno would declare only a handful of composers sufficiently original to qualify as modernists, Lambert satirized antipathy to tradition as an oppressive bandwagon:

> To the seeker after the new, or the sensational, to those who expect a sinister frisson from modern music, it is my melancholy duty to point out that all the bomb throwing and guillotining has already taken place . . . there are few composers who are not attached, either officially or unwittingly, to some revolutionary "movement."[71]

While remaining sympathetic to the desire to cast off the "shackles" of conventional musical form, Lambert insisted that "revolutionaries" ended up submitting to an even more debilitating restriction.[72] Three years later, Cecil Gray complained that "the possession of a wholly individual utterance, or mode of thought, quite unlike that of any one else" had come to be regarded as the artistic "sine qua non" in the wake of musical modernism.[73]

Even a cursory glance at early commentary reveals that the "official revolution" figured as a consistent presence in Britten criticism—an orthodoxy against which the composer was apparently in constant need of defense. In parodying the "cult of contemporaneity," Keller sought to do exactly that.[74] Elsewhere, recalling Adorno's disparaging remarks about the "new conformism," Keller complained that Schoenbergian standards were being applied with "dramatic lack of success, to the avant-garde and Britten (or Shostakovich or Hans Werne Henze) alike."[75] Defending Britten from charges of eclecticism, Charles Stuart offered a similar parody, rejecting extreme radicalism as a modernist cliché:

> Against extraneous manners and styles the composer sat on watch and ward year in and year out, with anxious biting of nails. Down went two pages of sonata first-movement or cantata to text by Walt Whitman at his hairiest. Then you went over what you'd written with a weedfork, uprooting reminiscences: here the ghost of a *Pelléas* phrase, here a stray bar from *Le Coq d'Or*, here a fleck of Franck, here, God help us, an echo of the Silver Rose music in *Rosenkavalier*. A man was mortally afraid to be anybody but himself. He defiantly flashed his identification card long before the thing had been invented.[76]

According to Keller and Stuart, Britten's critics fell victim to the "old fallacy of music history's straight line" (a mythical vision of artistic progress that prevented composers ever looking backward) and the "new fallacy that it is important for a work of art to express its own time."[77] Postwar anti-traditionalism was apparently so severe that, by 1953, critics and scholars were stirred to intervene with a scholarly volume defending Britten from charges of conservatism.[78]

If the composer's defenders were right, one might well have expected such charges to arise in discussions of *Albert Herring,* surely the record holder for the sheer variety of its borrowed musical voices. While Lady Billows delivers her diatribes in the voice of Handelian ceremony, the Vicar waxes lyrical on the nature of "virtue" in broad Victorian ballads.[79] Even Sid and Nancy, the opera's least obviously stylized characters, trade in pastiched popular song idioms. Yet, in actuality, the number of writers who described the opera as a patchwork was relatively small. Where one critic worried about the lack of an authorial voice beneath all the stylistic assimilations—"its parody is, indeed, so terribly clever that there are grounds for fears concerning the possible development of a composer to whom so many styles and emotions are fair game"—another limited his concerns to "moments when the music suddenly shifted from authentic Britten to a kind of generalized operatic world of sentiment."[80] But except for such mild and infrequent critiques, charges of conservatism were raised exclusively by those at pains to deny them.

Justification of pastiche was sought in characterization.[81] "Each character," one critic wrote, "has his own musical accompaniment, from the bassoon obbligato which speaks for the village policeman, the cool Anglican melodies of the Vicar, the vigorous Handelian percussion for the awe-inspiring Lady of the manor, to the lyrical scena of Albert's long self-examination."[82] Meanwhile, Shawe-Taylor had fun identifying the codes, as if practicing a kind of stylistic listening:

> The downright "old English" character of Lady Billows comes out in frequent bursts of Handelian polyphony and an addiction to bluff rhythms and diatonic tunes; the schoolchildren acclaim Albert in a song as square as the toes of their boots; the Vicar's characteristic melodic contours suggest a Shropshire or Devonshire origin; and Albert's "Mum" contemplates a seaside photograph of her son to the strains of a pier-head valse.[83]

Yet even as he reveled in the familiar styles, Shawe-Taylor felt the need to denigrate them, laying the blame for "bluff rhythms and diatonic tunes" at the characters' rather than the composer's feet. By doing so, he could create a layer of narrative distance between Britten and his flagrantly conventional musical material.

Irony could also serve to rationalize pastiche. In commending Britten's "burlesque of grand operatic strokes," for example, Dyneley Hussey appeared to invoke an exclusively musical form of irony, as if the composer were making a point about operatic tradition quite apart from the specifics of the tale.[84] Some critics even attempted to steer *Herring*'s music away from the affectionate realm of "parody" or "burlesque" toward a more self-consciously modernist form of irony. This meant

EX. 7. *Albert Herring* (Act I, Scene 1)—"Rejoice, My Friends".

comparing it with the "rib-nudging" music of Prokofiev and Shostakovich in order to capture "all the leg-pulling and italicizing Britten indulges in."[85] Such was the pressure to find a guiding authorial voice that many of the composer's staunchest supporters denigrated his music in order to defend it. While Keller described the opening music as "intentionally idiotic," Hussey observed that the score "at one moment lapses ridiculously into the lush manner of Puccini and at another resolves into a four-square Handelian ensemble ... [and] vocal floridities in the old oper-atic style."[86] To the common vocabulary of "parody," "burlesque," and "satire," some added adjectives like "banal," "pompous," and "absurd" to foreclose the possibility that something as eclectic as "Rejoice, my friends" (Ex. 7) might also be sincere.

Some commentators, however, found it difficult to reconcile this cynical rhet-oric with Britten's charming music. Already by 1949, the Earl of Harewood had grown tired of the tendency to denigrate the music as if parody and pleasure were mutually exclusive: "Parody has its place in *Albert Herring,* but there is a far a more important side to the score and that is Britten's genuine comic musical inven-tion, which is copious, tuneful, sustained and to the point."[87] "Albert's coronation anthem," Harewood insisted, "is *both* irresistibly funny and musically enchant-ing." Others echoed this defense: "In spite of such links [to musical tradition], the whole score remains immensely characteristic of its composer."[88] Phoebe Douglas engaged in a more extreme form of reverse psychology, hailing the opera as a les-son in musical timeliness and originality:

> There are many who dislike modern music, finding it weird and dissonant, and pre-fer to pacify their hearts and ears with older, smoother melodies. But the certainties of other days are gone; we no longer believe in the Divine Right of Kings, or go to bed happily bolstered by a sense of superiority over those who work for us. Britten's music is of our age; its tapestries depict our search for beauty and integration, and are an artistic contribution toward the resolution of the doubts and confusions that hedge us about.[89]

For Douglas, it was not despite but because of its traditionalism that *Herring* spoke successfully to the age's uncertainties. Concentrating on the dissonances sporadi-cally added to the pastiche forms, she concluded: "Britten has given the musical threads of tradition a new and more virile twist. His use of melodic line, spurned by many recent musicians as 'old fashioned' and redolent of a supposedly decadent classicism, reaches a new and modern power of interpretation."[90] Cardus likewise pointed to "shadows of harmony" as the sites of the composer's idiosyncratic musi-cal "signature."[91]

If there was a point at which the composer's originality was most palpable, it was in the Act 2 monologue, marked, as everyone agreed, by psychological depth. To evoke the memories and conflict that make up Albert's interior crisis, Britten recapitulated a medley of themes from the previous scene, adding dissonances and exaggerating their characteristic features. The most prominent musical mate-rial comes from Albert's coronation anthem ("Albert the Good"), first introduced by the Vicar before being taken up as a choral finale to the banquet scene. In its original form (Ex. 8), the pseudo-baroque melody appears in a largely unsul-lied B♭ major. Already by the beginning of the following interlude (Ex. 9), it is transformed from its ceremonial character into a more playful fugue subject. Although the fugue begins regularly enough, the formality is quickly undermined as the counterpoint veers off into aimless sequences before borrowing a con-spicuously "modern" voice. (See Ex. 10.) Together with the attenuated tonality, displacing the theme's intervals over several octaves mimics a Second Viennese *Klangfarbenmelodie* while maintaining the cadential gestures of the original. Any

EX. 8. *Albert Herring* (Act II, Scene 2)—"Albert the Good".

EX. 9. *Albert Herring* (Act II, Interlude)—Fugue.

EX. 10. *Albert Herring* (Act II, Interlude)—"Klangfarbenmelodie".

doubts as to whether the interlude is a metaphorical challenge to the coronation music are erased when Albert takes over the theme in the following scene (Ex. 11). As he enters the shop, inebriated from his lunchtime cocktail, he mangles the coronation anthem, repeatedly bashing the door and extending the tail to the fitting words "and again, again, again." The final stage of this literal and musical rebellion comes just before the protagonist skips off for his night of debauchery. As he mocks his own subservience to his elders (Ex. 12), the block chords accompanying the coronation anthem are spiced with dissonant major seconds, standing at a tritone's remove from the tonic key.

For the *Times* critic, this was the "scene of real dramatic tension in which Albert finds his soul."[92] After worrying that it "may seem a trifle out of place in this rollicking farce," another commentator concluded that the music "succeeded in investing Herring's experiences with a certain poignancy," thanks to the "melancholy echoes of Grimes."[93] Lockspeiser went even further, suggesting not simply that the monologue was original but—more radically—that it was "about" originality itself, "a lesson . . . of artistic independence, which an artist must continually strive to achieve and maintain."[94]

EX. 11. *Albert Herring* (Act II, Scene 2)—Opening of Monologue.

EX. 12. *Albert Herring* (Act II, Scene 2)—End of Monologue.

In focusing on a single scene as the site of Britten's true voice, commentators exemplified a critical proclivity diagnosed in T. S. Eliot's oft-cited "Tradition and the Individual Talent" (1918): "the tendency to insist . . . upon those aspects of [a poet's work] in which he least resembles anyone else."[95] On the contrary, Eliot maintained, "if we approach a poet without this prejudice we shall find that not only the best, but the most individual parts of his work may be those in which the dead poets, his ancestors, assert their immortality most vigorously."[96] While Eliot's essay has often been seen as a reactionary response to modernism—a nostalgic attempt to rescue the past—a more nuanced reading may help to explain *Albert Herring*'s paradoxical reception. Far from simply valorizing one side of a binarism, Eliot reframed the opposition as a dialectic: it was not simply that the most "traditional" parts of an artwork often turned out to be the most "individual," but that the two concepts depended on each other for their definition.[97] Already by the

1930s, this idea was being invoked by mainstream music critics in order to challenge "the official revolution." According to Lambert, for example, the innovation that modernists prized could only be perceived as such if set against tradition: "a background of classicism (like realistic style of surrealist painters) provides the essential norm without which much of the abnormalities would pass unnoticed— a discordant harmonization of a familiar tune like 'God Save the King' would be much more of a shock than any given fourteen bars in an atonal work."[98] Herring's monologue, with its discordant version of his anthem, could have been written to illustrate the point.

In staging the composer's originality less as an authorial presence than as a rhetorical gesture of deformation, the monologue bears out this dialectical reading powerfully. On the one hand, framing tradition as a "mere" pretext for innovation allowed critics to overlook the bulk of the opera's musical language. On the other hand, the "twists," "shadows," and "angles" to which they redirected attention ended up pointing to the conventions they sought to erase. Whenever critics spoke of the composer's "modernisms," it was always in relation to the conventions Britten had apparently transcended. While such a dialectical account may appear simply to reframe an outmoded aesthetic binary that today's sensibilities would sooner have us throw out, it has the potential to clarify and defuse the critical dilemmas that *Albert Herring* provoked. The very fact that critics have found it impossible to resist trying to locate within it an original voice that has consistently eluded them suggests that modernist oppositions between tradition and innovation are much easier to denounce than to displace. While it is commonplace to comment on the "inimitable" quality or "distinctiveness" of Britten's voice, writers have had a tough time describing it.[99] Just as Crozier implied hermeneutic surplus by highlighting a lack, we might hear the composer marking out his musical originality by foregrounding tradition.

MODERNIST TRADITIONS

Toward the end of *Between the Acts,* the audience can be overheard debating the merits and meanings of the pageant they have just witnessed: while one enthusiastic spectator dubs it "brilliantly clever," another dismisses it as "utter bosh."[100] The only thing upon which they agree is that the play's meaning is less than clear; its eclectic patchwork of literary pastiche is just too random; its welter of disparate voices too incongruous. As Isa, Giles, and Mr. Oliver survey the pageant before retiring for the day, they too agree to disagree, each seeing something different in its "orts, scraps and fragments."[101] Given that Woolf's novel is as eclectic as the artwork it describes, it should come as no surprise that its reception mirrored the critical ambivalence it portrayed.[102] The novel thematizes and draws upon a number of conflicting styles and aesthetics, while ultimately favoring none, making it difficult to establish where its sympathies lie. Is it with the nostalgic "old fogies," who want to hear the same old stories sung to the same old tunes, or with the modernists, "the young, who . . . shiver into splinters the old vision; smash to atoms what was whole"?[103] More importantly, why has it mattered so much, whether to early critics or more recent scholars?

Although mid-century preoccupations with artistic timeliness were often clothed in politicized rhetoric, they rested on long-standing aesthetic concerns. By the early 1920s, Woolf was one of many to assert an artist's resistance to tradition as central to the value of his or her art.[104] By the 1930s, the Leavises were systematically mapping timeliness and tradition, along with other related oppositions—seriousness versus triviality, convention versus innovation—onto the "great divide." While popular fiction was said to exploit conventional pleasures—familiar story lines, characters, and phrases that offered escape from the problems of the modern world—its highbrow counterpart was supposed to disrupt them with radically new musical ideas.[105] Such disruption was often aligned with thematic timeliness, as if employing up-to-date styles and techniques necessarily got audiences pondering pressing themes of war, oppression, and lost innocence. In anxiously stressing the timeliness and seriousness of *Between the Acts,* critics and commentators were—in other words—making claims not just about political relevance but about Woolf's modernism too.

Something similar may be observed in the defensive reactions to *Albert Herring.* By explaining away elements of convention and redirecting attention toward more timely aspects, early critics sought to secure a place for Britten's opera on the "right" side of the great divide. What is more, this defensiveness has only increased in scholarship since. Before echoing all the old defenses, Peter Evans, for one, dismissed the possibility that "Britten's purpose in writing *Albert Herring* could have been *no more* than a wish to entertain by apt caricature of the familiar."[106] In framing his queer reading as an antidote to the opera's apparent nostalgia and conservatism, Philip Brett, for another, invoked them again: "if Britten had not reached, consciously or unconsciously, for something beyond caricature and condescension and had merely produced a cosy little provincial romp in the spirit of the escapist Ealing comedies of the period, the opera would not have survived so well."[107] Even as recently as 2003, Brian Young advanced a socialist interpretation in the same apologetic spirit, as if to uncover a "timely" response to postwar politics was necessarily to erase the opera's conventionality.[108] While mid-century critics were relatively candid about their aesthetic judgments, scholars have tended to couch their defenses in terms of political or social relevance. Their recourse to the same defensive rhetoric, withal, raises the possibility of "politics" serving as a proxy for aesthetic distinctions. Donald Mitchell concluded "The Serious Comedy of *Albert Herring*"—the essay that set the scholarly tone—with an absolute assertion of aesthetic value, suggesting that it was the composer's modernism all along that has been at stake.[109]

In continuing to pose critical problems for even recent scholars, *Herring* suggests that modernist oppositions between tradition and innovation, timeliness and tradition, live on in the way we structure our histories. But while defensive approaches to such ostensibly conventional works tend to reinforce modernist oppositions, *Albert Herring* shows how easily they broke down. Whether stressing affinities with more overtly timely operas, explaining away its traditionalism as ironic, or focusing on its more self-consciously modernist features, critics were torn between their enjoyment of and embarrassment at *Herring*'s flagrantly conventional tropes and styles.[110] Yet it was this very self-consciousness that allowed them to have it both ways. By combining an eclectic welter of old and new voices with critical defensiveness, *Herring*'s audiences could apparently enjoy both tradition and timeliness. While some critics cast Britten's comic opera as something of a middle ground between the dogmatic reverence to tradition and extreme revulsion against it, others cast its success in more dialectical terms: "Modern he [Britten] is—but into his modernity is crystallized a thorough knowledge of and respect for the music of his great predecessors."[111] As an opera that could carry the burden of such tensions and contradictions, in other words, *Albert Herring* acted as an unflattering mirror for musical modernism more generally, simultaneously reveling in and disavowing its own conventionality.

4

The Turn of the Screw, or

The Gothic Melodrama of Modernism

*The driver braked to what was almost a stop, turned round and slid the glass
panel back: The jolt of this flung Mrs. Drover forward till her face was almost
into the glass. Through the aperture driver and passenger, not six inches between them, remained for an eternity eye to eye. Mrs. Drover's mouth hung
open for some seconds before she could issue her first scream. After that she
continued to scream freely and to beat with her gloved hands on the glass
all round as the taxi, accelerating without mercy, made off with her into the
hinterland of deserted streets.*[1]

—ELIZABETH BOWEN, *THE DEMON LOVER, AND OTHER STORIES* (1945)

For a number of mid-century critics, *The Demon Lover* fell squarely within the
Gothic tradition. One of the best-known and most-anthologized of Elizabeth
Bowen's short stories, it tells the tale of a middle-aged housewife who discovers
a mysterious letter—from her undead childhood sweetheart—awaiting her when
she returns home. The letter concludes with a sinister warning: "You may expect
me . . . at the hour arranged."[2] When the clock strikes seven, the protagonist is
kidnapped and driven off into the distance by the eponymous demon. As in most
Gothic novels, the setting holds immense significance as a purveyor of suspense.
Most of the story is spent describing the desolate townhouse that, in spite of its
urban setting, has all the "unfamiliar queerness" of the Gothic castle: the warped
doors, the dark and narrow staircase, and the "cracks in the structure" all offer a
sense of impending horror. And then, in the final paragraph, the subtle hues of
the mysterious setting cede to a dramatic black-and-white; pregnant silence gives
way to deafening screams; and intangible phantoms become gaudy flesh, as the
sentimental heroine comes face to face with a monster.

This melodramatic conclusion was obviously *The Demon Lover*'s deepest bow
to Gothic tradition. While one early critic lauded the tale as one of the few "real" or
"old-fashioned" ghost stories, Hugh Bradenham lamented that an otherwise dis-
criminating writer should welcome "visitors from another world . . . whose normal

purpose in fiction is to bring about crude changes in a melodramatic plot."[3] Yet for every critic who acknowledged the story's Gothic melodrama, there were others who disavowed it entirely, claiming *The Demon Lover* as a paradigm of modernist restraint, an up-to-date ghost story whose specters were more symbolic than literal.[4] Perhaps unsurprisingly, defensiveness has only increased as scholars and critics have sought to secure a place for Bowen in the modernist canon. Seizing on aspersions cast on the narrator's sanity, commentators often maintain that *The Demon Lover* is more a tale of psychological delusion than of ghostly apparition.[5] Still other writers find additional means of demystifying the mysterious demon. As Sarah Dillon has pointed out, this apparently simple tale in the Gothic mold has become the focus of a complex and often heated hermeneutic debate, one that continues to rage on even today.[6]

Premiered less than a decade after *The Demon Lover* hit the bookshelves, Britten's *Turn of the Screw* (1954) has provoked many of the same debates. Based on Henry James's novella of the same name published in 1898, it tells the story of a Governess who, charged with the care of two young orphans at their country estate, becomes locked in a battle over their souls with a pair of resident ghosts. Aside from deploying many of the same sinister edifices and ominous objects as Bowen's story, the opera went even further in giving flesh to its phantoms. It was not just that James's ghosts were made "real" by transferring them to the operatic stage. More problematic still, they were given words to sing. But while commentators have often admitted the ghosts' solidity, they have sought to explain them away in the same defensive spirit as Bowen's devotees. After paying lip service to the tale's notorious "ambiguity," Wilfrid Mellers went on to insist that the "modern," psychological reading of the ghosts—as inventions of the deranged protagonist—was the only sensible one.[7] Nor was he the only critic to discount a more literal interpretation of the opera as a ghost story; in 1992, Philip Brett was still dismissing the opera's Gothic garb as the mere disguise with which it shrouded more "serious" concerns.[8]

Rather than attempting to resolve this dilemma—to determine whether *The Turn of the Screw*'s ghosts are real or psychological, melodramatic or cerebral—I want to excavate its stakes, to ask why this distinction has mattered so much to early critics and more recent ones. For while commentators have often framed the question as a hermeneutic one, whose answer lies buried deep beneath the surface of the opera itself, their rhetoric betrays much broader aesthetic and historiographical concerns, which struck at the heart of the relationship between twentieth-century modernism and Gothic tradition.

TWENTIETH-CENTURY GOTHIC

In the long run-up to the première of Britten's opera, ghosts had become a hot topic of critical conversation. In a review from 1953 of a new ghost story collection,

Charles Poore went so far as to diagnose a Gothic resurgence: "Don't look now, but I think we are having a flourishing revival of supernatural literature."[9] "Newfangled ghost stories," he elaborated, "are bringing fresh terrors to the common place. Oldfangled chillers are in renewed demand." This revival included works by such well-known authors as Walter de la Mare and Elizabeth Bowen, as well as less established writers like Laurence Whistler and Rosemary Timperley. Alongside the many ghost story collections arose a growing body of criticism, which sought to legitimize and contextualize this popular wave as part of a long-standing Gothic tradition. In 1917, Dorothy Scarborough was already declaring it "impossible to understand or appreciate the supernatural in the nineteenth-century literature and that of our own day without a knowledge of the Gothic to which most of it goes back."[10] This idea of Gothicism as a discrete, living tradition was reinforced by several book-length studies that had emerged by the mid-twentieth century, including Edith Birkhead's *Tale of Terror* (1921), Montague Summers's *Gothic Quest* (1938), and Devendra Varma's *Gothic Flame* (1957).[11]

For the most part, however, it was not such painstaking studies but broad-brush modernist attacks that set the tone for twentieth-century Gothic criticism. As Julian Petley has explained, long-term hostility toward the Gothic tradition was so heavily augmented by highbrow censure that the word "Gothic" became a term of opprobrium.[12] Responding to Birkhead's study from 1921, Woolf complained that the Gothic tradition was characterized neither by coherent aesthetic theory nor by stylistic convention but by bad taste: "it is a parasite, an artificial commodity, produced half in joke in reaction against the current style, or in relief from it."[13] Part of the problem was cultural belatedness—a reactionary desire to return to a superstitious, medieval past. This nostalgia often extended beyond the presence of ghosts to the setting: "Walpole, Reeve and Radcliffe," Woolf observed, "all turned their backs upon the time and plunged into the delightful obscurity of the Middle Ages, which were so much richer than the eighteenth century in castles, barons, moats, and murders."[14] If the Gothic novel was already obsolete at its eighteenth-century outset, it was doubly so by the early twentieth century, at odds with the rationalizing "progress" of literary modernism.[15] This cultural belatedness was matched by political obsolescence, as twentieth-century atrocities shifted horror's goalposts: "Nowadays," Woolf opined, "we breakfast upon a richer feast of horror than served them for a twelvemonth; we are tired of horror; we suspect mystery."[16]

A more common objection to the Gothic was its association with melodrama, as Bradenham's review of *Demon Lover* made clear. As Jacques Barzun suggested in his "Henry James, Melodramatist" from 1943, the term "melodrama" implied a crude moral opposition between good and evil, usually expressed in the stagiest fashion.[17] By the middle decades of the twentieth century, "melodrama" had become an even more scathing moniker than "Gothic" among highbrow critics and artists.[18] In putting the two aesthetic modes together, commentators alluded to a number of common sins. On the most basic level, they included a shared reliance on stock characters and settings. Woolf, after all, mocked "the skull-headed lady, the vampire gentleman, [and] the whole troop of monks and monsters" that peopled the Gothic novel, while Birkhead compiled a catalogue of tropes:

> The Gothic Romance did not reflect real life, or reveal character . . . It was full of sentimentality, and it stirred the emotions of pity and fear; the ethereal, sensitive heroine, suffering through no fault of her own, could not fail to win sympathy; the hero was pale, melancholy, and unfortunate enough to be attractive; the villain, bold and desperate in his crimes, was secretly admired as well as feared; hairbreadth escapes and wicked intrigues in castles built over beetling precipices were sufficiently outside the reader's own experience to produce a thrill.[19]

As Birkhead made clear, it was not merely the fact of conventionality but also the types employed that linked Gothic tradition with melodrama; theirs was a shared contrivance whereby events and characters were exaggerated in order to arouse emotions. Woolf joked that "run[ning] over the names of some of the most famous of the Gothic romancers" would elicit "smil[es] at the absurdity of the visions which they conjure up," while another critic derided Gothic novels as "tales of terror, of sentiment and sensibility, but rarely if ever of sense."[20]

In its appeal to emotion instead of intellect, the Gothic offered a popular alternative to the realism and rationalism of the modern novel: "There must have been something in the trash that was appetizing, or something in the appetites that was coarse," wrote Woolf, denigrating not just the pleasures on offer but also those who enjoyed them.[21] While the Gothic market had "flourished subterraneously all through the nineteenth century," it had apparently re-emerged in the twentieth century as a shameless cog in the mass cultural wheel.[22] After accusing the nineteenth-century ghost story of spawning "'the unhealthy and unwholesome rubbish' that is the detective novel and thriller of to-day," another commentator went as far as to suggest that the Gothic novel "laid the foundations of circulating library popularity," as if its ghosts and ruined castles had singlehandedly galvanized mass literacy.[23]

Ultimately it was emerging mass technologies that proved the most popular outlet for twentieth-century Gothic melodrama. Many of those who had previously borrowed or purchased ghost story collections turned to the wireless or to cinema for their daily dose of the supernatural.[24] Radio series like the BBC's *Appointment with Fear*, which dramatized ghost stories old and new between 1943 and 1955, were popular with listeners, but it was film that emerged as the most "avid, unashamed plagiarizer of earlier, literary forms of the Gothic," as Misha Kavka has recounted.[25] Hollywood's Universal Horror films swept Britain throughout the 1930s and 1940s, and British imitations were just as popular.[26] Even before the release of the iconic "Hammer Horror" movies in the late 1950s, there existed a distinctive British tradition, every bit as melodramatic as the American original.[27]

But the tentacles of the Gothic tradition stretched far beyond the horror genre, as Ian Conrich has argued; such was the power and familiarity of Gothic codes that could add tension or suspense to a whole range of film genres, from supernatural thriller to murder mystery, comedy, or romance.[28]

Britten came of age during this crescendo of Gothic forms and imagery, evincing a deep interest in the supernatural from early on. In the introduction to his *Simple Symphony* (1934), he recalls being punished at school for "nocturnal expedition[s] to stalk ghosts," and a diary entry from 1931 records: "Fool[ing] about in [the] drawing room after dinner play[ing] 'Murder' game & telling ghost stories—and so I am going to bed in a very suitable frame of mind!!!"[29] In literature, Britten was drawn not only to nineteenth-century classics of a supernatural bent but also to the "cheaper" ghost story collections that highbrow critics loved to hate.[30] One day in October 1931 saw Britten devouring an unnamed collection of ghost stories; the next August, he spent an evening engrossed in Thomas Ingoldsby's Gothic tales.[31] As with most of his generation, his Gothic experience was not limited to the written word. The young composer's enthusiasm for A. J. Alan's "clever" ghost story broadcasts may have been somewhat muted, but his reaction to Rodney Ackland's dramatic adaptation of a Horace Walpole novel included melodrama of its own: "it was eerie & frightening beyond belief—so much so that I go back to Beth's to sleep!"[32] While he seems not to have seen the notorious Universal Horror films in his cinema visits throughout the 1930s and 1940s, many of Britten's favorite films drew heavily on the tropes and techniques of Gothic cinema, whether for the purposes of satire (as in Clair's *Ghost Goes West*, 1936) or suspense (as in Hitchcock's *Man Who Knew Too Much*, 1934).[33] When it came to trying his hand at composing for the commercial cinema, it was a Gothic melodrama—Rowland Lee's *Love from a Stranger* (1937)—to which Britten turned.

These early encounters left a permanent mark; from the *Serenade* (1943) to the *Nocturne* (1958), the *War Requiem* (1962) to *Owen Wingrave* (1970), ghosts and Gothic imagery suffused Britten's oeuvre. Nevertheless, most commentators agree that the most provocative of Britten's supernatural encounters came over the airwaves on the evening of June 1, 1932, as his diary reports: "listen to the Wireless . . . a wonderful, impressive but terribly eerie & scarey [sic] play 'The Turn of the Screw' by Henry James."[34] By January 1933, Britten had read James's original novella, reporting: "Read more of James' glorious & eerie 'Turn of the Screw'" on the 6th and "Finish the 'Screw.' An incredible masterpiece" on the 7th.[35] Although Britten re-encountered the tale in America, it was apparently not until 1952—after a screening of *The Tales of Hoffmann*—that he thought of making an operatic adaptation.[36] According to Myfanwy Piper, the opera's librettist, it was she who first put forward *The Turn of the Screw* as the basis for an opera-film, one with which the English Opera Group might surpass Powell and Pressburger's spectacular creation.[37] In the end, however, it was an altogether different venture that saw James's novella pressed into service: the fulfillment of a joint commission—by the

Venice Biennale and the 27th International Festival of Contemporary Music—of a live opera, not a film, to be staged at Teatro La Fenice on September 14, 1954.[38]

THE TURN OF THE SCREW AND GOTHIC MELODRAMA

In fashioning the plot of their opera, Britten and Piper stuck relatively close to James's original. It revolves around a young and innocent Governess, who is employed to care for a pair of orphans (Flora and Miles) at their isolated country-side estate. After a promising start, the Governess begins to encounter the ghostly reincarnations of a former governess (Miss Jessel) and valet (Peter Quint), who have returned to corrupt the children's innocence in ways that are not entirely clear. While most of her time is spent trying to extract information from the reti-cent housekeeper (Mrs. Grose), the action peaks with a series of confrontations between the protagonist and the undead intruders. By far the most melodramatic one comes in the final scene, in which the Governess incites Miles to renounce Quint, but only—it becomes apparent—at the cost of his own life. On the most literal level of the plot, then, *The Turn of the Screw* was deeply implicated in Gothic traditions. From its mysterious apparitions to demonic possessions and dramatic exorcisms, here was an opera essentially "about" ghosts: "ghosts are no innovation in opera," Erwin Stein admitted, "but I do not remember one in which ghosts play a principal part."[39]

It is not surprising, then, that many critics were squeamish about the subject. With the exception of one superstitious critic who observed gleefully that "the garish opera house . . . seemed to be covered by a ghostly light," first reactions to Piper's libretto read like a catalogue of contemporary objections to the genre. One sticking point was its morbidity: "In this absurd struggle between the spirits, the children and [the Governess]," Luigi Pestalozza complained, "there is no final salvation."[40] According to another, "reservations [were] expressed by most review-ers on the subject of the libretto. Though the libretto itself appeared to them quite good, the subject, they thought, was complicated and morbid."[41] For most, however, the whimsical superstition was the problem.[42] As one critic warned that "skeptics" would "fail to attain the suspension of disbelief necessary for the enjoyment of a ghost story," another offered a telling anecdote: "An Italian lady in the Fenice the-atre at Venice at the first performance of *The Turn of the Screw* was heard to ask whether Mr. Britten was an Englishman, for surely it was only Irishmen or such whimsical Celts who believed in ghosts."[43] When returning to his own voice, the critic proposed: "the imagination and the intellect are reverse and obverse of the same coin and cannot, therefore, both be uppermost at the same time. Mr. Britten's imagination[,] at any rate, accepts Henry James's story and its ghosts, whatever his intellect may say to their existence."

The mise-en-scène solidified the Gothic connection. As Misha Kavka put it, "there is something peculiarly visual about the Gothic."[44] Ever since the mid-eighteenth century, Gothic novelists and artists had relied on the symbolic potential of setting to heighten suspense. James's *Screw* remained faithful to this tradition: the first chapter is almost entirely devoted to describing Bly's country estate, from the "broad, clear front" and "cloistered tree-tops" on the outside, to the dull corridors and crooked staircases inside. This visual imagery no doubt appealed to the opera's creators. Both Piper and Britten turned to scenic locations—"The Tower and the Lake"—when selecting a provisional title.[45]

Tower and lake were also Gothic stereotypes, perfectly emblematic of the production at large. In translating James's densely descriptive prose into an actual stage design, Basil Coleman (the producer) and John Piper (the designer) magnified the novella's Gothic imagery. "The action," we are instructed, "takes place at Bly, a country house, about the middle of the last century."[46] When Piper's set was unveiled, however, audiences could be forgiven for thinking they had stumbled into a ruined medieval castle. While the exterior spaces (see Fig. 5) were adorned with Gothic details—from pointed arches and turreted rooftops, to imposing tombstones and shadowy branches—the domestic interior emphasized darkness and decay. Other visual tropes to which Coleman and Piper appealed—the "spiral staircase" (Fig. 6) and the "face at the window" (Fig. 7)—were so deeply enmeshed in Gothic tradition that they had served as the titles of well-known horror films.[47]

These visual clichés proved less embarrassing than the work's story line. With the exception of Virgil Thomson, who found the "Victorian Gothic" imagery neither apt nor convincing, most critics were wholeheartedly enthusiastic about the set designs.[48] One critic praised the "momentary shiver[s]" that the backdrops sent down his spine, while another enthused: "John Piper has captured the phantasmagorical atmosphere of Bly, with its turreted towers, dream-like decors which, partially dissolving into each other, contribute to that sense of ambiguity and flux which characterizes the story."[49]

The appearance of the ghosts on stage was another matter, making critics nervous from the very beginning. The flagrant materiality of opera, many suggested, could only simplify the subtle psychology of James's masterpiece and coarsen its famously "ambiguous" symbols.[50] It was doubtless this sort of criticism that compelled Piper to claim, twenty-five years later, that it was not the "action" but, rather, the "words between the action" that drew her and Britten to James's *Screw*.[51] Contrasting her libretto with William Archibald's *Innocents*, a stage adaptation of the same novella from 1950, Piper purported to have abjured melodrama, capturing instead the original "sense of time passing, the shifting of places, the gaps in the action, the long months when nothing and everything happened."[52] "Dramatic" events in James's novella are indeed relatively few and far between. In the first half particularly, weeks and months go by without incident, with characters simply going about their daily business in the domestic setting. In crafting their scenes, Britten and Piper retained some of the ostensibly trivial details and descriptions with which James had filled his pages. While Archibald's play omitted James's

FIG. 5. Production Photograph of *The Turn of the Screw*, 1954: Act 2, Scenes 1 and 2. Photographer: Angus McBean. © Harvard Theatre Collection, Harvard University. Image courtesy of the Britten–Pears Foundation.

"bumping swinging coach" journey completely, Britten and Piper expanded it to fill the opening scene:

> THE JOURNEY
> *[The lights go up on the interior of a coach. The Governess is in a traveling dress]*
>
> GOVERNESS
> Nearly there.
> Very soon I shall know, I shall know what's in store for me.
> Who will greet me? The . . . children . . . the children.
> Will they be clever? Will they like me?
> Poor babies, no father, no mother. But I shall love
> them as I love my own, all my dear ones left at home,
> so far away—and so different.
> If things go wrong, what shall I do? Who can I ask,
> with none of my kind to talk to? Only the old
> housekeeper, how will she welcome me? I must not
> write to their guardian, that is the hardest part of all.
> Whatever happens, it is I, I must decide.
> A strange world for a stranger's sake. O why did I come?

FIG. 6. Production photograph of *The Turn of the Screw*, 1954: Act 2, Scenes 4 and 5.
Photographer: Angus McBean. © Harvard Theatre Collection, Harvard University.
Image courtesy of the Britten–Pears Foundation.

> No! I've said I will do it, and—for him I will.
> There's nothing to fear. What could go wrong?
> Be brave, be brave. We're nearly there. Very soon I
> shall know. Very soon I shall know.[53]

Journeys in opera usually happen between scenes, with characters having already arrived by the time the curtain rises. But far from inducing yawns, this uneventful episode is freighted with sinister foreboding. Combining cryptic questions

FIG. 7. Production Photograph of *The Turn of the Screw*, 1954: Act 1, Scene 5. Photographer: Denis de Marney. Copyright: Getty Images.

with rhetorical excess, Piper instills her text with a sense of mystery and suspense, heightened by Britten's musical atmospheres.

Yet even after conceding that "for the theatre, Myfanwy Piper had no choice but to fill in, even to elaborate, what James surely deliberately left unexpressed in the nature of the ghosts," Martin Cooper could still complain that "They appear too often in this foreshortened version and say too much to maintain the effect of what should be nameless horror."[54] While Britten and Piper curtailed the Governess's monologues, they increased the frequency of the ghostly apparitions, and gave the originally silent ghosts words to sing. Even sympathetic critics were perturbed: "It is obvious that in the opera they would have to speak," conceded Massimo Mila, "but one sometimes one feels that they speak too much, that they are very talkative ghosts."[55]

While Quint's "possession" of Miles was merely implied by James's original protagonist-narrator, it is given strikingly literal representation in the opera's tension-filled encounters. Toward the middle of the second act, we see Quint poised theatrically over Miles (see Fig. 8), directing his movement by pointing and goading him to steal the Governess's letter: "Take it! Take it! Take!" While one commentator defended the scene as "very well done," others bemoaned its naïve and "literal-minded" take.[56] An even more pantomimic staging of this underlying theme comes at the end of the opera, where the Governess's metaphorical battle with Quint over the young boy's soul is staged literally (see Fig. 9), each character tugging on one of Miles's outstretched arms. If melodrama was said to thrive on an overly simplistic moral code—a worldview in which right and wrong, good and evil, were easily distinguishable—then this dramatic tug of war, between villainy and virtue, would appear to be its epitome. One critic blamed the composer for turning James's story "into a morality play, a struggle of Good . . . and Evil for the children's souls," while others chalked the melodramatic conclusion up to downstage positioning and exaggerated acting: "Objections would largely vanish if the production were more careful to keep the ghosts far back on stage and dimly lit."[57]

Two scenes were not so easily redeemable. Even if Peter Pears had stood further back on stage and donned "a more plausible red wig," Shawe-Taylor joked, the last scene of Act I and the first scene of Act II would still have raised eyebrows.[58] As the scenes in which the ghosts were given extended passages of song, they of course departed radically from the original. But critics voiced misgivings not just about fidelity but also about their poor taste, especially when it came to the libretto's obviousness and rhetorical excess. Attempting to represent the unrepresentable—to distill the "nameless horror" of the supernatural into words—Piper adorned the ghosts's speech with gaudy verse:

> QUINT
> I am all things strange and bold,
> The riderless horse
> Snorting and stamping on the hard sea sand,
> The hero-highwayman plundering the land.
> I am King Midas with gold in his hand.
>
> MILES
> Gold, O yes, gold!

FIG. 8. Production Photograph of *The Turn of the Screw*, 1954: Act 2, Scene 5. Photographer: Denis de Marney. Copyright: Getty Images.

QUINT
I am the smooth world's double face,
Mercury's heels
Feathered with mischief and a god's deceit.
The brittle blandishment of counterfeit.
In me secrets and half-formed desires meet.

MILES
Secrets, O secrets!

QUINT
I am the hidden life that stirs
When the candle is out;
Upstairs and down, the footsteps barely heard.
The unknown gesture, the soft, persistent word,
The unknowing gesture, the soft, persistent word,
The long sighing flight of the night-winged bird.[59]

Early audiences were left scratching their heads at this string of Gothic clichés and mythological allusions: "The last scene in Act I," Colin Mason complained, "is

FIG. 9. Production Photograph of *The Turn of the Screw,* 1954: Act 2, Scene 8. Photographer: Denis de Marney. Copyright: Getty Images.

expanded into a quartet in which the relationship between the children and the ghosts is made crudely explicit, and yet no more intelligible."[60] While one critic appreciated the scene's "melodramatic pathos," others saw it as having fallen flat on its face: "Quint's stanzas . . . faintly reminiscent of Midir's Luring Song in *The Immortal Hour,* are quite too harmless for a devil whose utterances ought almost to scare the Lord Chamberlain. And the music, at this point[,] cannot supply (what music could?) the evil element missing in the words."[61]

The second of the two scenes, the "Colloquy and Soliloquy," which opens the second act, was plagued by similar problems. While the Night Scene had merely introduced words to an existing scenario, the Act II duet is entirely new: a lovers' quarrel between the two ghosts. After Miss Jessel accuses of Quint of having betrayed her love, he replies that it was her own passions that deceived her, before reenacting his betrayal all over again:

> QUINT
> I seek a friend.
>
> MISS JESSEL
> She is here!

QUINT
No!—Self-deceiver.

MISS JESSEL
Ah! Quint, Quint, do you forget?

QUINT
I seek a friend—
Obedient to follow where I lead,
Slick as a juggler's mate to catch my thought,
Proud, curious, agile, he shall feed
My mounting power.
Then to his bright subservience I'll expound
The desperate passions of a haunted heart,
And in that hour
"The ceremony of innocence is drowned."

MISS JESSEL
I too must have a soul to share my woe
Despised, betrayed, unwanted she must go
Forever to my joyless spirit bound
"The ceremony of innocence is drowned."

QUINT AND MISS JESSEL
Day by day the bars we break,
Break the love that laps them round,
Cheat the careful watching eyes,
"The ceremony of innocence is drowned."
"The ceremony of innocence is drowned."[62]

Toward the end of their colloquy, Quint spurns the renewed advances of Miss Jessel, preferring a "curious" and "agile" friend (Miles). Together they vow to pursue the young children to satisfy their own selfish needs—Quint, the need for power, and Miss Jessel, the need to share her woe—as they come together in the climactic refrain, famously borrowed from Yeats's "The Second Coming."

For a number of commentators, the scene took theatrical explicitness to an even less acceptable level, having the ghosts act out a supposedly mysterious past in such summary fashion. One writer mocked the dialogue as "perhaps a little obvious," before complaining that the "first scene of the second act, where the two ghosts sing of their private affairs left me rather puzzled . . . One has the impression that both the composer and the librettist have condensed into this scene all the explanations and the symbolic ideas of the work."[63] Others viewed the meeting as a pretext for more melodrama; while one critic lamented that "they open[ed] the second act with a melodramatic scene during which [the ghosts] proclaim their evil aims," another denounced the scene, "in which Quint and Miss Jessel behave like two solid stage villains," as an "unnecessary inclusion."[64] It was not just the morbid preoccupation with evil that reeked of melodrama. That the librettist had added yet another dramatic conflict to an already creaky plot, one wrote, "makes too big a demand on our ordinary theatrical credulity."[65]

MODERN GHOSTS

Not that the opera was poorly received. On the contrary, most accounts of the premiere began with reports of rapturous applause: "the audience politely brought the fine English cast back for eight curtain calls," noted one commentator.[66] This enthusiasm was apparently shared by critics and commentators from all over Europe. The director of La Fenice described the occasion as "one of the great nights of our historic Venetian theatre," while the London *Times* critic dubbed the opera "masterly."[67] The reaction was especially significant, for, as commentators were keen to point out, the Venice Biennale had become one of the leading showcases of contemporary European opera. Invoking a list of recently performed works, several critics cast *The Turn of Screw* as Britain's answer to *The Rake's Progress* and *Lady Macbeth of the Mtsensk District*. Its combination of "refined music" and "obscure Jamesian plot," they agreed, advanced the cause of new opera.[68] When the English Opera Group's production returned home to Sadler's Wells, it was cast as a victory lap in the British press.[69]

Commentators were, however, only too aware that the opera's supposedly sophisticated style fitted oddly with the melodramatic features to which they occasionally alluded. For this reason, they tended to describe those features as exceptions that proved the rule: an atavism that only highlighted the *Screw*'s distance from Gothicism proper. After noting the crude explicitness of the two "problem" scenes, one commentator pushed them aside: "From this single flaw, which could quite easily be removed, it is a pleasure to turn to the extraordinary virtues of [the] text."[70] "These calculated misjudgments, however," another critic agreed, "do little to mar the theatrical effectiveness of the piece."[71] Virgil Thomson went even further, disavowing the "misjudgments" entirely:

> In this work the numerous faults of dramatic taste that have weakened the punch of [Britten's] recent operas seem to me almost wholly absent. On the contrary, two changes in the Henry James story were bold and are, I think, advantageous, though either *could* have changed the whole tone and meaning of it had they not been done with a sure hand . . . The turning of James' furtive and silent ghosts into overtly-singing ones . . . risked making of the establishment a banal "haunted house," of which there are thousands in the world . . . That they did *not* vitiate the terror of the tale is proof of somebody's sound literary sense.[72]

While most commentators stopped short of such unequivocal denial, they invoked the same rhetoric of overriding fidelity. For each one who lamented that "what Myfanwy Piper has done with [the story] takes it quite out of the Jamesian sphere," there was another who emphasized absolute fidelity to the opera's source.[73]

After admitting that Piper had "occasionally been insensitive to some of Henry James' silences and reticences," another nevertheless insisted: "she has been very faithful to the original."[74] Never mere factual observations, such statements were marshaled in aesthetic defense, as Desmond Shawe-Taylor's response makes clear: "Practical disadvantages, however regrettable, must not obscure the aesthetic issue—the unquestionable truth, as it seems to me, that . . . the little opera is a consummate work of art: a work of art in quite the high sense of James himself."[75] Invoking James in this way, commentators could make Britten the beneficiary of some high-profile struggles over the Jamesian legacy, particularly the author's status as a forefather of twentieth-century modernism.[76]

Defending James's oeuvre from Jacques Barzun's provocative "Henry James, Melodramatist," Q. D. Leavis had, for example, stressed the subtle detail and ironic detachment of his novella.[77] The opera's defenders were just as keen to stress these aspects. After observing that "the 'curious story' that the Prologue promises has even as an opera preserved the character of a narrative," one critic elaborated: "Neither the immediacy of the stage nor the emotional directness of music has excluded a certain detachedness of approach."[78] Another critic, writing for the Italian press, went so far as to praise the opera for "bring[ing] back the subtle agony of James," demonstrating "nobility of style and detachment from overt and simple complicity with the salacious subject."[79]

Another defense borrowed from Jamesian criticism was that of hermeneutic ambiguity. Gothicism and melodrama being associated with an uncomplicated binary worldview, praising "obscurity" or "ambiguity" was an easy means of steering the opposite way. Indeed, commentators were surprisingly keen to stress their own bafflement at what was otherwise a relatively straightforward haunted house tale. While one admitted, "It is very difficult to establish even approximately what *The Turn of the Screw*. . . was supposed to mean," another asked: "What should an Italian audience make of a sung version in the original language of a story which English readers have been reading for years without ever really finding out what it means?"[80] Such bafflement could only imply praise at a time when "ambiguity" was a mark of distinction, implying complexity and richness of meaning on the part of the work, and intelligence on the part of its interpreters.[81] Of this, the first-night audience appears to have been all too aware, reportedly falling over themselves to demonstrate that they could rise to the "ambiguous" tale's challenge: "Unlike the French at 'Billy Budd,'" one commentator explained, "[this audience was] not unresponsive. Clearly their practice in Pirandello stood them in good stead, and they fell outside into dozens of little groups gamely, ingenuously, or obscurely explaining and counter-explaining, and all ready to die rather than look blank."[82]

Such an emphasis was a central part of the novella's mid-century reception too, set out most famously in Edmund Wilson's essay of 1938, "The Ambiguity of Henry James." The real horror behind the story line's "ostensible" one, Wilson suggested, was that the novella's devotees had missed its deeper meaning. Following the work of Edna Kenton and Charles Demuth, he argued that the story's ghosts were best understood as products of the protagonist's imagination. His Freudian reading cast the novella as a tale of psychological delusion and sexual repression, rather than a supernatural thriller in the Gothic mold: "The poltergeist, once a figure of demonology, is now a recognized neurotic type."[83] For all Wilson's loudly trumpeted talk of "ambiguity," in other words, he appears rather confident of the story's meaning, sternly refusing to read it as a ghost story.[84] A number of the opera's critics appear to have picked up this kind of critical doublethink, championing ambiguity in one breath, explaining it away in the next. While one review praised the opera as a lodestar of a "new psychological aesthetic," another was titled "Governess as Ghost": "Both the libretto by Myfanwy Piper and the composer's musical treatment of it seem to have opted for that theory of the tale in which the ghosts are an invention of the Governess."[85]

These defenses were not without foundation. James was arguably in on the interpretive game, encouraging critics to disregard some of his novella's most striking features and influences. On the most basic level, the story often draws self-conscious or ironic attention to its own Gothic conventions, thereby subtly discrediting them as interpretive frameworks. After encountering Quint for the first time in chapter 3, James's Governess appears to mock her own gullibility while parodying Gothic convention: "Was there a 'secret' at Bly—a mystery of Udolpho or an insane, unmentionable relative kept in an unsuspected confinement?"[86] Elsewhere, she casts even greater aspersions on the Gothic clichés: "[Miles] could do what he liked . . . so long as I should continue to defer to the old tradition of the criminality of those caretakers of the young."[87] While these particular references were not retained in the opera, Piper's libretto found comparable means of throwing audiences off the Gothic scent. At the start of the fourth scene, the Governess parodies her own susceptibility to Gothic cliché: "My foolish fears are all vanished now, are all / banished now / those fluttering fears when I could not forget the letter / when I heard a far off cry in the night / and once a faint footstep passed my door."[88] Later on, immediately after the controversial Act 2 Colloquy, the Governess devotes an entire monologue to imaginative delusion:

GOVERNESS
[The lights fade out on Quint and Miss Jessel and fade in on the Governess]
Lost in my labyrinth I see no truth
Only the foggy walls of evil press upon me.
Lost in my labyrinth I see no truth.

O innocence, you have corrupted me,
which way shall I turn?

I know nothing of evil
yet I feel it, I fear it, worse—imagine it.
Lost in my labyrinth which way shall I turn?[89]

Thus, no sooner had the opera manifested its ghosts in a stagey, domestic quarrel than it moved to dematerialize them, using both text and lighting to reinterpret the Colloquy as a product of the Governess's imagination. While the opera's audience cannot actually witness events through the eyes and ears of the Governess, as in James's novella, it is nevertheless encouraged to identify with her and share her interpretative dilemmas. She is, in other words, cast as the symbolic spectator. This sense of the Governess mediating the narrative, even though she is not the narrator, is heightened by the opera's prologue, which casts the work as a retelling of testimony "written in faded ink, a woman's hand, governess to two children, long ago."[90]

Nor is it just the Governess who casts doubt on her testimony. The other characters also have inconsistent faith in the Governess and ghosts. While she alone witnesses Quint's first appearance on the tower in scene four, her detailed description appears to be enough to convince Mrs. Grose that the former valet had indeed come back to life. By the second-act lake scene, however, Mrs. Grose has changed her mind, unable to see the ghost standing right beside her: "Indeed Miss," she insists, "there's nothing there."[91] Yet such incredulity does not last; by the beginning of the following scene, she mysteriously repents and reaffirms her faith in the Governess's visions. The children's position is even more contradictory. Much ink has been spilled trying to determine the extent of their knowledge of (and complicity with) the opera's ghosts. On the one hand, we witness Flora and Miles conversing with Miss Jessel and Quint respectively (as, for example, in Act I, Scene 8). On the other hand, they often appear completely ignorant of the ghosts, even charging the Governess with imagining them:

> FLORA
> I can't see anybody, can't see anything
> nobody, nothing.
> I don't know what she means.
> Cruel, horrible, hateful, nasty,
> we don't want you! We don't want you!
> Take me away, take me away from her!
> Hateful, cruel, nasty, horrible.[92]

Throughout both the novella and its operatic adaptation, there are frequent attempts to pathologize the protagonist, raising questions about her sanity and her testimony. As commentators have often pointed out, the novella's long and complicated prologue introduces the Governess as a "fluttered, anxious girl out of a Hampshire vicarage," whose sexual repression and inexperience engender an infatuation with her prospective employer. For Wilfrid Mellers, this was proof enough of psychological subtext: "since there never was a less adventitious writer than James, I find it difficult to credit that, were not the Freudian interpretation basic, he would have stressed the Governess's infatuation for the Guardian, who is presented as a figure of unattainable sexual glamour."[93] When Britten and Piper finally decided to have a prologue of their own, it was this detail that they placed at its center: "She was full of doubts / But she was carried away: that he, so gallant and handsome / so deep in the busy world, should need her help."[94] This infatuation reappears throughout the opera, particularly in connection with the ghostly encounters. In the tower scene (Act I, Scene 4), for example, the Governess longs to see her employer immediately before Quint appears:

> GOVERNESS
> Only one thing I wish, that I could see him—
> and that he could see how well I do his bidding.
>
> The birds fly home to these great trees, I too am at
> home.
> Alone, tranquil, serene.
> [Quint becomes visible on the tower.]
>
> Ha! 'Tis he!
> [He looks steadily at her, then turns and disappears]
>
> No! No! Who is it? Who?
> Who can it be?[95]

Combining signs of sexual longing with expressions of isolation, the scene encouraged audiences to don psychoanalytic spectacles. Critics were only too happy to take the bait, steering the opera away from the Gothic mold into a more modern, psychological thriller. In wielding psychology against Gothic melodrama, however, these critics were not as modern as they may have thought. The tension between physical and psychological terror, reality and fantasy, had been endemic to the Gothic genre from the start, and was still at play in the most popular Gothic tales of the early- and mid-twentieth century.[96]

GOTHIC MUSIC

None of these discussions about the opera's ambivalent relationship with modernism and Gothic melodrama would have been so fraught had they not had significant implications for the music. Opera was regarded as a musical genre first and foremost, and it was Britten's integrity and legacy that critics were most concerned to protect. It was for this reason that they often tried to separate the music from other operatic components. Even Ernest Newman, who dismissed the libretto because "what Myfanwy Piper has done with it takes it quite out of the true Jamesian sphere," defended Britten's music to the hilt: "But when we come to consider the music there would seem to be a different story to tell."[97] The music supposedly did not partake of Gothic melodrama's crude tricks, and commentators devoted considerable energy to directing the audience's attention toward its more cerebral—even modernist—aspects.

One of these was the opera's widely publicized gestures toward musical formalism, particularly serialism. As a number of critics and analysts pointed out even before the premiere, the principal "theme"—first introduced after the prologue—included all twelve notes of the chromatic scale.[98] This theme became the basis for a protracted theme-and-variations structure, stretching across the entire opera's scenes and interludes, which expands upon the opening theme. Furthermore, as one critic pointed out, each interlude fixes the key of the following scene in ways that foreground even greater structural and symmetrical logic: "The sequence of key rises in the first act and descends in the second."[99] "Although each key has its own mood and colour," the same critic continued, "a unifying thread runs through the ritornelli."[100]

As this response makes clear, it was not just symmetry but unity that the opera's critics were touting. Indeed, the idea of an underlying motivic unity beneath the musical surface—a common means of stressing formal integrity and warding off charges of eclecticism—was a central trope in the opera's reception. After admitting that Britten's "use of the note row is also very free," one critic equivocated: "although it would not be an exaggeration to say that the entire opera is based on it."[101] Stein concurred: "almost the entire music of the opera is based on only two themes."[102] The combined effect of this motivic unity and variation technique, he concluded, was to provide large-scale formal coherence to a seemingly episodic structure. Elsewhere, Stein was even more candid in suggesting that listeners hear musical unity rather than melodramatic eclecticism:

> The themes of the opera are closely related with each other, not in character, but by the motives of which they consist. They are derived chiefly by way of variations from the theme of the screw. It so happens that a child's song and ghost's incantation occasionally use similar melodic turns.[103]

Occasionally, critics resorted to stronger rhetoric, discrediting surface stylistic heterogeneity entirely: "It sounds on first hearing improvised and facile, casual and only superficially brilliant. But it is not. It is, in fact, rather elaborately constructed out of well-chosen themes and formal variations on them."[104] Other commentators—no less defensively—invoked comparisons with "purely" instrumental genres as a means of stressing the primacy of musical form. One insisted that the music "stands on its own every bit as firmly as a symphony or a set of variations," while another concluded: "Britten can also let music take charge of a whole situation, music that is not just interesting for its dramatic values, but strikingly compelling in a purely symphonic kind of way."[105] This trope of musical purity, unspoiled by dramatic or illustrative considerations, also came out when a critic enthused that James's prose had proven "stimulating to the composer's *purely* musical instinct."[106] One critic even went so far as to subtitle his review "masterly construction," while yet another described the whole work as "the most difficult and tightly unified of Britten's operas."[107]

EX. 13. *The Turn of the Screw* (Act I, Scene 7)—"The Dead Sea".

This focus on "purely musical" matters of form, unity, and symmetry provided a musical equivalent to the libretto's psychoanalytic perspectives.[108] But like the opera's textual codes and ciphers, these musical clues were neither well hidden nor particularly consistent. As Philip Rupprecht has observed, although the "screw" theme's claustrophobic ubiquity seems to endow it with even greater power and agency than a Wagnerian leitmotif, it lacks a Wagnerian sense of physical or metaphysical reference: "its function is not tied to specific elements of plot or character, but to the way in which these are presented to the audience; the Screw is less a part of the story than of its telling."[109] One might even think of the opera's formal patterns and connections as a kind of Gothic game—a Radcliffean secret, in which underlying meaning and logic is constantly toyed with, and just as constantly undermined.

Yet, with only a few telling exceptions, Britten's music outside the interludes eschews extended musical forms and set pieces in favor of a more fluid, musically enhanced declamation, halfway between recitative and aria. When some critics described the vocal writing as melodramatic, they meant it as much in a historical sense—harking back to a nineteenth-century recitation with heightened musical accompaniment—as in an aesthetic one.[110] When Flora interrupts her song of the seas (see Ex. 13) and fixates upon the "Dead Sea" with macabre obsession, Britten almost brings musical time to a standstill as he repeats the sinister half-step interval with relative abandon. In the controversial Act II Colloquy (Ex. 14), the flexible vocal lines veer between the speech-like monotone of the opening measures and the hysterical screams of "No, self-deceiver." In the orchestral accompaniment, moreover, Britten gives sonic flesh to his phantoms: underneath their melodramatic declamation, we hear contrasts of volume and orchestration, which not only differentiate but also seem to physicalize the two ghosts, literalizing their conceptual struggle as a material one. While Miss Jessel reproaches her former lover to the barely audible accompaniment of murmuring strings and timpani rolls, Quint responds with the backing of high, trilling woodwinds (at Figs. 9, 11, and 13). At the same time as choreographing the ghost's movements, however, these striking gestures and timbres go even further to pictorialize their imagery: at Fig. 9, the clarinet's chalumeau trills are hardly subtle in evoking the "terrible sound of the wild swans' wings," while the flute patter after Fig. 11 mimics Miss Jessel's "beating heart."

Elsewhere Britten's melodramatic literalism "stoops" to announcing various characters' entrances and underscoring their movements. The most frivolous instance of such musical "mimomania"—to borrow Nietzsche's term—comes in the second scene, when Miles and Flora practice their bows and curtseys to the synchronized sound of harp glissandi.[111] A more telling example may be drawn from the final scene with Britten's trademark passacaglia, or "wrong-footed funeral march," as one critic described it. This passage does not merely symbolize the unstoppable march of death, but also seems to choreograph the entrances (first of Miles, then of Quint), before serving as a visceral backdrop to the stagey battle over the boy's soul.[112] Other intensely rhythmic numbers such as "Tom, Tom, the Piper's Song," from Act I, Scene 5, likewise set the pace for stage movement, choreographing the children's bounding around the stage on their toy hobbyhorse. Indeed, the fact that the opera's most expansive musical forms are all diegetic songs and numbers—from Flora's "Lavender's Blue" to Miles's piano sonata—seems, at first hearing, to assign the music a literalistic or mimetic role. Even the supposedly "pure" interludes and variations, which critics praised enthusiastically with formalist rhetoric, bore pictorial connotations, from the "crunch of the [carriage] wheels on the gravel" in the first interlude, to the bird-like flute arpeggios of the third, to the rippling lake sounds of the sixth.

That such musical mimeticism or sonic literalism fitted oddly with critics' formalistic defenses and psychoanalytic explanations was by no means lost on them. One commentator highlighted the paradox of a score that was "icy, cerebral and artificial" on the one hand, and "directed at the senses" on the other: "It tries to plumb no depths yet the effects are sure, although they hit the solar plexus more than the ear."[113] In a number of accounts, however, these "ingenuously illustrative" aspects of the score caused considerable concern, one critic denigrating the score for its "skirt[ing] the fringes of the action, ranging from moments of movie-score

SCENE I. Colloquy and Soliloquy
The lights fade in on Quint and Miss Jessel - nowhere

EX. 14. *The Turn of the Screw* (Act II, Scene 1)—"Colloquy".

EX. 14 (continued).

drama to *Peter and the Wolf* simplicity, including a lilting harp passage to accompany the children and wailing sirens for the ghosts."[114] Although the film music comparison chimes well with the composer's own remarks that *The Turn of the Screw* was his "most suitable [opera] for television," it was not intended as a compliment.[115] In drawing attention to Britten's "wailing sirens," this commentator brought the discussion back to Gothic melodrama. Riccardo Malipiero went further, drawing explicit connections between Britten's illustrative music and a crudely literal reading of James's story: "instead of rising to the peak of the harsh mountain of psychopathic revelation," he explained, "[the expressive crescendo] stops short halfway and remains in the literal, narrative rather than musical and poetic level."[116]

The more sympathetic critics, however, forgave the crude and melodramatic literalism for the sake of Britten's subtle "moods" and "atmospheres." "The fact that all [of the interludes] are variations on one theme . . . does not impress one over-much," wrote one "What is delightful is their dramatic effect . . . they set the atmosphere for the next scene, and they are never just arbitrary essays in pure music."[117] Like many others, he praised Britten's subtle attention to sound—color, orchestration, and timbre. "It is evident," another commentator insisted, "that he does not . . . first 'compose' a work and then orchestrate it, but that for him the act of creation is a single process."[118] One Italian commentator dubbed the music "a masterpiece of timbral images," while another enthused: "mature and imaginative command of instrumental timbres seemed entirely successful in creating the various moods."[119]

Despite all the talk of formalism and literalism, then, Britten's music often blurs the boundaries between these extremes. In the markedly "atmospheric" music of the seventh interlude (see Figs. 70–71 in the published score), Britten seems precisely to play with this dividing line. The "screw" theme, singing from deep out of the murky textures, is nothing if not a musical symbol or hermeneutic clue; yet the unusual textures and instrumental effects seem to draw attention to the sonic surface, as if to demand a more immediate response. The celesta arpeggios crystallize this wider ambivalence: they have a partial melodic and motivic identity—as the opera's "second" theme—even as they mimic the lake's rippling waves. Similar in effect are Quint's apparently wordless vocal melismas to Miles at the beginning of the "Night" scene (Ex. 15), an obvious nod to the Gothic "humming and groaning" that Britten and Piper were anxious to avoid.[120] As the supposedly solid ghost is hidden from view, his voice takes on the air of an *acousmêtre*, residing—in the words of film theorist Michel Chion—"neither inside nor outside" the narrative.[121] Like the uncanny sounds of the "Night" interlude from which it springs, the glassy celesta accompaniment, the subtle undulations of the melody, and the soft dynamic swells suggest physical presence and absence by turns.

Even the diegetic songs are repositioned in the space between the literal and the symbolic by a range of musical devices. In "Tom, Tom, the Piper's Son" it is the

EX. 15. *The Turn of the Screw* (Act I, Scene 8)—"Miles".

exaggerated physicality and violence of the accompaniment—the harsh timbres and dissonant chord clusters—that simultaneously gesture toward literalism and beyond it, to symbolic excess. In the Act II "Benedicite," the realistic sounds of the church bells and canticle melody are rendered uncanny by chromatic trills, sustained, syncopated chords, harmonic recontextualization, and melodic distortion. Uncanny children's songs, of course, have a considerable history, running from Schubert's death lullabies through Mahler's First Symphony and Berg's *Wozzeck* to Gothic film scores. More to the point, they played into a broader ambivalence of musical surfaces that both reveal and conceal, whose source and identity raised pressing questions in the listener. Such "atmospheric" music seems to put the audience in the Governess's position, tasked with interpreting a subtle and contradictory sign system that is realistic and obvious on the one hand, and elusive and coded on the other.

Critics who admired the libretto's subtlety found in Britten's "timbral images" comparably redeeming details: "every nuance of action and character finds expression in the timbre of the instruments," wrote one.[122] Another found in these atmospheric timbres the sonic equivalents of the subtle mannerisms with which James had sidestepped Gothic convention: "Mr. Britten . . . elicited from [the ensemble] just such disturbing tones and tonalities, figures and drum-taps, . . . as the equivalent of James's mannered periods in the creation of a sinister atmosphere."[123] Yet these effects stretched back to the literary soundscapes of the earliest Gothic novels: from the wind sighs that double as ghostly whispers in Walpole's *Castle of Otranto* (1764), to the spectral music and evanescent chanting in Ann Radcliffe's *Mysteries of Udolpho* (1794), to the oscillation between subtle murmurs and melodramatic laughter at the center of Charlotte Brontë's *Jane Eyre* (1847).[124] Perhaps even more important for our present purposes, this literary play between exaggerated sound effects and subtle sonic symbolism was actualized in a number of Gothic soundtracks from Britten's own time: from the BBC's *Appointment with Fear* (1943–1955) to Hitchcock's *Rebecca* (1940), and the Hammer Horror series that ran in the late 1950s and 1960s.[125]

GOTHIC MODERNISM

In emphasizing these largely overlooked aspects of *The Turn of the Screw*'s mise-en-scène, text, and music and tying them to Gothic melodrama, my intention has not been to answer *the* question that has preoccupied most scholars: whether the work's ghosts are real or imagined, supernatural or psychological. It has been instead to open up a window on the aesthetic stakes, exposing the opera's challenges to the modernist critical tradition. While modernist readings of the opera have generally prevailed in recent scholarship and criticism, reactions to the premiere reveal a more complicated situation, wherein such interpretations were unsettled by associations with Gothic melodrama. The fact that contemporary commentators embraced mutually exclusive interpretations suggests that the problem resided less in the interpretations than in the binary categories to which they appealed.

The wider significance of the opera's fraught reception may be sought here. In their attempts to draw sharp distinctions between a modernist, psychological tale and an old-fashioned, melodramatic ghost story, defenders of Britten in 1954 were participating in a much broader critical trend. By 1921, Birkhead had already predicted that science and psychology would fundamentally remake the Gothic novel for the twentieth century.[126] By the early 1950s, this transition was supposedly complete:

> Ghosts have grown up. Far behind lie their clanking and moaning days; they have laid aside their original bag of tricks—bleeding hands, luminous skulls and so on. Their manifestations are, like their personalities, oblique and subtle, perfectly calculated to get the modern person under the skin. They abjure the over-fantastic and the grotesque, operating, instead, through series of happenings whose horror lies in their being just, just out of the true. Ghosts exploit the horror latent behind reality.[127]

Such a distinction between the modern, subtle, psychological ghost story and the Gothic melodrama was almost ubiquitous in early- to mid-twentieth-century criticism. Indeed, for all her attacks on the crudities and excesses of the Gothic novel, even Woolf made room for its supposedly subtle, modern, psychological descendant, inaugurated by the novels of Henry James:

> Henry James's ghosts have nothing in common with the violent old ghosts—the blood-stained sea captains, the white horses, the headless ladies of dark lanes and windy commons. They have their origin within us. They are present whenever the significant overflows our powers of expressing it; whenever the ordinary appears ringed by the strange.[128]

This desire to erect overdetermined boundaries was not entirely ingenuous. After all, the modernist canon—from the poetry of Yeats and Eliot, to the novels of Joyce and Forster—hardly lacked ghosts, apparitions, and mysterious voices. Even as Woolf attacked the Gothic supernatural, she penned stories like *Mrs. Dalloway* (1925) and *To the Lighthouse* (1927)—not to mention "The Haunted House" and "A Mark on the Wall"—which flirted, sometimes subtly, sometimes not so subtly, with Gothic tropes and conventions. In one of her more candid moments, Woolf admitted that the distinction was less clear-cut than highbrow critics might have imagined. "It would be a fine exercise in discrimination," she remarked, tongue firmly in cheek, "to decide the precise point at which romance becomes Gothic and imagination moonshine . . . [A] gift for romance easily escapes control and cruelly plunges its possessor into disrepute."[129] She then elaborated:

> In our days we flatter ourselves that the effect is produced by subtler means. It is at the ghosts within us that we shudder, and not at the decaying bodies of barons or the subterranean activities of ghouls. Yet the desire to widen our boundaries, to feel excitement without danger, and to escape as far as possible from the facts of life drives us perpetually to trifle with the risky ingredients of the mysterious and the unknown.[130]

It would seem, then, that the difference between the two categories she had worked so hard to separate was a matter of degree rather than kind. What is more, Woolf apparently admitted that any lines drawn between them were a matter more of self-flattery than reality. Just as old-fashioned ghost stories were never completely devoid of psychological implication, so it is equally true that modernism's psychological images and projections were never totally free of superstition, excess, and externalized horrors.[131] Indeed, in its notorious attempts to shock and unsettle audiences, one might even describe modernism as the epitome of Gothic melodrama.

The Turn of the Screw highlights this overlapping of aesthetic oppositions particularly vividly. On the hermeneutic level, it foregrounds both the material reality and psychological invention of James's ghosts, simultaneously invoking and undermining these popular binaries. On an aesthetic level, it navigates between suspense-filled subtleties and melodramatic eventfulness. At the same time, Britten's opera also drives home a related musical point: that the archetypes of high modernism and Gothic melodrama could often sound remarkably alike. Many of the score's distinctive features—its atmospheric dissonances, its play with gestural immediacy and formalist abstraction, its loyalties divided between subtle timbral effects, and transgressive rhetorical excess—were as characteristic of musical modernism as of its rejected Gothic other. One recalls that, even as they denounced film composers for reducing musical modernism to the status of a Gothic soundtrack, Adorno and Eisler praised Berg's *Lulu* for doing something similar: "suspense," they insisted, "is the essence of modern harmony."[132] Cast as both modernist psychodrama and Gothic melodrama, Britten's *Screw* arguably did not reconcile aesthetic opposites so much as reveal the unsettling commonalities between two traditions, which commentators fought hard to—but could never quite—separate.

5

The Burning Fiery Furnace and the Redemption of Religious Kitsch

There was a dramatic silence only broken by the clank of the censer chains as incense was put on and a column of blue smoke began to rise. Then a rather cracked voice intoned, "Let us proceed in peace," but peace was not to be the order of the day, for the tympani began to roll and then with a crash of full organ and orchestra the procession set off singing "Hail thee festival day" in a tumult of sound. I was spellbound by all this and delighted when they came past me so that I could get a proper look at them.[1]

—COLIN STEPHENSON, *MERRILY ON HIGH*, 1972

Near the opening of his novelistic memoirs—a chronicle of a long career as an Anglo-Catholic priest—Colin Stephenson looks back at one of the defining moments of his religious life: his first experience of High Mass at St. Bartholomew's, Brighton. Here the stage was set for a lifelong religious aestheticism, an epicurean obsession with monumental processions, intoxicating incense, and kitschy icons. For High Mass at St. Bart's was apparently less a solemn service than an awe-inspiring spectacle. If detractors disparaged the occasion as a "den of iniquity"—or, worse still, the "Sunday opera"—even visiting clergy viewed their own contributions as interludes between the *Gesamtkunstwerk*'s main acts. "I preached there not long ago," Fr. Davies reported: "'It's not a sermon you have but an interval while the wind performers empty their instruments.'"[2] Writing in the wake of Vatican II and related protestant reforms of the liturgy, this aestheticism had come to seem increasingly untenable: "looking back on it now," Stephenson reflected, "one realizes that it had about as much chance of appealing to the average Anglican as the Folies Bergères to the Mothers' Union."[3] Yet, for all aestheticism's baggage, it is depicted with deep affection, with an ambivalent sense of mourning for this powerful but increasingly obsolete form of worship.

Premiered at around the same time that Stephenson penned his novel, Britten's *Burning Fiery Furnace* (1966) touched upon much the same ambivalence. The story line, adapted from the *Book of Daniel* by the librettist William Plomer, revolves around the Babylonian king Nebuchadnezzar and the three Israelites (Ananias, Misael, and Asarias; renamed Shadrach, Meshach, and Abednego), who were thrown into his furnace for refusing to worship his golden idol. While the story's central message is one of unwavering faith—for God ultimately delivers the young men from the furnace unharmed—Britten's and Plomer's dramatic setting foregrounds its aesthetic implications: the questions it raises about the proper relationship between aestheticism and asceticism, ostentatious worship and austere faith. This chapter will explore this aspect of the church parable's meaning, using the fraught relation between the work and its reception to shed light on how mid-century audiences negotiated the fault lines of contemporary theological aesthetics. If the story line appears straightforwardly to reject religious aestheticism in ways that line up neatly with contemporary trends in liturgy and aesthetics alike, this chapter will offer an alternative perspective, in which Britten's *Fiery Furnace* risked burning down the very boundaries that it staged.

BELLS AND SMELLS

As the tale of King Nebuchadnezzar and his golden statue clarifies, the putative tension between monumentality, sensuality, and luxury in worship, on the one hand, and authentic faith, on the other, has a long and complicated history that goes back to (and even predates) the Bible.[4] Yet, as Stephenson's novel implies, twentieth-century divisions in the English church had more distinctive roots in the English Reformation, with its puritanical rejection of Catholic religious services. In the eyes of aesthetes like Stephenson, the break with Rome was "a complete disaster [which] deprived the ordinary Englishman of the full practice of the Catholic religion which was his by right."[5] One of the defining aspects of the Anglican tradition from this point on was opposition to ritualism and aestheticism, practices heavily associated with the Roman liturgy; and so, as Stephenson lamented, "the Church of England got deader and deader and the sacraments fell into disuse," until "a gallant group of men in Oxford decided to change all this and they were subjected to terrible persecution." The heroes of Stephenson's account were of course the mid-nineteenth-century Anglo-Catholics, who cleared a space for Catholic ritualism and aestheticism within the Established Church once again.

Far from extinguishing English antipathy to religious aestheticism, however, the movement arguably fanned its flames, as liberal, evangelical, and puritan branches of the Church of England charged themselves with upholding Protestant principles.[6] Even in its late-nineteenth- and early-twentieth-century heyday, when Anglo-Catholic practices entered the Anglican mainstream, such aestheticism was often still coded as "Catholic" in the most derogatory senses of the term. For some Evangelicals, high liturgy signaled moral depravity and sensual indulgence, and was often "associated with 'worldly' activities such as dancing, drinking, gambling and Sabbath-breaking."[7] Such links were strengthened by a native tradition of literary aestheticism, stretching from Oscar Wilde to Evelyn Waugh and beyond, which associated high liturgy with moral decadence and class privilege.[8] Writing in 1968, Anthony Burgess—an English Catholic of a self-consciously puritan stripe—denounced the spirituality of Waugh and other aesthetes as "disturbingly sensuous, even slavering with gulosity, as though God were somehow made manifest in the *haute cuisine*."[9] For Burgess and others, such a self-indulgent model of Christianity verged on sacrilege, with the sensual pleasures of worship ("religious good feeling") replacing genuine faith.[10]

In addition, religious aestheticism had strong associations with authoritarian governance and conservative cultural politics. For many, powerfully prescriptive rites were inseparable from dogmatic forms of clericalism and papalism, both of which ran counter to Britain's constitutional heritage. As one commentator, railing against the Anglo-Catholic liturgy, put it in 1935: "Evangelical Churchmen have no desire that the English should submit to the Pope, or that the Roman Catholic conception of Christianity should be adopted in this country."[11] For T. S. Eliot, flying in the face of the English mainstream, this commitment to hierarchy, authority, and dogma was high liturgy's most compelling facet, serving as an antidote to modern society's ills. Railing against liberal visions of spirituality as a personal choice, Eliot cast faith as a corporate affair, requiring absolute subservience to Catholic dogma and ritual.[12] According to him, it was only through obedience and observance that Christian authority and the coherence of English society more broadly could be guaranteed.[13]

If such a corporate vision went against the grain in the 1930s and 1940s, when Eliot penned most of his polemics, it was even more of an irritant by the time Britten's *Burning Fiery Furnace* was premiered. Particularly as postwar immigration from the Empire and Commonwealth rose, Eliot's notion of a unified Christian culture seemed increasingly tenuous.[14] The 1960s famously bore witness to an unprecedented cultural revolution targeted at the kind of authoritarian traditions and hierarchies that religious aestheticism seemed to symbolize. While many disavowed religion entirely, others looked elsewhere for decentered models of spirituality.[15] Christian churches and institutions were not immune from these trends.[16] Writing in 1960, John Robinson, Bishop of Woolwich and a popular theologian (with whom Britten expressed sympathy), called for services that emphasized liberalism, ecumenicalism, and pluralism: the church as a community of equals instead of a hierarchy.[17] Such reforms, he implied, would leave more "elaborate or heavily ritualistic" forms of worship out in the cold.[18] These changes were matched by even greater revolutions in the Catholic Church, as the Second Vatican Council's introduction of vernacular texts and music radically re-shaped the Roman liturgy.

This rising tide of theological opposition to aestheticism was paralleled by a much broader trend in twentieth-century aesthetics. One of the driving currents of British modernism was, after all, an explicit rejection of romantic aestheticism.

Even Eliot, who would later embrace liturgical sensuality and sublimity, was instrumental in outlawing these qualities from poetry, considering them effusive, anti-intellectual, emotional, and exaggerated.[19] For T. E. Hulme, another Anglo-Catholic poet and critic, the austere "classicism" of modernist writing was likewise a welcome bulwark against the pseudo-sublimity of late Romanticism: "In the classic," he wrote approvingly, "it is . . . always perfectly human and never exaggerated: man is always man and never a god."[20] If English theologians viewed aestheticized religion as a compromised and indulgent expression of faith, prominent literary critics apparently found aestheticism's sacred aspirations equally damaging to art. While Eliot stressed the inadequacy of language to articulate spiritual truths, Hulme insisted: "The instincts that find their right and proper outlet in . . . their own [religious] sphere are spread over, and so mess up, falsify and blur the clear outlines of human experience. It is like pouring a pot of treacle over the dinner table."[21] It was here in the aesthetic sphere, in other words, that "high" liturgical aestheticism reversed into its opposite: the lowest of the low. "The original convention which underlies kitsch," Hermann Broch wrote in 1950, "is exaltation, or rather hypocritical exaltation, since it tries to unite heaven and earth in an absolutely false relationship."[22] For Broch, this conjunction of lowbrow sensuality and metaphysical pretention lay at the root of the twentieth-century kitsch: "the stars, and everything else that is eternal," he insisted, with echoes of Hulme, "are obliged to come down to earth."[23]

These dismissals were particularly pronounced in the world of opera and theater, where sensuality and spectacle had long reigned supreme. As Adorno suggested in 1955, opera's characteristic gaudiness and exaggeration stemmed from this quasi-religious sense of overreach: "This original ideological essence of opera, its besetting original sin," he explained—with a revealing metaphor—"can be observed in decadent extremes, as in the comic affectations of singers who fetishize their voices as if they truly were the gift of God."[24] In his well-known discussion of "holy theatre," the famed English theater director Peter Brook made a similar point, denouncing romantic opera and ballet for debasing theater by striving toward an excessive, gaudy, and materialistic kind of sublimity:

> The tendency for centuries has been to put the actor at a remote distance, on a platform, framed, decorated, lit, painted, in high shoes—so as to help persuade the ignorant that he is holy, that his art is sacred. Did this express reverence? Or was there behind it a fear that something would be exposed if the light were too bright, the meetings too near? Today, we have exposed the sham.[25]

If Adorno denounced aspirations to metaphysics tout court, Brook sought to revive the theatre's original "holy" function in the most abstract sense—to allow people to experience the invisible reality behind the world of appearances and to transcend the drabness of everyday life. "It is foolish," he insisted, "to allow revulsion from bourgeois forms to turn into a revulsion from needs that are common to all men."[26]

While Brook avoided specific prescriptions for what an authentic "holy theatre" might look and sound like, the exaggerated and moribund conventions of Romantic theater were clearly anathema to his cause. This often made for a set of anxious, if not seemingly paradoxical, commitments: to transcend the drabness of everyday life without succumbing to escapism; to make the invisible incarnate without material props and effects; to take performers and audiences out of themselves without Wagnerian browbeating; to free up communication by severely restricting actors' means. Surveying the three figures that apparently got closest to his ritualistic ideal—Cunningham, Grotowski, and Beckett—Brook identified small means, intense work, and rigorous discipline as key ingredients. According to him, this resulted in an asceticism that foreswore the popularity that theater directors and composers had come to expect: "the very purity of their resolve, the high and serious nature of their activity inevitably brings a colour to their choices and a limitation to their field. They are unable to be both esoteric and popular at one and the same time."[27] "There is no crowd in Beckett, no Falstaff," Brook went on to explain, "These theatres explore life, yet what counts as life is restricted." If audiences usually reacted to the theater with "stamping and cheering," the most appropriate response to holy theater was a much more solemn and understated one: silence. "We have largely forgotten silence," Brook complained, "another form of recognition and appreciation for an experience shared."[28]

BRITTEN AND RELIGIOUS AESTHETICISM

As a prominent composer of sacred music, known especially for his dramatic rendering of biblical narratives, Britten was all too aware of the power and pitfalls of religious aestheticism. One might even go as far as to suggest that, having been raised a Christian of a "puritanical" stripe, he had it in his blood.[29] As reports from youthful diaries and letters confirm, his low-church background left an indelible impression on him. His first experience of High Anglican Morning Prayer at Gresham's School in 1928 was met with an ambivalent sense of fascination: "We went to into Chapel to a sort of glorified Morning Prayer. It is a high service, anyhow they sing plainsong, and in the Creed turn to the East and bow and nod etc."[30] Nor had this ambivalence subsided three years later, when he was studying at the Royal College of Music. After attending church at St. Mark's, North Audley Street, Britten opined: "V[ery] nice service altho' it is too high for my liking."[31] Britten's simultaneous attraction and repulsion to liturgical aestheticism were even more evident in reactions to the Catholic liturgy. After describing the mutability of her brother's spiritual sympathies, Beth Welford (née Britten) noted that he was sporadically drawn to the Roman Catholic Church, more for aesthetic than for theological reasons: "I think he felt that their religion seemed more alive than did our Church of England; and he considered their music better."[32] As early as November

1930, Britten wrote enthusiastically of attending High Mass at the Roman Catholic Westminster Cathedral: "The service is very bewildering, but the music superb, & also the choir."[33]

It was not just Britten's early encounters with liturgy that were shaped by these tensions, but also his understanding of "religious music" in a more general sense. After listening to Wagner's *Parsifal* and Stravinsky's *Symphony of Psalms* in April 1936, he contrasted the two approaches, invoking a distinction between religious aestheticism and sacred austerity. "Wagner," he noted, was "attracted to the sensuous side of the subject—the incense, ritual, beauty of sound & emotion, Stravinsky by the moral, psychological side, yet tremendously influenced by the ritual side as well."[34] Closer to Britten's home, it was Anglo-Catholic hymnody and its choral and even orchestral spin-offs that stood as the English equivalent of Wagner's brand of religiose sensuality. For, as this chapter's epigraph makes clear, the musical analog of the golden icons was the full textures, propulsive harmonies, march-like rhythms, and stirring melodies of the Victorian and Edwardian hymn. If Nietzsche famously complained that Wagner's music "has the pressure of a hundred atmospheres," Britten's generation often felt similarly about hymnody.[35] Writing in 1947, Auden described his experience of the hymn with a mixture of nostalgia and embarrassment, speaking as it did to his narrow and coercive Anglo-Catholic upbringing.[36] Yet it was precisely because hymns evoked—even demanded—such a powerfully emotive sense of submission that Auden could not help but look back with embarrassed affection: "It is difficult," he apologized, in introducing John Betjeman's poetry, "to write seriously about a man one has sung hymns with."[37]

When it came to Britten's own forays into English church music, the composer proved himself just as ambivalent. As Heather Wiebe has argued, early choral works such as *A Boy Was Born* (1933) and *A Ceremony of Carols* (1942) embodied a relatively new kind of sacred austerity, diverging from the Romantic aestheticism of the English choral tradition, each in different ways: the former with its jarring dissonances, challenging vocal lines, and technical virtuosity; the latter with its pared down textures and modal harmonies.[38] This austerity was by no means lost on contemporary critics. While one critic remarked that *A Boy Was Born* "needed some broad tune, something in nature of a chorale, massively harmonized," Edward Sackville-West championed *A Ceremony of Carols*'s eschewal of sentimentality and aestheticism: "This is not a nineteenth-century Christmas: there is no plum pudding, no jollification."[39]

If Britten often seemed to follow what he saw as the Stravinskian path, however, he was not always so abstemious. While a penchant for religious kitsch was already noticeable in *Saint Nicolas*'s (1948) stirring, final hymn—complete with crashing cymbals and rolling timpani—it reached a peak in the late 1950s and early 1960s, with his most popular works of public spirituality. In *Noye's Fludde* (1958), the monumental hymns and dramatic processions of the cantata from

1948 became louder and more exaggerated, as did their browbeating accompaniment.[40] Indeed, the hymns included in this setting of the Chester Miracle Play from 1958—"Lord Jesus, Think on Me," "Eternal Father, Strong to Save," and "The Spacious Firmament on High"—are all sung in stirring unison with full orchestral and percussive accompaniment.

The ritualistic portions of *War Requiem* (1962) were often understood as the culmination of this trend, a pinnacle moment in which Britten "stooped" to a whole new level of monumentality and aestheticism. As Wiebe has pointed out, the composer's works had "rarely tapped into so blatantly theatrical a mode," pulling out all the nineteenth-century stops in order to reflect the *Requiem* text's extremes of violence and consolation.[41] One of the most obvious examples of "sensory overload" comes in the "Dies Irae," especially when it reappears in the "Libera Me" (see Fig. 113 in the published score). After a gradual buildup—including a dominant pedal, textural expansion, dramatic crescendos, snare drum ostinato, trumpet fanfare, and glissando anticipation—the entire orchestra erupts with a series of musical explosions, symbolizing not only the power of the Almighty but also the detonations of modern warfare. While most critics were effusive, Robin Holloway was not the only one to cast aspersions on the "noisy and banal trumpeting of the Dies Irae" and the "saccharine 'In Paradisum.'"[42] It was doubtless these extremes, among other things, that prompted Stravinsky to dismiss the work as a form of religious kitsch—less an embarrassment of riches than a straightforward embarrassment.[43] If his principal objection was to the high-minded and coercive rhetoric with which critics lauded the work, he also implied that it had its roots in Britten's bombastic music.[44]

According to many, it was only against this backdrop that Britten's subsequent works could be understood—as a step back from the contentious aestheticism and monumentality of his mass for the dead from 1962. While Peter Evans announced a major aesthetic shift in Britten's post-*Requiem* music, most critics were more specific in declaring a new austerity or asceticism, in his sacred works especially.[45] In a review of the *Songs and Proverbs of William Blake* (1965), Colin Mason explained that the cycle "shows to an extreme degree the asceticism which has lately become increasingly marked in [Britten's] music":

> It well suits the bitter message of the Blake texts, although there is a strong feeling, also, of self-denial on the composer's part for purely musical reasons. The thrilling harmonic thickening and intensification at "God is Light" in the last song is one of very few examples of his old sensuousness of harmony in a work that makes his Hardy cycle "Winter Words" seem positively optimistic.[46]

If aestheticism was associated with musical indulgence—thick textures, brightly triadic or richly chromatic harmonies, sweeping melodies—asceticism implied disavowal of all these things: "the new emphasis on austerity," Jeremy Noble noted in 1966, "has shown itself in thin textures, in the virtual abandonment of functional triadic harmony, and in an increased reliance on primitive technical devices such as ostinato and pedal-point."[47]

In *Curlew River* (1964), the first of his "Parables for Church Performance," this asceticism became the basis of a new genre. As the director Colin Graham explained in his production notes, extreme sparsity, economy, concentration, and control were central to its aesthetic and spiritual conception.[48] Far from eschewing ritual altogether, however, it turned to more ascetic and disciplined forms, from Japanese Noh Theater to medieval Christian monasticism. While *Noye's Fludde* opened with timpani roaring and congregation bellowing, *Curlew River* began with unaccompanied chant. As the parable continues, this Western asceticism quickly gives way to equally rigid postures and austere music drawn from the East. As Anthony Sheppard has argued, such appropriations were part of a broader turn in modernist dramaturgy away from the illusionism and exaggeration of bourgeois theater.[49] At the same time, they responded to the ecumenical trends outlined above. By combining Western and Eastern asceticism, *Curlew River* nodded toward the kind of cultural and spiritual diversity that Eliot sought to forestall.[50] If religious aestheticism's overwhelming power, sensuality, and indulgence were associated with dogma and authority, asceticism, in its modesty, came to represent spiritual alternatives. One of the reasons that people turned to asceticism throughout this period—in practices from avant-garde theater to Yoga, Transcendental Meditation, and beyond—was the promise of a more authentic transcendence: a freer form of spirituality gained, paradoxically, through physical discipline and contemplative self-control.[51] This was not lost on contemporary critics. If several speculated that *Curlew River* had "carried austerity too far," one defended the church parable in Zen terms: "The intense, spare repetitive nature of the music will probably not make it one of the composer's more popular creations, but under the best circumstances . . . the work exerts a quiet, hypnotic spell that leaves the sympathetic listener strongly moved."[52]

STAGING ASCETICISM

It was in complex and self-conscious response to this backdrop that *The Burning Fiery Furnace* was conceived. If *Curlew River* wore its asceticism on its sleeve, its successor went one step further by elevating style into subject matter—staging a contest between religious asceticism and aestheticism in its story line. On one side of the parable's central conflict are three young Israelites, whose abstemiousness and austerity testify to the authenticity of their faith. On the other side are the Bablyonians, whose self-indulgent worship is associated with fetishism and idolatry, with the most superstitious and authoritarian kinds of established religion. Ultimately, it is the humble and austere faith, in need neither of pomp nor of ceremony, that seems to prevail, with even gaudy King Nebuchadnezzar giving up his golden statue and offering praise to the God of Israel.

Lying close to the narrative surface, then, was an almost Puritan opposition to pleasure, indulgence, and sensuality. While this was perhaps too obvious for most critics to mention, Robin Holloway was eager as ever to highlight the elephant in the room: "In the depiction of Babylonian gold-lust, a tone can be heard that is not so much ascetic as prim and even priggish."[53] In the scene where Nebuchadnezzar puts on a feast, the Israelites' refusal sets this priggishness in sharp relief:

ANANIAS
Great King! We value deeply
All your gracious favours—

MISAEL
We feel honoured vastly
To be here at your table—

AZARIAS
Guests at this royal table
Of the great King of Babylon.

ALL THREE
But we beg your Majesty
To excuse our frugality.
We are very small eaters.

NEBUCHADNEZZAR
Do you live then on air?
When in Babylon, dine.
Dine as the Babylonians dine.

ALL THREE
Sir, pray excuse us.

NEBUCHANDEZZAR
Come now, we cannot have you living only
On your excellent reputations.
Never let it be said
We let our guests go empty.

ASTROLOGER
Why are they not eating?

COURTIERS
They are making excuses.

ASTROLOGER
They are not even drinking.

COURTIERS
Not drinking—they are not even drinking!

NEBUCHADNEZZAR
What, you refuse even to drink with us?
Take care lest you offend us.

AZARIAS
O King, though greatly tempted
By this royal meat and wine—

MISAEL
So graciously pressed on us—

ANANIAS
Your majesty will understand—

ALL THREE
Partaking is forbidden
By the sacred laws of Israel
[The three draw apart][54]

It was doubtless scenes such as this that had Holloway complaining of "the drab-
best stoicism": "Make do, knuckle under, hold fast, carry your burden, forgive and
forget, dutifully kill the fatted calf. This is cold comfort at best, and at the worst,
not bread but a stone."[55] For Holloway, this was an especially strange message for
an artist to impart. Yet, besides swimming with mid-century theological and aesthetic tides, Britten's stoicism had important precedents. If Britten and others saw
Wagner's music as an embodiment of Babylonian decadence, *Parsifal*'s narrative
appears to come down on the Israelites' side. In Schoenberg's *Moses und Aron*—
premiered in Britain just one year earlier—there was an even more immediate
forebear; not only was Moses the Israel to Aron's Babylon, but this dichotomy was
borne out in the opera's style.

The same was true of Britten's *Furnace*, as Robin Holloway, among others,
pointed out. Its most obvious manifestation lay on the dramaturgical level, with
its opposition to theatrical luxury and excess: "The movement and production
details," Graham insisted, echoing the *Curlew River* preface, "should be as spare
and economical as possible, . . . [the] lighting as simple as possible; no attempt
should be made to achieve theatrical effects."[56] This objective was evident in such
foundational decisions as the setting in Orford Parish Church. This humble stone
building not only foreswore the decadent décor of more elaborate churches and
bore the literal scars of puritanism, but also signaled rejection of the lavish theaters
and opera houses that Brooks and others loved to hate.[57] According to some, this
denial was matched in the mise-en-scène. While the Babylonian component forced
Britten and Graham to loosen their ban on extravagant scenery, the simple stage
design, paucity of props, and plain monks' vestments (Fig. 10) nevertheless set an
ascetic baseline. As one critic observed approvingly, *The Burning Fiery Furnace*
begins and ends on a "simple, curtainless platform . . . with the singers, dressed

FIG. 10. The Abbott (Bryan Drake): "We Come to Perform a Mystery" (Orford Parish Church, June 1966). Photographer: Zoe Dominic.

as monks."[58] If this commentator glossed over much of what came between, some were more brazen, extending diagnoses of simplicity to the production's more lavish aspects. After reluctantly conceding that *Curlew River*'s simplicity was tempered by a series of theatrical moments, Edward Greenfield defended the latter as actually quite simple.[59] Goodwin took an almost identical tack, praising the "simple primary colours" of the costumes and stage props as a rule to which even the giant golden statue and fiery furnace were apparently not exceptions.[60]

Some commentators understood the music in a similar vein. Desmond Shawe-Taylor described it as stylistically of a piece with Britten's other "austere" works of this period, turning to the "furnace music" (see Ex. 16) to explain why.[61] Part of the reason was doubtless its "difficult" musical surface, as Britten skirts

EX. 16. *The Burning Fiery Furnace*—"Furnace Music".

expressionism—chromatic tremolos, awkward leaps and false relations, unusual and exaggerated timbres—to fashion forbidding musical sounds.[62] While the orchestral whip literally mimics the crackling flames, it might also be read as a metaphor of modernist aesthetics of flagellation, as if experiencing Britten's music meant feeling the characters' pain. According to Shawe-Taylor, however, it also meant sharing in their hunger, surviving on Britten's lean musical fare:

> Imagine how almost any other composer might have reveled in the orchestral depiction of the furnace heated "seven times more than it was wont to be heated." Britten has just two string-players; but with an eerie *sul ponticello* harmonic on his double-bass and a low, husky trill and upward and downward chromatic scales from the viola, he gives us the wicked seething and cracking of the heat.

If this diagnosis of musical abstinence seems strained—leaving out instruments such as piccolo, horn, trombone, organ, and whip—there were more unequivocal examples of asceticism. The most striking come in the prologue and epilogue, when the monks process in to the sounds of the *Salus Aeterna,* an unaccompanied plainchant hymn. As Peter Stadlen pointed out, this "lean, ascetic style" spreads to other parts of the score:

> An hour's music is once again largely derived from a plain-chant melody, the beautiful "Salus aeterna." The technical principle is of course familiar from Renaissance times. But in a sense Britten's lean, ascetic style remains truer to the spirit of the chant than did the ever more luxuriant polyphony of the 15th and 16th centuries.[63]

While assertions that the entire score was derived from the opening chant were exaggerated, talk of a "lean, ascetic style" was not wholly without foundation. One potent example directly follows the procession, as the Abbot announces the story to the congregation (see Figs. 1–4 in the published score): here the dry recitative borrows the chant's melodic and tonal contours, while the light organ and drum accompaniment continue its textural minimalism. In the robing music that follows (see Figs. 5–7 in the published score), Britten's heterophonic elaboration adds subtle textural and instrumental colors even as its muted dynamics, crystalline textures, and meandering harmony preserve the austere sense. This musical abstinence recurs throughout the work, usually as an accompaniment to Jewish prayer. In the Israelite's trio before the Babylonian procession (Ex. 17), Shadrach, Meshach, and Abednego invoke both strands of this musical asceticism, shuttling back and forth between organum-like treatment of the *Salus Aeterna* melody and an equally simple heterophonic elaboration. Not everyone approved. "Artistically," Holloway complained, "the result is a severe impoverishment, even a denial, of the free spirit that could once set Rimbaud and Michelangelo, and write the *Spring Symphony* and *The Prince of the Pagodas.*"[64]

While some viewed this asceticism in terms of self-denial or even pain, most gave it a more positive spin, associating it with the new religious solemnity that Britten's church parables had inaugurated. If reverential silence was—according to Brook—the response to which holy theater aspired, the humble setting and musical sparsity were apparently key: "the audience," one commentator observed pointedly, "naturally did not applaud in the religious setting."[65] Goodwin was even more explicit, assuring those disappointed "that Britten should have diverted his talent for the theatre into the more restricted surrounding of the church" that "the experiment has, if anything, enlarged . . . our own capacity for experience that can touch our hearts and minds very deeply."[66] Invoking "simplicity" as a touchstone of authentic spirituality, he praised "the musical and dramatic conception" as "marvelously balanced and proportioned, conveying an effect of divine simplicity allied to a far-reaching depth of expressivity."

For many, the climax of solemnity came when the angel descends to rescue the Israelites from the furnace (see Ex. 18). Here the noisy and exaggerated bombast of

EX. 17. *The Burning Fiery Furnace*—"Israelites Trio".

Babylonian chanting gives way to the Israelites' Benedicite, set to an unassuming organum texture with a treble descant on top. While Anthony Lewis praised the "contrastingly simple music and beautiful number for three boys," Goodwin was confident that "divine simplicity" had prevailed: "the Benedicite is taken up by the full company of men and boys' voices in a triumphantly eloquent paean. It is a climax of great dignity and spirit."[67] Andrew Porter was just as emphatic, insisting

EX. 18. *The Burning Fiery Furnace*—Benedicite.

"in its very simplicity must lie part of the power: the Angel sings shining unelaborated notes, almost as if catching the overtones of, and casting a steady celestial radiance on, the song of human praise rising below."[68] For Peter Stadlen, however, the passage's virtue was not in simplicity per se but in allowing listeners space to think: "the deceptively spare score," he enthused, "makes in fact acute demands on the listener's ingenuity and powers of detection; so much is left to be filled in, a beatific ellipsis."[69] If bombastic hymns and dramatic processions were associated with mindless dogma, this simple hymn of praise apparently encouraged a more thoughtful, rational, and even intellectual faith, appealing—as Goodwin pointed out—to listeners' minds as well as their hearts.[70]

Just as stripping the musical altars was supposed to encourage free, spiritual contemplation, so too was careful choreography. As Graham noted, the "simple, frieze-like" movements were both symbol and model of meditative self-control: "Every movement of the hand or tilt of the head should assume immense meaning . . . This requires enormous concentration on the part of the actor, an almost Yoga-like muscular, as well as mental, control."[71] In foregrounding this aspect, he was paying homage to spiritual trends as well as experimental theatrical traditions; Yoga and other "alternative" spiritualities were said to model a direct, personal, and reflective relationship with the divine. While the Babylonians prepare themselves to be carried away with intoxicating hymns and dazzling images, the Israelites focus their minds in quiet supplication and prayer, emphasizing not just the importance of meditation but of staying true to one's spiritual self:

> ALL THREE [TOGETHER]
> Lord, help us in our loneliness.
> The idols of the heathen
> Are silver and gold,
> But Jehovah, Most High,
> Has armed us with salvation.
> In the armour of faith
> Lord, help us in our loneliness.
> We defy our enemies.
> Lord, help us in our loneliness.
>
> HERALD
> By the Royal decree
> Of the great King of Kings,
> Nebuchadnezzar,
> There shall be set up
> In the province of Babylon
> An Image of Merodak,
> The great god of Babylon.
> O people, nations and languages,
> At what time ye hear the sound of the cornet,
> Flute, harp, sackbut, psaltery, dulcimer,
> And all kinds of music,
> Ye fall down and worship the image of gold.
> Whoso falleth not down and worshippeth.
> Shall be cast into the midst
> Of a burning fiery furnace.

[The three pray aloud and are interrupted by the instrumentalists preparing for the procession]

> ALL THREE
> Blessed art thou, O Lord God of our fathers,
> Let thy name be glorified for evermore.

For our sins we are in the hands of an unjust king,
But thy ways are just and true.
O deliver us not up wholly,
Cause not thy mercy to depart from us.
They shall not be confounded
That put their trust in thee.
Lord, help us in our loneliness.

[Led by the Herald the Musicians circulate in procession, then return to the acting area where the Courtiers have gathered. The image rises in the background, and Nebuchad-nezzar and the Astrologer come towards it.]

ASTROLOGER
O hearken, all ye people!
I speak for the King of Kings.
Now fall ye down and worship –
Worship the image of gold –
Or fear the penalty!

[While the Three remain aloof, still praying to their own God, all the others worship and sing a hymn of adoration to the Image][72]

As one commentator pointed out, "the individual's conscientious resistance to tyranny" was a timely theme in the 1960s, one arguably brought out in Britten's music too.[73] In setting the foregoing text to music, the composer pitted the flexible temporality of Jewish prayer against the coercive rhythms and constant meters of Babylonian decree.[74] In the ceremonial robing music that frames the drama (see Figs. 5–7 and Figs. 91–92 in the published score), Britten's subtle heterophony musicalized this point, evoking the "radical religious individualism" of mid-century spiritualism in musical texture and time. Compared with the thick hymnic textures and propulsive harmonies associated with Babylonian corporatism, this flexible heterophony and ambling modality naturally struck a freer, more individualistic tone.

In its combination of Western chant and Eastern heterophony, moreover, this robing music served as an emblem as much of cultural and religious pluralism as of individual liberty. Elsewhere, this connection is made even clearer, as the register accompanies the Israelites' talk of cultural difference, as they respond to the courtiers' chauvinistic remarks (see Figs. 46–49 in the published score). Accordingly, many critics heard the supple asceticism of Jewish prayer as a cipher for the pluralism that the parable seemed to promote. Jeremy Noble insisted that the "radical pride and racial hatred" of the Babylonian chorus were "all the more telling for being set against the calm dignity of the music of the three Jews."[75] Goodwin went even further, casting Britten's music, for the Israelites especially, as an "eloquent protest against intolerance and racial prejudice."[76]

Alongside the push to establish the new church parable's ascetic credentials went recognition that it stepped back from the brink of austerity in various ways. Plomer described it as "less severe in mood and incident" than *Curlew River*, and Britten's original conception was of a work "for the same instruments . . . probably using the same kinds of technique—but something much less sombre, an altogether gayer affair."[77] Despite all the talk of austerity and asceticism, even Peter Stadlen described Britten's *Furnace* as something of a *Meistersinger* to *Curlew River's Tristan*.[78] According to most commentators, this difference was down to the plot. Where *Curlew River* portrayed a mother's inner turmoil and grief, the biblical narrative staged an altogether more "dramatic" battle.[79] Noble remarked that, "for all their similarities, *The Burning Fiery Furnace* makes a more extrovert, less private impression than *Curlew River*," while Stadlen elaborated on the "wealth of coloristic, descriptive invention that mirrors the confrontation of the worlds of Babylon and Israel."[80] Thus, even as the narrative's progress rejects aestheticism explicitly, it also carved out space for it. Representing the Babylonian foil to ascetic spirituality meant depicting its contrasting qualities and features in full.

According to Graham, the more "outgoing, fantastic and colorful" elements were in the first place visual.[81] As he explained in his production notes, the "rich purples, reds and golds" of the Babylonians set them apart from the Jewish heroes in their austere hues (see Figs. 11–12).[82] This can be seen as well in the gaudy icon that the Babylonians worship (Fig. 13). "On the bare platform," one critic observed, "much of the dramatic effect comes from the costumes that the monks don. Most spectacular is a gold and orange robe for Nebuchadnezzar, with a train perhaps 10 yards long carried by two pages."[83] Another commentator made the point by comparison:

> Visually, [the production] is much less austere—the golden image, a blaze of purpureal radiance, the fire, the vision of the four men and the fabulous sinister splendour of Nebuchadnezzar's appearance, his face and fingers masked in gold, his train a billowing mask of gold and orange.[84]

This increase in vivid colors was apparently mirrored in Britten's score: "even the orchestration, though Britten has added only one instrument, an alto trombone, to the *Curlew River* complement, sounds richer and more colourful," noted one critic.[85] "To his earlier ensemble of chamber organ, flute, viola, horn, double-bass, harp and small bright percussion instruments," Porter reported, "Britten adds an alto trombone, which somehow miraculously enriches the musical texture—not least in the passages associated with Babylonian splendour."[86] Just like the reds, purples, and golds of the mise-en-scène, these "colourful" musical timbres symbolized hedonism, self-indulgence, and excess. But critics and audiences did not necessarily turn away in disgust: "Britten," John Warrack noted, "finds room for much more colour and incident than in *Curlew River*, and if that work's transfixing intensity is loosened, there is a gain in richness and humanity."[87]

FIG. 11. The Three Israelites: (from left to right) Azarias (Victor Godfrey), Misael (Robert Tear), and Ananias (John Shirley-Quirk) (Orford Parish Church, June 1966). Photographer: Zoe Dominic. Image reproduced courtesy of the Britten-Pears Library.

It was not just the sheer pleasure of Babylonian timbres that appealed but its dramatic potential too: "The scoring expands accordingly," as one critic enthused, "most thrillingly in a Babylonian march of stamping pagan violence around the church, in the flickering sting of the fire music, in the lash of the added range of percussion."[88] Another commentator followed Warrack and others by singling out the furnace music (see Ex. 16) for its evocative colors: "the evil crackle as the furnace is heated is appallingly evoked by flutter-tonguing on the muted horn, with the lick of flames in flute arpeggios."[89] To some extent, the foundations of these effects were already laid both in the Bible's rhetorical maximalism—with the furnace "heated up seven times more than was customary"—and in the libretto's spectacular gaze: "See what happens . . . See them all / Go up in smoke! . . . See them burning!"[90] But even as Shawe-Taylor described Britten's music as a modest (even abstemious) response to this imagery, most heard it as a timbral feast, with

FIG. 12. Nebuchadnezzar (Peter Pears) and His Golden Mask and Vestments (Orford Parish Church, June 1966). Photographer: Zoe Dominic. Image reproduced courtesy of the Britten-Pears Library.

the cracks of the whip, viola and flute tremolos, chromatically inflected swells, and muted trombone ostinati coming closer to indulgent musical spectacle than the champions of asceticism allowed.

Elsewhere, the portrayal of the Babylonians struck a frankly "theatrical" tone. As Edward Greenfield observed:

> With "Curlew River" the Noh-play adaptation was largely the antithesis of opera. In "The Burning Fiery Furnace" Britten . . . has found a compromise, keeping the bald structural simplicity and the sense of slow measured progress of "Curlew River," but implanting a series of striking theatrical moments—the spectacular entry of Nebu-chadnezzar in costume of red and gold with an enormous train borne by the acolytes, the appearance and later the equally instantaneous disappearance of the golden idol.[91]

In the Babylonian "entertainment," the libretto thematizes precisely this turn from solemn ritual to theatrical spectacle:

FIG. 13. Nebuchadnezzar's Golden Idol (Orford Parish Church, June 1966). Photographer: Zoe Dominic. Image reproduced courtesy of the Britten-Pears Library.

All sit down and begin feasting, except the Three, who politely refuse what is handed to them. Attention is distracted from this by the Entertainers, who dance and sing.

ENTERTAINER 1
The waters of Babylon,
The flowing water,
All ran dry.
Do you know why?

ENTERTAINER 2
Of course I do!

ENTERTAINER 1
And so do I!

COURTIERS
Good cheer indeed!

ENTERTAINER 1
The people of Babylon,
The thievish people,

Ate the figs,
They ate the melons and ate the grapes—
The thievish people of Babylon ate the grapes—
Do you know why?

ENTERTAINER 2
Of course I do!

ENTERTAINER 1
And so do I!

ENTERTAINERS 1 AND 2
The reason the waters all ran dry
Was that somebody had monkeyed with
the water supply;
The reason the gardens grew like mad
Was because of all the water they'd had:
The reason they gobble up the melons and figs
Was that Babylonians are greedy pigs!
If pigs had wings then pigs would fly
Far above Babylon. Babylon, goodbye!

COURTIERS
Good cheer, good cheer!
If every change of name
Leads to a royal feast . . .

ENTERTAINERS
Goodbye!

COURTIERS
Good cheer indeed!
[Suddenly the Astrologer notices that the Three are not eating and drinking, and addresses them][92]

This sendup of theatrical divertissement is introduced in the stage directions as a "distraction" from the issue at hand, and elicits rowdy inattention from the onstage audience. Indeed, so taken are the Babylonian revelers with the spectacle that they remain blithely ignorant of its insulting content. But while most critics got the message, denouncing its "deliberately childish," "prep. school" aesthetic, some reveled in its spectacle along with the Babylonians.[93] One noted that its "charming music" made up for the meaningless frivolity, while another declared himself grateful that Britten and Graham had made "more room for spectacle and diversions."[94] Still another breathed a sigh of relief that "the story, if not unremittingly gay, provides scenes of feasting, comic entertainment, idolatrous ceremony and spectacular miracle, a range of moods so much ampler than that of *Curlew River*'s shadowy world."[95]

When it came to the adoration of the Golden Image, the ambivalence was even more extreme (Ex. 19). After the Astrologer urges everyone to fall down and worship, the chorus drops to its knees in "hysterical wailing," chanting music that represents not only the Babylonians' sinister corporatism, but also the literal swooning of the worshipers as they prostrate themselves before the Gold. Ascending sequences, constant crescendos, and extreme timbral effects choreograph their loss of individual control. While Peter Stadlen praised the "wealth of description, coloristic invention," Shawe-Taylor compared the Hymn with *Moses und Aron*'s infamous pagan dance: "Aided by a mere handful of instruments Britten's suggestions of a corrupt, hysterical Paganism far surpasses Schoenberg's 'Dance Round the Golden Calf.'"[96] It was "much more than ingenious," Noble wrote:

> Built up out of the glissando fourths with which the trombone had earlier set its official seal on the Herald's pronouncements, it grows irresistibly into an ecstasy of mindless self-abasement. Dynamics and tessitura mount together, at the prompting of N[ebuchadnezzar] and [the] A[strologer]. Gradually all the instruments, all the voices but those of the Jews, are drawn into the wallowing mass of sound, and when the trombone finally lurches in, at the top of its register, the sense of nausea is almost unbearable.[97]

Nor was he the only one to invoke "ecstasy," "nausea," and "intoxication." This simultaneous repulsion and attraction were even more pronounced in responses to the Babylonian procession (Ex. 20). Here we encounter the full range of instruments in sight as well as sound: this "most spectacular" set piece, one critic reported, "is an orchestral interlude, midway in the piece, in which the players walk in procession through the church playing such instruments as hand harp, alto trombone, a glockenspiel, a French horn and a flute."[98] As critics were quick to note, this array of sounds and instruments had its origins in the biblical source— in "the sound of the cornet, flute, harp, sackbut, psaltery, dulcimer, and all kinds of musick"—so it was hardly surprising that the composer responded with the richest, most indulgent textures in the score.[99] After the bass drum, horn, and trombone pull together the rigid march pattern, Britten superimposes a variety of decorative lines, each of which work independently and contrapuntally to give an impression of opulence and complexity: the erratic viola arpeggios; the syncopated flute pattern; the intricate rhythms of the glockenspiel; the meandering pentatonicism of the little harp. "The exotic instruments come into their own," noted one critic, in "an astonishing feat of counterpoint": "each instrument has its own characteristic theme (or rhythm) and at the climax of the March all the themes are simultaneously combined."[100]

But despite its attractive sonic surface, the Babylonian procession, in its quasi-militaristic rigidity, was like Babylonian law and scripture itself: a monumental imperative that allowed no space for individual reflection, deviation, or compromise. While one commentator insisted that "no one could fail to be stirred by

EX. 19. *The Burning Fiery Furnace*—Hymn to Merodak.

EX. 19 (continued).

EX. 20 and Ex. 20 (continued). *The Burning Fiery Furnace*—Babylonian Procession.

the episode," another explained: "the effect of this pagan march, a contrapuntal web of multi-colored tone, is jubilant—yet menacing and sinister."[101] Still another made reference to the "arresting web of sound," as if listeners were ensnared in the silky but deadly threads of Britten's musical texture.[102] But only the most candid reviewers admitted its invidious appeal: "The musical image is so compelling that we hardly need the text to specify the ideology before which the Babylonians are prostrating themselves: nationalism; with its concomitant evils of conformism, intolerance, racial hatred."[103]

REDEEMING RELIGIOUS AESTHETICISM

As these responses to the Babylonian ceremonies and processions suggest, Britten's setting threatened the very hierarchies that the parable staged. The problem was not just that the Babylonian music and spectacle could be quite alluring, but also that Israelites' asceticism struck some as bland. After juxtaposing the Babylonian hymn of praise with the "calm dignity" of the Israelites' chorus, Noble demurred:

> I have a feeling, though, that this is one more case where Babylon gets the best of it musically. Though others may not (in fact do not) agree, I found the final setting of the Benedicite oddly ineffective. The texture, with the three Jews chanting in organum-like parallel chords and the solo treble supplying a halo descant at the octave above the tenor line, . . . seemed the very reverse of triumphant.[104]

After elsewhere insisting that "this moment of revelation demands a musical image of goodness as powerful as that of the evil that has gone before," the critic sighed: "the setting of the Benedicite . . . seems not to do what is asked of it."[105] Nor was he the only one to sense anti-climax. Another critic described the Benedicite as "the only point at which the music itself seems not quite to rise to the occasion."[106]

But there was yet another, perhaps even more disturbing, way of reacting to the Benedicite. According to a handful of critics, the literal representation of the angel amid the fire was as stagey and indulgent as the Babylonian spectacle it supplanted:

> But—a miracle! The three young men are standing in the midst of the fire, and there is a fourth figure (a protective angel of God) at their side which grows in incandescence as the temperature rises. The flames part to reveal the youths unharmed and singing the Lord's praises from the heart of the furnace . . . The youths step out, summoned forth by the astonished Nebuchadnezzar, untouched by fire.[107]

While one critic listed the moment among the parable's stunning *coups de théâtre,* another compared it to the miracle at the end of *Curlew River,* often regarded as a kitschy intrusion into an otherwise abstemious drama.[108] "One could wish," one commentator complained with quasi-puritan disdain, "that the apparition of the Spirit might be left invisible; it looks painfully like the most sanctimonious Roman

Catholic oleographs."[109] In a context in which external icons were pitted against individual faith, such a literal staging of divine power seemed to clutter the parable's picture.

For many, moreover, connections between powerful Babylonian spectacle and the supposedly ascetic denouement were reinforced by the music. Much as in discussions of the mise-en-scène, these putatively opposed musical moments often drew comment in the same breath. Among the richest and most thrilling musical moments, John Warrack insisted, were "the Babylonian march of stamping pagan violence, . . . the flickering sting of the fire music, . . . [and] that of the clear treble that pierces the texture to make the fourth voice in the furnace."[110] Another critic offered a similarly revealing list:

> The processional march is one of the musical highlights of the score. Another is the song of the three young men in the furnace, the *Benedicite,* with their divine companion, a treble: Britten had already made a memorable setting of this in the *Turn of the Screw;* the new one is necessarily much more solemn and when, at the end of the play within a play, the Babylonian court unites in a reprise the effect is climactic, a moment of musical as well as dramatic glory.[111]

As this commentator reminds readers, the simple organum of the Benedicite is not confined to the Israelites from whom it originates, but is ultimately passed to the entire cast of Babylonian worshipers in a grand reprise. Whether arranged in one gigantic homophonic chorus or in multiple dispersed choirs with staggered entries—with the viola, flute, horn, and trombone now bolstering the organ accompaniment—it infuses the originally sparse texture with a richness and monumentality that seemed to undermine the ascetic point.

Yet even in its leanest, most austere guise—when it first interrupts the chaotic noise of the furnace with its solemn sound and overwhelming calm (Ex. 18)—the Benedicite still exhibits connections and affinities with the most striking moments of Babylonian aestheticism. One reason for this, perhaps, is the strict regularity of the homophonic refrain, which, for all its vaunted stillness and simplicity, and its treble descant, was as rigidly uniform as the authoritarian march.[112] There were also more specific musical or motivic connections, which—as Peter Evans pointed out—acted throughout as "bridges" between otherwise distinct musical worlds.[113] One such connection, the melodic outline of a fourth, is particularly relevant here: as if to echo the Hymn to Merodak (Ex. 19), the interval appears throughout the Benedicite, marking the outer limits of the Israelites' musical paeans. The opening of each vocal phrase, with chromatic appoggiatura on an open vowel ("O") carried an even clearer sense of Babylonian provenance, suggesting something of their characteristic swooning even as it drew local connections between the respective vocal styles. In this particular passage, the accented half-step is as much a feature of the Astrologer's music (see "True, O King") as of the Israelites's hymn, thus cutting cleanly across the scene's musical battle lines.

It was not, however, just textural affinities and motivic connections that united the supposedly austere Benedicite with the gaudy Babylonian ceremonies: it was also, paradoxically, their differences. For, at the limits of their respective registers, such aesthetic opposites tend to converge; simplicity and complexity, asceticism and aestheticism, in their extremes, often look and sound remarkably alike. This was a point made in the original program notes, where it was suggested that the starkness of the contrast drew the two parts of the furnace music together: "The sudden stillness—the cessation of the 'fire' music," the commentator observed, "is as moving as the brilliant instrumental depiction of the tongues of flames has been exciting."[114] Indeed, if the march of the procession or noise of the furnace is so rich, dense, or elaborate as to almost fall out of music entirely, the Benedicite appears to have had a similar effect for the opposite reason. In the latter, it is the extreme minimalism and simplicity—the chant-like repetition of the choral parts, the paucity of distinct melody or harmonic progression, the sustained notes in the organ and treble line—that focus attention on the sensual aspects of the sound itself.

It would seem, then, that even as *The Burning Fiery Furnace* embraced and rejected the aestheticism associated with Babylonian worship, it found a way of constructing an altogether more acceptable form. In passages such as the Benedicite, we encounter a kind of aestheticism that retained its otherworldly quality while appearing less indulgent and authoritarian; more modern, individual, rational, and even—paradoxically—more ascetic. At a time when liberal Christians and theologians were casting off high and low church divides, new age spiritualists were searching for more pluralistic modes, and the theatrical avant-garde were looking for authentic rituals, confusing these boundaries performed timely cultural, spiritual, and aesthetic work. In combining the extremes of religious aestheticism and asceticism, *The Burning Fiery Furnaces* allowed mid-century audiences to have it both ways.

At the same time, it suggests that the fault lines were by no means clear. It was arguably because of its problematic associations, and the self-conscious irony and exaggeration with which it was treated, that the Babylonian worship had such a powerful effect. Indeed, the very fact that the *Furnace* and its reception sought to redeem such registers implies that it was not just authoritarian zealots who longed for tangible access to the divine. Quite the contrary, as the Israelites' Benedicite makes clear, extreme asceticism signaled comparable excess. Something similar might be said of *Curlew River* and more uncompromising examples of modernist austerity, as one critic was at pains to suggest: "No doubt the avant-garde will condemn the experiment for its 'reactionary' qualities, but in some ways Britten is here as close as any of their avant-garde (with their own brand of jingles and clonks) to achieving the new 'complex of sounds' which is the confessed ideal of Pierre Boulez."[115] If modernism has often been credited with carrying the secularism, rationalism, and scientism of modernity to its logical extreme, derailing music into mere noise or sound, we might conclude by implicating even—or perhaps especially—the most extreme instances of modernist asceticism in the aspirations of religious kitsch. The very fact that some critics had trouble separating the two—or even deciding which they found the more compelling—suggests that there was more than one way to "bring the stars down to earth."

6

Death in Venice and the Aesthetics of Sublimation

We got into the auditorium, Julian now pulling me, and found our seats, half-way back in the stalls. People stood up to let us in. I hate this. I hate theatres. There was an intense subdued din of human chatter, the self-satisfied yap of a civilized audience awaiting its "show": the frivolous speech of vanity speaking to vanity. And now there began to be heard in the background that awful and inimitably menacing sound of an orchestra tuning up.[1]

—IRIS MURDOCH, *THE BLACK PRINCE* (1973)

At the crux of Iris Murdoch's *The Black Prince* (1973) stands a musical orgasm— an "operatic" gesture that resounds throughout the novel. From the overture to Strauss's *Der Rosenkavalier*, it is doubtless familiar to Covent Garden regulars. Yet this sound is related by Bradley Pearson, a self-styled highbrow who would not ordinarily be found in such vulgar company. The only reason he is there is because he was invited by Julian Baffin. In accompanying this young girl to the Royal Opera House, Pearson reveals the depth of his infatuation; for him, a night at the opera represents a prospect more daunting than hell.[2] Indeed, operatic spectacle is the only thing worse than the trashy novels that Julian's father churns out. Even as it draws on the lewd and inane, opera apparently harbors pretensions to greatness and sublimity. As he takes his seat in the stalls, he can only imagine the high-minded rhetoric to which this bourgeois audience will turn, once the interval drinks arrive, in order to sublimate opera's "cheap" thrills and mindless entertainment.

As it turns out, Pearson does not even make it that far, for Strauss's gaudy fare proves literally impossible for him to stomach. While the prelude makes him writhe in his seat, the love scene has him throwing up in the nearest alley. Yet despite Pearson's contempt, this reaction results as much from pleasure as from pain, with his uncontrollable urge to vomit serving none too subtly as a metaphor for sexual release. Neither is this the first nor the last time that Pearson is delivered into erotic frenzy. For all that he fancies himself a modern-day Apollo, an ascetic

147

man of letters and paragon of moral virtue, he seems to have little self-control. Throughout the first half, he struggles to impose order on his rampant sex drive. After an illicit affair with Rachel Baffin, he turns his affections to her young daughter, drawing on all the Platonic clichés he can muster to sublimate his desires. The only difference between the opera audience's ponderous platitudes and his own is that theirs succeed where his fail. Where they are able to maintain an air of decorum, Pearson is set on a downward spiral into the Dionysian abyss, as he takes the young and innocent Julian to his bed.

In thematizing the gulf between the highbrow's lofty words and his prurient deeds, Murdoch's novel suggests that cultural boundaries were more a matter of sublimation than of essence. Nevertheless, if *The Black Prince* shines a light on this process of translating art's disreputable pleasures into intellectual reflection, it reflects back onto Murdoch's novel itself.[3] Notwithstanding all the ironizing techniques, the book and its readers are implicated in the aesthetic of sublimation it diagnoses. Even as the tale teems with "lowbrow" preoccupations—sex, slapstick humor, contrived narrative twists, and melodramatic thrills—it shrouds them in the highbrow intellectualisms and abstractions that were supposedly the stuff of high art. While this mixture of intellect and sensation endeared Murdoch's stories to late-twentieth-century readers, criticism has rarely been so balanced. Apparently unable to resist the philosophical nattering, commentators have ignored their more immediate pleasures.[4] To treat such high-minded "novels of ideas" as one would most other fiction of the period would apparently be to risk seeming narrowly literal, if not crude. Much like the operas it vilifies, *The Black Prince* offers its readers deniability: the chance to revel in the "cheap" pleasures of popular fiction while simultaneously disavowing them.

In the same year that the fictional Pearson was invented, Gustav von Aschenbach, one of his close relatives, was resurrected in Britten's *Death in Venice* (1973), an opera based on Thomas Mann's novella from 1912. Like Pearson, Aschenbach is an aging novelist and intellectual who, in the midst of a bout of writer's block, turns his attention to an adolescent, this time a young Polish boy holidaying with his family on the Venetian Lido. He too summons all the philosophical wisdom he can muster in order to control and rationalize his infatuation, but his sublimation proves unsuccessful and he succumbs to his bodily desires. Britten's opera resembles *The Black Prince* in form as well as content, for it is similarly fragmented, broken up into passages of spectacular melodrama and abstract philosophical monologues, which meditate self-consciously on foundational aesthetic oppositions.

Just as telling were the parallels in how the two works were received. The reception of Britten's opera appears to have replicated the aesthetic of sublimation staged as its subject matter. In a review of the first production, John Robert-Blunn parodied this high-minded response in a vignette strongly resembling Murdoch's opera scene:

"Intense intellectual approach to the emotions," said one young man gaily, to another, after experiencing Benjamin Britten's new opera *Death in Venice* at the King's
Theatre, Edinburgh, last night . . . When everyone else can see the Emperor's new
clothes, I feel that I should be able to see them, too. But I can't. This gripping English
Opera Group production . . . has many merits, but there seem to be so many mes-
sages to be understood or misunderstood. In a long introduction for the likes of me,
Andrew Porter discussing Mann's novel (on which Myfanwy Piper's libretto is based)
writes: "The story, dealing with art and life, . . . is a complex and many-layered composition. So is Britten's opera." The art of understatement is not dead.[5]

Like Pearson, Robert-Blunn was troubled by the discrepancy between the work's
idealistic reception and its less-than-ideal spectacle, which included "a bit too
much of boys sporting loincloths."[6] And with good reason: critics often forced self-
conscious gaps between the opera and its interpretation, warning audiences that
there was more to the opera than meets the eyes and ears. "It's not only what happens," John Amis insisted, "but why and how and what passes through the mind
of Aschenbach that makes the story interesting."[7] Roger Baker went even further,
dismissing literal interpretations as ignorant: "Those who hadn't done their home-
work could be forgiven for seeing him as a cruising predator but it is, of course, a
mistake to see *Death in Venice* as an opera about a homosexual situation."[8] Martin
Cooper came closer still to Robert-Blunn's highfalutin critical stereotype:

> The subject of Britten's "Death in Venice," which had its first performance at the
> Maltings at Aldeburgh on Saturday night, is the artist's nature and, in a profounder
> sense than Strauss's "Capriccio," the nature of art itself. In Myfanwy Piper's libretto
> the different levels of Thomas Mann's story are skillfully dramatised . . . The boy Tad-
> sio [sic] is no more than an agent, and in Mann's story the sex is almost irrelevant.[9]

Cooper was just one of many to reference the different hermeneutic "levels" to
which the opera was susceptible, arranging them in such a way as to render the
most immediate unmentionable in anything other than a negative sense.[10] To read
Britten's opera as a tale of erotic infatuation, in other words, was to misread it. Yet,
for all that early critics warned of the likelihood of narrowly sexual interpretations,
such readings remained conspicuous by their absence.

With most critics following Aschenbach in "spouting pondering platitudes
about art and life and the creative artist," it fell to queer theorists, almost twenty
years later, to point to the elephant in the room. In 1994, Philip Brett identified
"allegorization" as the method by which the powerful, unequivocal homoeroticism
of *Death in Venice* was neutralized. It was, he suggested, as part of a concerted effort
to keep the composer closeted that "music critics fell over themselves to adopt and
elaborate upon the Apollonian/Dionysian allegory with which Mann himself had
clouded some central questions."[11] While Brett was right to stress that the dominant
mode of reception had served to "mask, parry, or render ridiculous [its] homosexual content," this was only one symptom of a much broader selectivity.

Unlike Brett, I view the response to *Death in Venice* as formed not only by the epistemology of the closet but also—like the other operas discussed throughout this study—by the logic of the "great divide." It was this logic that propelled Pearson's snobbery, compelling him to reject all but the most difficult and intellectual artworks as "mere" entertainment. It was also what moved Murdoch's devotees to their own selective readings. If the novel so uncomfortably straddled the great divide that it could only be rescued by the most abstract of philosophical meditations, the position of opera in the 1960s and 1970s was more precarious still. Not only fictional intellectuals like Pearson but a large number of critics regarded opera as one of the lowest artistic forms, denigrating it as both unseemly and unviable in the twentieth century.

Death in Venice's reception reflects this context, relying as it did on the stock oppositions of contemporaneous anti-operatic discourse: between abstraction and immediacy, the intellectual and the visceral, form and rhetoric. In styling the opera's charms as more intellectual than visceral, there was a lot a stake. Critics were attempting to secure not just Britten's place on the "right" side of the divide—as we have seen time and again—but also that of the genre more broadly. Yet they were never able to erase fully the opera's powerful spectacles and visceral music, making for a reception just as full of defensiveness, ambivalence, and contradiction. Like the other operas examined hitherto, *Death in Venice* invited precisely the selectiveness it resisted. At once staging and confounding oppositions at the heart of operatic criticism, *Death in Venice* shows how composers, directors, critics, and audiences responded to opera's troubled twentieth-century reputation.

STAGING ABSTRACTION

> *When, almost forty years ago, audiences began to chuckle about Lohengrin's swan and the Germanic beards in the Ring . . . [o]ne sensed that, artistically, things just could not go on like this, that this very stylization was making opera into a marketable specialty item. The music of Figaro is of truly incomparable quality, but every staging of Figaro with powdered ladies and gentlemen, with the page and the white rococo salon, resembles the praline box, not to mention the Rosenkavalier and the silver rose.*
>
> —T. W. ADORNO, "OPERA AND THE LONG-PLAYING RECORD" (1969)[12]

As scholars have often observed, the twentieth century was a troubled time for opera; when not being denounced as a bastion of elitism, it was charged with prefiguring "some of the worst abominations" of the culture industry.[13] Yet even so, the late 1960s and early 1970s represented a real low point. In the same year that Peter Brook denounced opera as the embodiment of everything wrong with the theater, Pierre Boulez recommended that opera houses be blown up.[14] This last suggestion caught the imagination of the British music press; after reprinting the original article in translation, *Opera* debated the modern opera "problem" in depth.[15] "When I go to a performance now," Boulez elaborated:

> I ask myself why are they singing! I feel too a contradiction between the convention of opera, which is pure convention, and the realistic gestures of singers, which are conventional in the bad sense ... When I see the Japanese Nō theatre or Banraku [the puppet theater], each of which is still more conventional, more stylized than opera, it is all so far away from realism that I am not disturbed at all. What I don't like in opera is the perpetual reference to the world of everyday.[16]

Echoing a critique already voiced by Bertolt Brecht in the 1930s, Boulez's explanation would appear to confirm that anti-operatic sentiments were united in opposition to the realistic traditions of the nineteenth century.[17] However, while some lamented opera's aspirations to realism, others bemoaned the stylization that Boulez advocated. After complaining of "artificiality" in the epilogue to *Opera: A Modern Guide,* Arthur Jacobs and Stanley Sadie diagnosed "widespread impatience with a form so stylized" in their postscript from 1969 to the same publication.[18] Writing elsewhere the same year, Jacobs appears to have shouldered the burden of opera's contradictions as he denigrated the genre for being both too realistic and not realistic enough.[19]

If such criticisms appear paradoxical, Jacobs's prescriptions offer some clarification. According to him, it was the "gramophone record" that heralded the way forward, offering scope for a "music theatre of the mind," "untrammelled by theatrical compromise, untroubled by singers' difficulties in withstanding the orchestra, unconcerned with the audience's sight-lines or drinking habits."[20] In casting technology in the role of deus ex machina, Jacobs echoed the sentiments of Adorno's "Opera and the Long-Playing Record," published just eight months earlier.[21] After complaining of a mode of reception that focused on the minutiae of operatic production, Adorno asked: "What's the point? Why even bother doing it on stage? One wants to spare Mozart from this."[22] For Adorno, no less than for Jacobs, the long-playing record promised to force "concentration on music as the true object of opera . . . comparable to reading, to the immersion in a text."[23] Implying that opera would be better served without live performance's material distractions, these accounts suggest that the "problem"—while often framed as a question of realism versus stylization—ran deeper, indicating wider suspicions of the genre's flagrant materiality. As Martin Puchner has suggested, modern anti-theatricalism drew on much older idealistic traditions.[24] The "problem," in other words, was as much a question of reception as of production; whether reveling in the details of magnificent mise-en-scène or enjoying the empathy of realistic representation, audiences were deemed to be stuck in Plato's cave.

Far from delivering the final nail to opera's coffin, this crescendo of anti-operatic discourse coincided with a revival of interest in opera and music theater. While some composers, such as Nicholas Maw, Richard Rodney Bennett, and Malcolm Williamson, continued to produce relatively traditional, large-scale operas, an even greater number attempted to remedy the maladies that detractors diagnosed.[25] Britten occupied a precarious place along this aesthetic divide. From a relatively early age, he acknowledged the need to modernize even while composing works that kept operatic traditions alive. As early as 1944, while still at work on his first and most "realistic" opera, Britten lamented the paradoxes of operatic realism using precisely the terms Jacobs and Boulez would employ more than twenty years later: "I feel that with the advent of films, opera may turn its back on realism, and develop or return to stylization—which I think it should. It is an art and it should be 'artificial,' for, after all, people don't usually use singing as their usual method of communication in real life."[26] When he later turned his attention to more experimental forms of drama, he framed them as long-awaited solutions to opera's "problem."[27]

As we learnt in the previous chapter, *Curlew River* (1964) and the other church parables represented his most sustained attempt to construct a "drama of ideas." In fusing elements of Japanese Noh theatre with Christian liturgy, they mobilized ritualistic representation to encourage a reception more symbolic than literal.[28] As the producer Colin Graham made clear, the aim was, above all, to avoid "theatrical effects": "The movement and production details should be as spare and economical as possible; the miming, which plays an integral part, is symbolic and should be pared down to its quintessence."[29] In addition to heavy restrictions on gesture, Graham eschewed the extravagant set designs that Adorno and others decried. It was doubtless *Curlew River* that Sadie and Jacobs had foremost in mind when they wrote:

> That Benjamin Britten has written some operatic works which are not for the opera-house at all is symptomatic of the suspicion with which many composers of different countries have viewed the old-fashioned operatic form and conservatively-inclined managements and audiences of established opera houses.[30]

On the other side of Britten's operatic equation, and even more than *Owen Wingrave* (1971), *Death in Venice* appears to have signaled a return to a more traditional form of opera: not only was it written for an opera house but it also reverted to a larger and more conventional orchestra than the church parables. Nevertheless, as commentators have often emphasized, the composer's operatic swansong absorbed many of the anti-operatic characteristics of the works that preceded it.[31] It shared directors with the church parables, thus emerging with several similarities of mise-en-scène. Although Graham's original intention to "entirely do away with the straight-line stage & the proscenium" was thwarted, the production still sought to avoid resembling traditional theater: "it's a totally unrealistic approach, in fact, scenically, and it's a very cerebral piece, and we've tried to devise a way of designing that is rather like a camera—the inside of a camera—a man's mind, with images growing out of the darkness and retreating into it."[32] In seeking to dematerialize the Venetian setting, Graham even followed Jacobs and Adorno in turning to technology:

> It won't be really until we get to Covent Garden that we will be showing the piece entirely as we want to show it because we'll be able to put up a lot of back projections there, whereas here at Snape, we've had to put a gantry where we can use five or six separately backlit backcloths instead of the twenty five or so projections that we'll be able to use later on.[33]

Apparently even more remarkable than the use of backlit backcloths was the extreme economy of means: through most of the production, very little attempt was made to draw audiences into a scenic illusion. Recalling the minimalism of the church parables, there was often little more to sustain visual interest than the downstage protagonist set against a black backdrop (see Fig. 14). William Mann praised "Colin Graham's spare, pointed, highly theatrical production which conjures marvels from black drops and a few people," while Edward Greenfield lauded the "restraint [which] may be judged in that only after 50 minutes does John Piper's full Venetian canal-scape emerge for the first time, swiveled into view on enormous triangular columns."[34]

Although some backdrops gestured toward a realistic sense of place, most of Piper's set designs followed the minimalist aesthetic that Graham had described. With the exception of Greenfield, critics got the point. Martin Cooper praised "John Piper's spare but evocative scenery," while John Falding reported: "The opera lasts more than two and a half hours, but its two acts contain 17 scenes which designer John Piper achieves mainly through backlit paintwork and photographs. We are kept to the barest essentials."[35] Nor was this minimalism's significance lost on them. Even the most conservative of commentators, lamenting that the "black, depressing set creates no illusion of the splendour of one of the world's most beautiful cities," admitted: "if *Death in Venice* is an illusion imprisoned in Aschenbach's imagination, perhaps the set is perfectly illustrative."[36]

Far from limited to the opera's staging, however, this anti-literalism was fundamental to all aspects of the opera's conception, as Greenfield pointed out. One of the ways, he explained, that Britten and Piper sought to "enhance the symbolic elements" was by "having a single singer take on the incidental parts."[37] On the most basic level, this allowed the creators to undermine the direct association between individual performers and specific characters, contradicting a key tenet of dramatic realism. However, it also allowed them to flesh out, quite literally, these characters' symbolic roles as representations of fate. According to Cooper, this dramaturgical technique marked them as Dionysian impulses within the protagonist himself:

> By giving seven of the smaller roles to a single singer (John Shirley-Quirk) and thus suggesting their single identity, Britten emphasises the existence of a Kafkaesque plot against Aschenbach, finally revealed when the listener recognizes in the voice of Dionysus those of the Traveller, Fop, Manager, Barber and Leader of the Players.[38]

FIG. 14. *Death in Venice* (Act I, Scene 1)—Aschenbach (Peter Pears), Snape Maltings, Suffolk, June 1973. Photo: Nigel Luckhurst. Image reproduced courtesy of the Britten-Pears Foundation.

In casting the Polish family as mute dancers, the creators added another level of separation to this "complex and many-layered composition."[39] For Ned Rorem, writing for *The New Republic,* this dramaturgical decision was the only responsible reading of the novella's symbolism: "If the Silent Ideal must be depicted within a medium whose very purpose is noise, then mime, while a bit illegal, is probably the only solution."[40]

According to Greenfield, an even more forceful way of encouraging abstract readings was through dramatic minimalism—a dearth of action—to parallel the abstemiousness of the staging. In banishing the kind of narrative events associated with traditional drama, the creators forced audiences to dig for "deeper" symbolic levels. As Kenneth Loveland explained:

> Even in the most dramatic operas, such as *Peter Grimes* and *Billy Budd,* Britten is concerned with mental plight, and no matter how widespread the background, the focal

point is often narrowed down to man's inner conflict with himself . . . Here [in *Death in Venice*], to achieve what is essentially an examination of introspection, Britten reduces the opera to almost a personal narration; it is von Aschenbach we hear, and very nearly everything that happens is a musical or visual representation of his thoughts.[41]

Loveland was not the only critic eager to grasp this significance: while Stephen Walsh concluded that "Aschenbach is not merely the hero of the story: he is the story," Jeremy Noble explained that "the bald formality with which Aschenbach announces his preoccupations . . . takes a little getting used to as a convention but proves not inappropriate for so initially stiff and detached a figure."[42] "The actual incidents of the story," he continued, "are seen merely as an intermittent background to the ceaseless reflective monologue." After admitting "in at least three of Britten's earlier operas the action is surrounded by an element of separate commentary in the form of prologues and epilogues," Bayan Northcott lauded the monologue's originality: "I can think of no operatic precedent for the almost complete reversal of traditional narrative priorities in *Death in Venice*."[43]

The desire to coerce a more abstract appreciation of the work was as palpable in the monologue's content as in its form. In its patchwork of philosophical aphorisms, the opera wore its intellectualism proudly, as Robert-Blunn noted caustically: "in the course of the opera's 17 deftly changing scenes . . . Aschenbach emerges as a pompous twit, spouting ponderous platitudes about art and life and the creative artist."[44] Despite his vitriol, Robert-Blunn was not altogether wrong. In addressing abstract intellectual questions, *Death in Venice* formed part of a wave of "philosophical operas," designed to reinvent opera as a cerebral genre. In reflecting on artistic representation, moreover, it gestured toward the "artist opera," a notable subgenre of this broader type. As Daniel Albright explains:

> The philosophical opera and the opera that dissociates its media are both the products of a kind of self-consciousness . . . This acute attentiveness to the problematic aspects of opera—opera's tendency to the flamboyant and fatuous—sometimes expressed itself in meta-opera, that is, opera about opera.[45]

Although less overt than in *Ariadne auf Naxos* or *Capriccio*, *Death in Venice* takes a number of self-reflexive glances at artistic process. As Cooper pointed out, it is about an aging writer and his struggle to create.[46] Yet while critics and scholars have been quick to characterize the work as an "artist opera," one could just as easily describe it as an "audience opera." Aschenbach is a spectator as well as an artist. Indeed, his creations often seem to be little more than a means of sublimating his gaze. By staging the struggle and fatal failure of Aschenbach to abstract his experience, *Death in Venice* offered a warning to its audiences. If, as Conrad Wilson suggested, an opera "with an author as its hero" smacked of didacticism, one about a spectator did so all the more.[47]

Most critics heeded the less-than-subtle hints that an intellectual response was required. Although both novella and libretto speak of a Nietzschean balance between the Apollonian and Dionysian, the opera's reception was more one-sided, with most critics confident that Britten had managed to equal, if not surpass, the intellectualism of his source. Borrowing his terms from the opera, Andrew Porter interpreted *Death in Venice* as a "moral fable": whereas "Gustav von Aschenbach . . . surrenders wholly, at last, to Dionysus," Mann and Britten retained a firm footing on the idealistic pedestal.[48] Patrick Carnegy offered a similar opinion, albeit with a more negative spin: "Dionysus seems too much in thrall to Apollo—not least in the very well behaved choral dances."[49] After observing that "the platonic element is more fully developed" in the opera than in the novella, Alan Blyth compared the "Games of Apollo" scene with Luchino Visconti's film from 1971:

> Surely Visconti's vision of the visual and sensual delights of the city . . . was much more convincing than anything in the opera. Venice itself, a real hotel, the period clothes, a nubile, feminine boy, even (dare I say it) Mahler's *Adagietto*, were so much more suggestive of the permissive decadence intended.[50]

In contrasting the opera unfavorably with the film, Blyth swam against the tide. For most critics, eager to praise the opera's Apollonian abstraction, Visconti's film became a negative foil. Roger Baker found that "Visconti managed to repress . . . the element which clearly makes an appeal to Britten: the intellectual control of emotion," while Peter Heyworth observed: "the vulgar simplifications that Luchino Visconti in his film imposed on Thomas Mann's wonderfully subtle and many-layered story is not calculated to appeal to a man of Britten's acute literary perception."[51]

Although most agreed that Britten's *Death in Venice* was more cerebral than Mann's, there were signs that the opera was wobbling on its idealistic pedestal. The most obvious evidence comes from dissenters like Robert-Blunn, who questioned not only the "official" interpretation but also the unanimity with which it was endorsed. Perhaps even more revealing were the denials:

> In Mann's story the sex is almost irrelevant. In the opera a long choral ballet of Lido-bathing youths alters the emphasis, while Aschenbach's Bacchic dream is given correspondingly less importance. In Sir Frederick Ashton's choreography erotic suggestion is muted until the very end, when Aschenbach's death reveals the Tadsio-Eros equation, beautifully suggested by Robert Huguenin's dancing.[52]

In his eagerness to explain away eroticism, Cooper overstepped the mark, imagining "sex" even where none exists. In suggesting that Britten elevated the "choral ballet" (otherwise known as "The Games of Apollo") over the "Bacchic dream," Cooper rehearsed the common view of the work as more intellectual than visceral.[53] Cooper was not alone. Others found in the "Games of Apollo" proof of wider restrictions on sensuality in Britten's opera, praising the "poised movements" of the beach ballet as "calculated enough to be sensual without overstepping a very delicate frontier."[54] While these critics located the pinnacle of the opera's idealism in "The Games of Apollo," others denounced the same scene for compromising it.

These anxieties were already evident in the early correspondence between composer and librettist. By the summer of 1971, Myfanwy Piper struggled with a "second draft": "whereas the first beach ballet was domesticated and seaside [sic], this I think should be far more Hellenic and parodic of the idea just as Mann's language is."[55] As Piper's notes made clear, the problem was how to represent the fourth chapter's stylistic contrast as a theatrical one. At this point, Mann shifts from detailed realistic narrative to a more abstract meditation on the nature of beauty, in which setting and symbol, real and ideal, become almost indistinguishable. For all its lofty prose and erudite symbolism, however, the passage contains some of the novella's most erotic writing. One suspects that it was precisely because these "moments of reality" were so sensual that the author resorted to a litany of Platonic references in order to sublimate them, drawing upon the venerable tradition of abstracting Greek love. In the context of operatic action, whereby the pederastic gaze was embodied on stage, such abstraction became at once the more difficult and the more necessary. In a letter to his librettist from May 1971, the composer showed himself all too aware of this quandary:

> The scene in which I have come to a grinding halt, you know, is the big final one of Act I, the idyllic one. I couldn't get the tone right, relaxed enough after all that to-ing & fro-ing to Venice, & before the final climax, and *abstract* enough . . . *as if in Aschenbach's mind*, and I wanted to save Aschenbach before the big set piece.[56]

In fashioning this scene, Britten and Piper evidently grappled with the impossible goal of staging abstraction, resisting the very materiality of the theater. For Rodney Milnes, it was not simply that their solution failed to resolve an irresolvable dilemma. In casting the opening of Mann's fourth chapter as a ballet, the composer actually compounded it:

> Any external dramatic presentation . . . inevitably tends to coarsen the fable, render it fleshly, mawkish even. The pitfalls are almost avoided in Myfanwy Piper's libretto, though not in the act of staging; the symbol of a twelve-year old boy on the printed page is one thing, and would be something else on stage. But a well-developed nineteen-year-old dancer is quite another, and irrelevant, matter.[57]

If opera's "problem" was bound up with the materiality of performing bodies, adding dance to the mix would hardly seem like the best solution. What is more, as if the exhibitionism of ballet were not already enough to make critics shake their heads in disgust, Piper considered having the dance performed naked:

> I think the way to deal with the beach scenes is to have the . . . 2nd one [ballet], as far as the boys are concerned, really naked so as to remove the whole thing slightly from reality, as the whole of Aschenbach's attitude is removed from reality. It is a vision as well as an experience. At the end when T is mixed up with grownups he could simply have his white beach towel.[58]

Although the idea of a naked ballet was ultimately discarded for fear that "it might cause a certain interest that none of us really wants," the composer was initially receptive: "Your idea of the naked Ballet II section is excellent & could be wonderfully beautiful, Hellenically evocative."[59] The final version of the scene was staged as a compromise, with the dancers dressed in nothing but loincloths (see Fig. 15).

Piper's and Britten's intention certainly appears paradoxical: to stage the body in order to dematerialize it; to highlight the ideal by foregrounding the real; to soften the erotic charge by stripping everybody naked. In the rarefied genre of ballet, however, this paradox had a venerable lineage, as André Lepecki has pointed out: "Historically, neither 'presence' nor 'body' are central to Western choreographic imagination . . . 'the body is suspiciously absent.'"[60] In turning to ballet, Britten and Piper could depend on a long tradition of abstracting bodies into concepts of form, movement, and beauty. At the same time, as Albright explains, the move risked exposing dance's voyeuristic pleasures:

> A third function [of ballet in opera] might be to complement opera, to embellish the drama by doing the things that opera cannot do. Often, this entails display of the body. The premise of opera is nakedness transposed from the skin to the larynx: vulnerability, modesty, and wild abandon are all reseated in throat, all sex becomes oral sex . . . But from opera's beginning, it has been understood that an audience might also enjoy seeing a copulation that was more vivid and less metaphorical than two voices in parallel thirds.[61]

This "risk" was intensified by Britten's and Piper's apparent desire to push sublimation to its limit. They were so eager to mark the scene as transcending the narrative world that they did not even provide audiences with a plausible dramatic pretext. Like most operatic ballets, this one is staged as an intrusion on the otherwise closed Venetian narrative as figures from Greek mythology are embodied on stage. It was in response to this precarious situation that the composer framed the ballet with a pseudo-Greek chorus:

> What would your reaction be to having the "interpretations" of the boy's dances sung by the chorus as a kind of madrigal (again, your word)? Thinking of it visually, the chorus comes on at the beginning of the scene, & group themselves round as a kind of frame—then A[schenbach] comes on and does his introduction (ending in "live in Elysium"). Then lights dim on singers, leaving the boys brilliantly lit, with A. in the foreground. Ballet no. I followed by the chorus singing "And is that Phoebus . . . he lords in the air" either clearly visible, or in formalized groups, Aschenbach then singing "Ah, how the antique world possesses me, And everything I see prolongs the spell."[62]

By having the chorus chant snippets from Socratic dialogues and "interpreting" the dance as an ancient Greek pentathlon, Britten sought to dilute the scene's spectacular eroticism: by forcing home the perception that the protagonist's voyeuristic gaze was just a pretext for aesthetic reflection.

FIG. 15. *Death in Venice* (Act I, Scene 7)—Tadzio (Robert Huguenin) and Boys during the Games of Apollo. Snape Maltings, Suffolk, June 1973. Photo: Anthony Crickmay. Image reproduced courtesy of the Britten-Pears Foundation.

Yet for every commentator who bought this conceit there was another who expressed anxiety. Bayan Northcott's reaction was a relatively common one:

> The only real disaster in this whole scheme is surely the extended children's beach ballet. Coming at the end of an Act I running an hour and a half and glorifying Robert Huguenin's rather glum Tadzio, the pre-school nostalgia of this lengthy Ancient Greek sports day strikes me as both dramatically gratuitous and disturbingly at variance with what is for the most part so faithful a transposition of Mann's original.[63]

Objections were often framed as moral responses to the scene's eroticism. While Malcolm Rayment suggested that "perhaps the worst [scene] was the seemingly interminable balletic scene at the end of the first act [which] became positively embarrassing with the girls fully dressed and the boys in little bathing trunks," Andrew Porter declared:

> . . . my only serious reservations about the opera concern the Pentathlon that forms the climax of this suite [the Games of Apollo]. Right, that Aschenbach might have

FIG. 16. *Death in Venice* (Act II, Scene 13)—Tadzio (Robert Huguenin), Dionysius's Followers and Aschenbach (Peter Pears). Snape Maltings, Suffolk, June 1973. Photo: Nigel Luckhurst. Image reproduced courtesy of the Britten-Pears Foundation.

a vision of Tadzio, victor in every event; unhappy, that the form it takes should suggest sports day at an English prep. school with a fond infatuated master looking on.[64]

In adding "I suspect, the introductory 'classical' dances . . . would probably have
been enough to make the point," Porter belied his own aesthetic presumptions,
implying that the mise-en-scène should be no more than a window into a more
abstract domain, a principle often voiced in contemporaneous anti-operatic critiques.[65] The problem with the "Games of Apollo" lasting longer than "necessary,"
then, was that the scene allowed spectators to notice the dancing bodies in front of
them, compromising its symbolic function. Its dramatic "gratuitousness," "stasis,"
and "tediousness" were code for theatrical titillation. Peter Heyworth even went so
far as to denounce the ballet as "contrived," "allow[ing] an element of *divertissement* that is quite foreign to the nature of Britten's score," a lapse equaled only by
Aschenbach's dream in Act II (see Fig. 16): "A stagey device, even if it leads to a
scene that, musically, is among the most gripping in the opera."[66]

Such a comparison—between the "Games of Apollo" and Aschenbach's
Dionysian dream—is particularly provocative because, for all that they purported
to represent diametrically opposing aesthetics, there were several points—sore

points indeed—of similarity: both incorporated Apollo or Dionysus into their cast of characters and featured a scantily clad dancer illuminated center stage, while the protagonist looked on from the periphery.[67] While the genre's detractors would doubtless have interpreted the Act I finale's "lapse" into spectacle when it aspired to abstraction as a sign of failure—proof of opera's tendency to appeal to the body instead of the mind—we might prefer a more dialectical understanding, in keeping with Aschenbach's final thought speech:

> For mark you, Phaedrus, beauty alone is both divine and visible; and so it is the sense way, the artist's way, little Phaedrus, to the spirit . . . And by beauty we mean simplicity, largeness, and renewed severity of discipline; we mean a return to detachment and to form. But detachment, Phaedrus, and preoccupation with form lead to frightful emotional excesses, which his own stern cult of the beautiful would make him the first to condemn. So they too, they too, lead to the bottomless pit.[68]

In good Nietzschean fashion, Aschenbach's gloss on Plato's *Phaedrus* makes clear that Apollonian ideals of form and beauty strive to rise out of and fall back into Dionysus's sensual abyss. There can be no beauty without the senses, no order without chaos, no abstraction without immediacy. At once the most philosophically abstract and spectacularly visceral scene in the opera, "The Games of Apollo" bore this idea out in "operatic" fashion. When *Death in Venice* aspired to the ideal, it conjured up its conceptual opposite, deconstructing the very opposition that it stages. The stylization of the dances, the voyeuristic display of flesh, the ritualistic chorus, the musical climaxes and contrasts, the exotic orchestral and vocal colors (drums, wind machine, bells, and countertenor squealing high in his register)—all conjure up a phantasmagoric vision that both transcends and is pure theater.

HEARING ABSTRACTION

If bodily display was one reason why opera was regarded as suspect, the tradition of overwhelming and visceral music was another. As Bradley Pearson, Murdoch's fictional highbrow, put it:

> I do not wish to deny that there are some people—though fewer than one might think from the talk of our self-styled experts—who derive a pure and mathematically clarified pleasure from medleys of sound. All I can say is that "music" for me was simply an occasion for personal fantasy, the outrush of hot muddied emotions, the muck of my mind made audible.[69]

After endorsing Bertolt Brecht's idea of music as a narcotic, seducing audiences with theatrical illusions and cheap thrills, Eric Bentley went even further, excluding music from the intellectual drama he famously championed:

> Above all, music performs its dramatic functions very inadequately. Though Wagner and Richard Strauss have carried dramatic music to extraordinary lengths, they not

only cannot, as the latter wished, give an exact musical description of a tablespoon, they cannot do anything at all with the more baffling world of conceptual thought. They cannot construct the complex parallels and contraries of meaning which drama demands.[70]

Such a dismissive view could apparently not go uncontested. This notion that "opera cannot qualify ideas," "paradigmatic" in the 1950s, compelled Joseph Kerman to pen his polemic *Opera as Drama* in 1956.[71] In addition to being the most influential book on opera in the latter half of the century, establishing a set of criteria from which Anglo-American music critics could draw, Kerman's monograph laid bare the deep-seated ambivalence about the value and viability of the genre.

As many of Kerman's most often quoted aphorisms make clear, there is much in *Opera as Drama* to substantiate the view that in opera the body reigned supreme. In describing the music of Puccini and Strauss he draws heavily and disapprovingly on the language of sensual immediacy and physicality.[72] Among the specific musical characteristics associated with operatic immediacy was unmotivated lyricism, with *Tosca*'s shepherd's folk song and church scene cast as mere pretexts for melody.[73] Kerman's derogatory comments would soon be followed by Boulez's scorn at "voice for the sake of voice alone."[74] Not merely the primacy of melody but also the type of melody associated with opera attracted criticism. After describing *Turandot* as an aimless drift "from one pentatonic tune to the next, and from one sentimental phrase to its almost inevitable repetition," Kerman added: "Puccini clings to his limited ideas and repeats them protectively."[75] The constant and "indiscriminate" repetition laid bare Puccini's depraved priorities:

> What mattered was not [Cavaradossi's] plight, but the effect it could make on the audience. Puccini's faint emotionality is directed out over the footlights . . . Tosca leaps, and the orchestra screams the first thing that comes into its head; this loud little episode is for the audience, not for the play.[76]

Adorno, writing just a year before Kerman, agreed that these priorities compromised opera's dramatic integrity.[77] Bending to the whims of "an audience that always wants to hear the same thing" instead of persuading its audience by its structural logic, opera seduced through grand rhetorical gestures and the repetition of cheap thrills and culinary moments.[78]

Although all three critics lamented the musical immediacy of popular opera in identical terms, their motivations were poles apart. While Adorno's comments were part of a general assault on the pretensions and delusions of the middle class, Boulez's critique formed the background to imagining a utopian future for the genre, one in which his own "unwritten opera" played a revolutionary role.[79] Kerman's motivation was altogether different. Although his diagnosis of "flabby relativism" and "unintellectuality" in operatic culture might appear to be the epitome of anti-operatic discourse, it was actually intended as defense. Kerman's real antagonist was neither Puccini nor Strauss but rather those who regarded opera as a "low form of music" and "a low form of drama."[80] In denigrating his bêtes noires, he sought to rescue others from similar charges: "between Verdi and Puccini, between Wagner and Strauss, lies the decisive gulf between art and sensationalism."[81] Puccini and Strauss were, in other words, collateral damage in Kerman's fight to keep opera alive. Yet the rhetorical overkill with which the critic excoriated them suggests that cordoning them off from a more intellectual operatic tradition never convinced even him.

While the distinction between Puccini and Verdi, opera and drama, was occasionally cast as one of dramatic integrity, it was more often described in terms of musical form.[82] According to Kerman, the most important way that opera could supply the kind of conceptual meaning denied to it by literary critics was through the "dramatic" potential of musical form: "Opera is a type of drama whose integral existence is determined from point to point and in the whole by musical articulation."[83] Much as Boulez would later suggest "crack[ing] the discrepancy between symphonic music and operatic music," Kerman regarded organic development and symphonic form as solutions to the "problem" of operatic immediacy:

> The new dynamic [symphonic] style made it possible to join together elements in essential contrast—soon treated as elements in essential conflict: abrupt changes of feeling were at first juxtaposed, then justified and developed until a final resolution lay at hand. Music in a word became psychologically complex.[84]

At least in Kerman's ears, dramatic music was distinguished from its "theatrical" counterpart by its integrating each moment into a dynamic whole. This allowed for a mode of reception in which the listener apprehended meaning by actively following the dialectical process of the unfolding musical form. While remaining keen that commentators avoid the kind of analytic reductionism associated with Alfred Lorenz—the "*reductio ad absurdum* of certain valid insights"—Kerman urged critics to direct audiences to symphonic opera, in which formal argument took precedence over rhetorical gesture and musical satisfaction could be rationalized as a hard-won activity of the mind.[85]

Kerman was just one of a number who defended opera through the moderate formalism that came to dominate Anglo-American operatic criticism in the period. It is no coincidence that, in scouring the repertoire for a recent opera whose "arresting" musical climaxes were underpinned by organic structure, Kerman should have pointed to *The Turn of the Screw* (1954). As we have seen, from this gothic drama onward, Britten's operas served as lodestars for the structural listening that Kerman sought to champion. Even mainstream critics were so taken with matters of musical technique that they became almost indistinguishable from musicologists, often discussing the same passages in almost identical terms.[86]

Yet even in this formalistic context, *Death in Venice* elicited responses that were remarkably attentive to matters of motivic unity and large-scale form. This was partly the work of specialist previewers who instructed critics and audiences alike on how to listen. In an introduction published in *Opera* magazine almost a month before the premiere, Peter Evans attributed the opera's dramatic power to hidden musical connections, demonstrating—with detailed musical examples and reductions—that its most compelling moments were derived from identical motivic cells.[87] Styling the opera as a discourse of musical motifs, he stressed the "characteristic refinements of musical detail and motivic chain" with which the composer had replicated the nuances of Mann's novella. In his *Listener* preview, Jeremy Noble did much the same:

> What follows, then, attempts only to help the radio listener by bringing out some of the salient points in the music, and above all the images Britten has devised to embody the dualism that is the opera's central theme, a dualism of intellect and body, order and chaos, Apollo and Dionysus, life and death.[88]

Like Evans, Noble regarded the "density of the thematic relationships . . . [as] the musical equivalent of Mann's deliberately claustrophobic style."[89] Following the premiere, other critics were happy to get on board. Having suggested that the music's "ironies and thematic transformations are the musical equivalent of Mann's prose fabric," Patrick Carnegy praised the composer for "conjur[ing] deftly with a handful of closely related themes."[90] For Porter, such "careful, deliberate use of leitmotif techniques" was not only symbolic of the intellectualism of Mann's novella but also crucial to the listener's experience: "as the listener grows familiar with the score, he begins to respond consciously to the cross-reference and relationships of the close-woven, many hued tapestry."[91] Greenfield's review insisted that the music's emotional and symbolic content was supported by a larger sense of form:

> The result over a very long span (nearly two and a half hours of music with only one interval) is an intensification of emotion, which firmly establishes the composer's right to impose operatic form . . . Britten's music intensifies the symbolism on every level. For example, the arrival of the plague (symbol ultimately of Dionysiac indulgence) is felt subconsciously, long before the idea is made explicit in the text, through Britten's sinister use of the tuba in crawling bass figures . . . Even a brief study of the score shows how subtle the web of musical motifs is, but even an unprepared listener will note the broad contrast of chromatic contortions (temptation music of every kind) set against the relative purity, often pentatonic, of the music of true beauty.[92]

Gillian Widdicombe, by contrast, opted for sheer denial, insisting that there was no "grand climax, finger-tip lyricism, and blatant emotions," much as we saw critics do with *Peter Grimes*.[93] After concluding that "*Death in Venice* is one of those complex operas demanding and deserving time and thought for just appreciation [and] has nothing in common with the shallow, pretty-picture world of Visconti's film of the same name," Widdicombe exposed the stakes: the work had to be distanced at all costs from the "cheap" pleasures of operatic spectacle and film.

Yet while evaluations based on such restricted criteria do little justice to the opera's compelling theatricality, it is hard to deny that *Death in Venice* wears its formalism on its sleeve, right from the opening of the prologue. As audiences are plunged into the protagonist's philosophical monologue about the machinations of the intellect, Aschenbach's recitative traces a set of musical phrases that "calls attention," as Philip Rupprecht has shrewdly observed, "to its own rigor."[94]

Even as it retains a firm tonal orientation, Britten's opening (Ex. 21) thematizes serial construction by setting out its rows in clear and adjacent sets. The opening tetrachord (F—G—F♯—G♯), for example, is immediately transposed up three semitones (G♯—A♯—A—B), before the final hexachord of the row is sounded (B—E—D—C—D♭—E♭). In repeating the pattern in melodic inversion (E♭—D♭—D—C; C—B♭—B—A; A—E—F♯—G♯—G—F), highlighted by a parallel inversion of register, the composer flaunts his motivic rigor. Such ostentation was a gift to commentators anxious to exorcize musical viscerality. Already in his preview, Evans observed that these opening tetrachords introduced the "plague" motif's major and minor thirds, setting in motion a symphonic thread that would run below the entirety of the opera's "surface."[95] Porter likewise understood this "twelve-tone row" as signaling the beginning of the musical end by foreshadowing the motifs associated with the protagonist's eventual demise.[96] Even the opera's most distinctive and unique moments, he insisted, could be traced back to these opening seeds. John Evans went even further:

> If one is tempted to conclude that the twelve-note proposition and the modal resolution are unrelated strands of an eclectic score, one would be mistaken . . . The concept of *modulation* between the twelve-note proposition of the opening scene and the modal resolution of the opera's postlude acknowledges an extraordinary symphonic logic that permeates the score . . . The opening twelve-note proposition in *Death in Venice*, while encapsulating the dramatic image of intellectual sterility within Aschenbach ("My mind beats on, and no words come"), initiates the central major/minor third motivic cell of the score and, as I hope to demonstrate, highlights the tonal polarities that place the Apollonian/Dionysiac conflict in context throughout the opera.[97]

Although written later, Evans's discussion sheds light on the widespread insistence that there was a "symphonic logic" running from the score's first note to its last. In stressing the long-term structural significance of the opening music, Evans was ruling out two possibilities: that it might be no more than a pictorial effect, illustrating intellectualism; and that it might represent the kind of eclectic dabbling in serialism that was just then being stigmatized as "amateurish."[98]

But a narrow focus on motivic connections served also to obscure more prosaic affective and rhetorical conventions. The most obvious way in which the prologue grabs attention is through a textural and dynamic crescendo; each new textural strand emerges from a different register, building the passage up like a large-scale arpeggio, while the harp's *stretto* glissandi further enhance dramatic suspense. This sense of "unrest" is heightened by underlying "Tristan" chord (F—A♭—B—E♭), whose dissonances remain unresolved at the end of each mini climax. Such

EX. 21. *Death in Venice* (Prologue)—"My Mind Beats On".

gestures of anticipation and frustration had the advantage of suggesting an overriding form even while relying on a relatively loose musical rhetoric.

The risk of falling on the wrong side of the great divide was all the more potent in the first act's theatrical conclusion (Ex. 22), which sports the kind of "grand

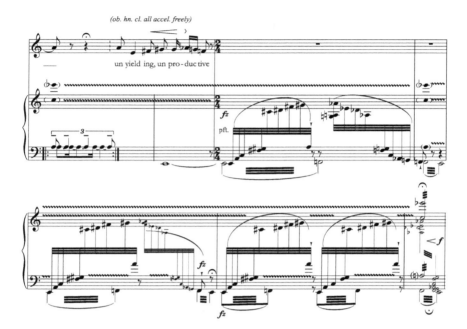

EX. 21 (continued).

climax" and "blatant emotion" that critics decried, and therefore denied. In musical terms, it might be described as a total crescendo—dynamic, rhythmic, textural, and registral—followed by a sudden, brass-punctuated climax accompanying Aschenbach's apparently wordless cry. Given opera's long-standing association with *jouissance,* we might well think of other terms here. The sustained bass drone, combined with the tenor's "almost spoken" descending third on the words "love you," perfectly captures a sense of postcoital relaxation. Indeed, this passage has unsurprisingly drawn comment in almost every discussion, for not only is it one of *Death in Venice*'s capital moments, it also issues the most potent challenge to any notion that "the opera's abstractness neutralises the story's more volatile implications."[99] Indeed, the passage's approximation of orgasm calls to mind the notion of "body music," coined by Daniel Albright in a discussion of *A Midsummer Night's Dream* (1960):

> Oberon's cries are sublimated in all sorts of artful ways, through archaisms, through vocal lines that pretend to be instrumental lines, and so forth; but behind all these dissimulations there is something raw—not far from Peter Quint's *Miles!,* not even far from Bottom's hee-haw. Oberon's music, despite the self-conscious strangeness, its cerebral quality, is *body music;* if Bottom is the opera's chief ass, Oberon is the opera's chief penis.[100]

As Albright's irreverent metaphor makes clear, Britten often relied on more visceral levels of musical representation than critics were willing to admit. But, as Albright also notes, Britten's "body music" often contained the seeds of its own sublimation, in both text and music, almost as if audiences were encouraged to write off this "operatic" finale as ironic or insincere. It was an invitation critics were only too happy to accept:

> Other stretches of music seem happy to stay on the level of, say, Puccini: and the closing line of Act One has Aschenbach proclaiming "I love you" to the receding figure of the boy, for all the world as if he were Don José singing his flower song to Carmen. Such banalities, however, seem sometimes to be planted deliberately in the score, so that Aschenbach can later comment self-critically on the state of his emotions.[101]

Those even less willing to admit the rhetorical grandeur of the opera's catharsis grounded the power of their reactions in structural "depths," not that they had to dig very "deep" to get there. In this respect, Evans once again led the way, rationalizing the significance of Aschenbach's outburst in terms of the "plague" motif and the major/minor third tension that flows from it.[102]

This tendency to focus on questions of long-term structure while blocking one's ears to the passage's immediate visceral dimensions persists even in the most recent scholarship. Listening for tonal progress as avidly as Evans had listened for motivic unity, Claire Seymour diverts attention from the music's bodily resonances to a more metaphysical meaning:

> It rises chromatically from a low E, gradually spanning an octave, signifying the unstoppable advance of both the plague and Aschenbach's sickness . . . The final phrase unequivocally establishes the E major tonality which Aschenbach has struggled to deny; but the final cadence is imperfect; suspended and unresolved: at the close of Act I spiritual transcendence remains a possible outcome.[103]

Ruth Sara Longobardi likewise advocates looking past immediate reactions at the deeper motivic significance of the protagonist's cry. After insisting "there has been little question as to the import of this passage," she offers an alternative to the supposedly common view: "The plague motive, because it derives directly from a Dionysian realm that functions beyond the protagonist's point of view, erodes the psychological realism of this moment, superimposing on Aschenbach's experience a layer of mythical significance."[104] Far from being unusual, as she implies, her suggestion has been a standard rhetorical move.

Yet this is a move that conceals as much as it reveals. Most of the motivic references to which critics customarily appeal actually occur before Fig. 187 (see Ex. 22), a passage set apart from the climax (beginning at Fig. 188) by a shift in texture and motivic material, not to mention the pause (at the upbeat to Fig. 188). Moreover, the sense of harmonic release (at bar 16) can be viewed as being as much a result of the cessation of the local dissonances as the resolution of the large-scale tonal tensions that critics preferred to highlight. Even this marked "resolution" is

EX. 22. *Death in Venice* (Act I, Scene 7)—"I Love You".

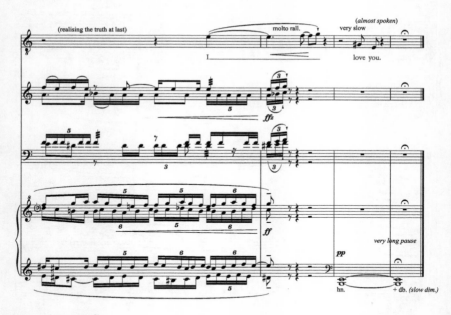

EX. 22 (continued).

hardly complete: while the horns and double-basses sound the root and fifth of the chord of an E major "tonic" in second inversion, the "almost spoken" utterance of Aschenbach lacks the audible strength to establish this key firmly. Indeed, given the speed of its buildup—from silence (just before Fig. 188) to a huge orchestral fortissimo (at bar 16) in the space of seven bars—the climax strikes a "performative" tone, creating the very tension that it appears to resolve. The accumulation of local dissonances thematizes large-scale tonal tension while the telescoping of textural lines provides the semblance of thematic density.

In an aesthetic context in which intellectual abstraction was valued over compelling immediacy, critics were granted a pretext to overlook other, less rarefied dimensions. The music obviously thrives on rhetorical juxtaposition and contrast; particularly within individual scenes, it is often constructed as a series of contrasting tableaux that approach the cinematic in the rapidity of their shifts. Not even the most rigid formalist could refrain from picking out outstanding musical "moments," even if they attributed their reactions to deep structure instead of compelling surface. Yet the opera's formal arrivals and rhetorical climaxes usually happened to coincide, suggesting that structural and atomistic modes of listening were two sides of the same coin, the former representing a sublimation rather than rejection of the latter. Far from a neutral mode of analysis, then, formalistic approaches to *Death in Venice* played into the broader aesthetic of sublimation sketched throughout this chapter, working alongside appeals to philosophical abstraction to redeem the opera's pleasures from the taint of the visceral.

BOURGEOIS OPERA AND THE GREAT DIVIDE

Opera has been in a precarious situation since the moment when high bourgeois society . . . ceased to exist . . . . At once barbaric and precocious, the newcomer who has not yet learned as a child to be bowled over by opera and to respect outrageous requirements will feel contempt for it, while the intellectually advanced public has almost ceased to be able to respond immediately or spontaneously to a limited stock of works, which have long since been relegated to the living-room treasure chests of the petit-bourgeoisie.
—THEODOR W. ADORNO, "BOURGEOIS OPERA," 1955[105]

In the final volume of his *Oxford History of Western Music,* Taruskin reflects on the "opera problem" that lies at this chapter's root.[106] At a time when modernist polemicists were declaring culture to be "polarized to the point of crisis"—between an alienated avant-garde and a pandering mass culture—the spectacularly public genre was dismissed as decadent. In setting out the logic of the "great divide," Taruskin appeals principally to Clement Greenberg's essay "Avant-Garde and Kitsch," published in 1939: "The title," as he explains, "stated categorical alternatives. One could be avant-garde, or one could produce kitsch, mere pseudo-art. There was no middleground."[107] In the operatic sphere, however, Theodor Adorno's "Bourgeois Opera" has often been said to mark the mid-century battle lines. Indeed, for a number of scholars, Adorno's diatribe from 1955 stands as a shining example of modernist attempts to consign the opera to the "wrong" side of the great divide: to dismiss it as a cheap form of mass culture.[108] With this in mind, Taruskin delineates the challenges that Britten operas pose: first, they kept the genre "viable through the leanest years of its existence, and prevented it lapsing into an exclusively 'museum' status"; and second, they remained popular with opera lovers while commanding the respect of critics "otherwise committed to modernism."[109] In devoting a large portion of his chapter to Britten's awkward position, Taruskin sheds light on *Death in Venice*'s stakes. In defending the work from the taint of immediacy, commentators were attempting to secure not just Britten's place on the "right" side of modernist historiography, but also the place of the operatic genre more broadly.

While this account highlights the importance of carving out space for seemingly paradoxical works like *Death in Venice*, it also demonstrates the difficulty in doing so. Despite setting out to show how Britten straddled the great divide, Taruskin's "standoff" between Britten's "Music in Society" and Elliot Carter's "Music in History" risks opening up the gap once again. Nor is this framework limited to the titles. In concluding his chapter with quotations from Britten's Aspen speech in 1964, spun as a "polemic against the other side of the mid-twentieth-century divide," Taruskin lays bare a thread that runs throughout his discussion of Britten's works. However, while he views Britten's operatic allegories as a way of serving society and renouncing modernist esotericism, we have seen that they often had quite the opposite effect. The real problem with presenting Britten as a populist foil to the contemporary avant-garde, however, is not simply that it glosses over these kinds of tensions and paradoxes, but that it reinforces the broader oppositions that this study has set out to challenge—between an art that serves society and one that scorns it.

If the complex case of *Death in Venice* demonstrates how Britten's oeuvre upended mid-century oppositions even as it drew on them, we might say the same of anti-operatic polemics like "Bourgeois Opera." We have seen throughout this study that the most forceful assertions of modernist oppositions often contain the seeds of their own deconstruction. In this respect, Adorno's and Boulez's diatribes were no exception. The historical distance may even allow us to recognize that their anxieties and complaints were shrewder and subtler than they at first appear. While scholars have often interpreted their attacks on opera as a straightforward product of snobbery—a dismissal of the genre as a cheap and indulgent progenitor of mass culture—*Death in Venice* may help us to tease out the deep-seated anxieties, tensions, and paradoxes that lurk between their lines.

In characterizing opera as "bourgeois," Adorno was, on the one hand, making a historical point: that the genre's inability to free itself from its origins in the "bourgeois era" had rendered it obsolete in the twentieth century. The period from which it hailed being one when "intellectual" concerns seemed to coincide with those of the people, opera now fell afoul of the great divide: "The esthetic conventions it rests upon, perhaps even the measure of sublimation it presupposes, can hardly be expected of the broad listening strata."[110] While the "unthinking" masses now turned to Hollywood for intoxicating spectacle, highbrows fancied themselves too sophisticated for opera's bargain-basement intellectualisms. It was in describing those who clung to opera throughout the twentieth century, on the other hand, that Adorno's use of "bourgeois" shifted from the largely neutral descriptor to a more pointed expression of social and aesthetic contempt: "Opera, more than any other form, represents traditional bourgeois culture to those who simultaneously fail to take part in that culture . . . It is frequented by an elite that is no elite."[111] Much like Bradley Pearson, Adorno thought that the opera "problem" lay not just in the immediacy of its pleasures—as with mass culture—but also in the high-minded rhetoric with which it was rationalized. It was, in other words, one of middlebrow sublimation.

This problem was apparently only exacerbated by attempts to modernize, intellectualize, or otherwise repackage the genre—a paradox seen throughout *Middlebrow Modernism*. "Opera," Adorno insisted, "has reached the state of crisis because the genre cannot dispense with illusion without surrendering itself, and yet it must want to do so."[112] "Forced attempts at innovation," he elaborated, were destined to fail, as making opera an honest genre would mean taking a Nietzschean hammer to its characteristic features.[113] Or as reiterated by Boulez: "even if one announces a modern opera, that is really deception, because the word 'modern' must be dropped first if you are to join it to the word 'opera.' It cannot be modern because it is opera!"[114] Whether serving as museums for a canon of tired master-works or showcases for a "superficial modernism," opera houses were catering to "bourgeois" audiences eager to buy their way out of the great divide.

Such vitriol can be difficult to swallow; yet, when approached critically and historically, this discourse sheds light on *Death in Venice* and its reception. Adorno's discussion of "an elite that is no elite," eager to demonstrate its cultural distinction, accords with the defensive and esoteric rhetoric that permeated responses to the opera, as does his suggestion that this criticism could serve to sublimate the genre's less rarefied dimensions. Just as astute were Adorno's observations about how "bourgeois" operas encouraged this sublimation. In response to the vilification of operatic spectacle, he explained, directors and designers embraced a repentant aesthetic of scarcity on the one hand, and exaggerated stylization on the other. As we have seen, the original production of Britten's last opera shuttled back and forth between the austere minimalism of Aschenbach's monologues and the spectacular excess of the beach ballets. Bourgeois operatic music, according to Adorno, featured a similar mixture of asceticism and grand climax, sewn together with "thinly motivic materials."[115] These too were in Britten's final opera, and even bled one into the other, making the eclecticism all the more pronounced. It was precisely the motivic markers at the score's most rhetorically compelling moments that allowed critics to defend its "operatic" climaxes as intellectual rather than visceral. Affinities such as these marked *Death in Venice* as an archetypal "bourgeois opera," at once forbiddingly expensive and irredeemably cheap.

In engaging with this view, it has not been my intention here—as elsewhere throughout this study—to pile on *Death in Venice* or its devotees but rather to encourage a more frank and nuanced discussion of the aesthetic values, tensions, and prejudices that shaped it. In diagnosing the failure of bourgeois opera as one of sublimation, critics like Boulez and Adorno highlighted its greatest strength: by moderating its intellectualism and asceticism with old-fashioned dramatic and musical spectacle, it offered a less abstemious form of modernism. As Begam and Smith have explained, opera's institutional strictures made it well suited to this task: "The operatic stage is a realm where function follows form more often than the other way around, and where avant-garde practices—twelve-tone composition, minimalist costuming, sets constructed entirely of light and show or else made shockingly au courant—tend to reify into mere gestures with peculiar rapidity."[116] These tensions were built into the genre's aesthetic makeup. While the play of musical motifs allowed critics to disavow the grand operatic climaxes, the libretto offered an extra layer of apologetic intellectualism and rationalization. To judge from mid-century discourse, in other words, we might cast opera as the quintessentially middlebrow genre, capable of threatening modernism's oppositions. It is hardly surprising, then, that Boulez concluded his "operatic" diatribe by quoting the anxious dictum that appears near this study's opening: "Schoenberg was quite right," Boulez opined, "when he said, 'The middle road is the only one that does not lead to Rome,'" as if his Viennese idol had been discussing opera specifically.[117]

For all the talk of opera's death, the genre seemed to have cleared itself a busy middle road by the time Adorno and Boulez penned their polemics, enough so that they worried about bourgeois operas ruining the audience for genuine modern music. While Boulez associated this with Henze's irredeemably "compromised" commissions for the Hamburg Staatsoper, which threatened something of an operatic revival, Heather Wiebe has recently identified a comparable trend in British opera.[118] Nor was the problem limited to opera. By the time *Death in Venice* reached the stage, many of those who had steered clear of the supposedly outdated genre were smuggling "operatic" theatricality and gesture into modernist compositions. In the realm of instrumental music, as Robert Adlington has pointed out, performative virtuosity, indeterminacy, and aleatoricism meant that even theoretically abstract modes of avant-garde composition "knock[ed] at the door of music theatre."[119] Much of the period's self-consciously anti-operatic music theater seemed to draw on the spectacular excess, stylization, or corporeality associated with opera. "While one must sympathize entirely," Rodney Milnes conceded in 1972, "with today's composers seeking a new name for the medium and jettisoning [opera's] excesses of duration, orchestral and choral forces . . . there is still a slight impression that they are stealing the emperor's clothes while pretending that they do not exist."[120] From the wild Dionysian gestures of Birtwistle's *Trageodia* (1965) to the nude male dancer at the center of Maxwell Davies's *Vesalii Icones* (1969), *Death in Venice* was by no means the only work to foreground "operatic" corporeality amid a pretense of intellectual abstraction.

By now, however, it should come as no surprise that Adorno and Boulez were hardly exempt from these strictures. Less than a decade after threatening to blow up the opera houses, Boulez descended into the Bayreuth pit to conduct the "Ring of the Century." Even within his attacks in 1968, he let slip that his own operatic museum—should he ever get to choose one—would be as compromised and eclectic as the "musty old wardrobe" he detested. "Some Verdi," he conceded, "you are obliged to do, because Verdi very much belongs to history."[121] Not even his more enthusiastic and daring selections were free of the taint of literal and musical spectacle: "C'est du Verdi seriel," one of his Darmstadt colleagues remarked of Boulez's beloved *Moses und Aron*.[122] While Adorno had less to do with the genre in practice, his critical ambivalence was no less striking. At the height of integral serialism, he glanced back nostalgically to the "flamboyant" and "dramatic" style of Strauss, Schoenberg, and Berg.[123] Elsewhere, his formalist defense of *Wozzeck*'s "operatic" mode veered close to the kind of sublimation he loved to jeer at.[124] One might even hazard that the reason why Adorno and Boulez regarded bourgeois opera as more pernicious than mass culture was that it mirrored their own ambivalent positions. For musical modernism was nothing if not a spectacular mixture of immediacy and abstraction. From some angles, the esoteric discourse of modernist circles—Darmstadt, IRCAM, even Boulez's imaginary theater—could look a lot like the pretentious nattering in the opera foyers, which modernists did their best to caricature.[125] As Adorno pointed out, opera, at least since Wagner, had been a domain in which spectacle and form, body and mind, had interacted in destabilizing ways. Perhaps the problem with bourgeois operas like *Death in Venice* was not that they reconciled supposedly irreconcilable aesthetic categories. It was, rather, that they exposed modernism's own acts of sublimation, laying bare the precariousness of the great divide.

1 MIDDLEBROW MODERNISM

1. Virginia Woolf, "Middlebrow" (1932), in *The Death of the Moth, and Other Essays* (London: Hogarth, 1947), 115.

2. "Paul Bunyan," *Time,* May 19, 1941; Virgil Thomson, "Musico-Theatrical Flop," *New York Herald Tribune,* May 6, 1941.

3. W. H. Auden, "Opera on an American Legend," *New York Times,* May 4, 1941.

4. Auden.

5. W. H. Auden, "Paul Bunyan: An Operetta in Two Acts and a Prologue" (1941), in *The Operas of Benjamin Britten,* ed. David Herbert (London: Herbert, 1979), 77.

6. On one occasion, Britten imagined himself sharing in Inkslinger's dilemma—a connection several scholars have pointed out—writing to Wulff Scherchen: "I may have to go to Hollywood, which I should hate; but if I had the chance I must take it, since it is a grand way of making a lot of money quickly." Britten to Wulff Scherchen, October 8, 1940, in *Letters from a Life,* vol. 2, ed. Donald Mitchell and Philip Reed (London: Faber, 1991), 876.

7. Olin Downes, "Official Opening for 'Paul Bunyan,'" *New York Times,* May 6, 1941.

8. E[ugene] B[onner], "Opera in English: Paul Bunyan," *Monthly Musical Record* 2, no. 1 (1941): 12.

9. Downes, "Official Opening."

10. Robert Bagar, "Britten Work Has Premiere at Columbia," *New York-World Telegram,* May 5, 1941.

11. Downes, "Official Opening."

12. Thomson, "Musico-Theatrical Flop."

13. Thomson. See also William Mann, "Paul Bunyan," *Times,* June 7, 1976.

14. Van Wyck Brooks, "Highbrow and Lowbrow," in *America's Coming-of-Age* (New York: B. W. Huebsch, 1915), 7.

15. Brooks, "Highbrow and Lowbrow," 8.

16. Dwight Macdonald, "A Theory of Mass Culture," *Diogenes* 3 (1953): 1.

17. See Melba Cuddy-Keane, *Virginia Woolf, the Intellectual, and the Public Sphere* (Cambridge: Cambridge University Press, 2003), 16–33.

18. J. B. Priestley, "To a High-Brow," transcript of broadcast, October 17, 1932, BBC Written Archives Centre, reprinted in *John O'London's Weekly*, December 3, 1932.

19. See Cuddy-Keane, *Virginia Woolf*, 25.

20. F. R. Leavis, *Mass Civilisation and Minority Culture* (Cambridge: Minority, 1930), 25.

21. Q. D. Leavis, *Fiction and the Reading Public* (1932; London: Chatto & Windus, 1968), 270.

22. For elaboration, see Leavis, *Mass Civilisation*, 25; and Leavis, *Fiction and Reading Public*, 33.

23. The "men of 1914" label was coined by Wyndham Lewis to describe a modernist quadrumvirate comprising T. S. Eliot, Ezra Pound, James Joyce, and himself. Wyndham Lewis, *Blasting and Bombardiering* (London: Eyre & Spottiswood, 1937).

24. Arnold Schoenberg, "Foreword to Three Satires for Mixed Chorus, op. 28" (1925–26), in *A Schoenberg Reader*, ed. Joseph Auner (New Haven: Yale University Press, 2003), 186.

25. Arnold Schoenberg, "Heart and Brain in Music" (1946), in *Style and Idea*, trans. Leo Black, ed. Leonard Stein (Berkeley: University of California Press, 1984), 154.

26. Theodor Adorno, *Philosophy of Modern Music*, trans. Anne G. Mitchell (New York: Seabury, 1973), 3. Originally published as *Philosophie der neuen Musik* (Frankfurt am Main: Suhrkamp, 1949).

27. Adorno, *Philosophy of Modern Music*, 133.

28. L[ouis] Fleury, "Pierrot Lunaire," *Music & Letters* 5, no. 4 (1924): 354.

29. M. Du Pré Cooper, "Atonality and 'Zwölftonmusik,'" *Musical Times* 74, no. 1084 (1933): 497.

30. Constant Lambert, *Music Ho! A Study of Music in Decline* (1934; London: Penguin, 1948), 198.

31. Lambert, 207.

32. Andreas Huyssen, *After the Great Divide: Modernism, Mass Culture and Postmodernism* (Bloomington: Indiana University Press, 1986), vii.

33. Susan McClary, "Terminal Prestige: The Case of Avant-Garde Musical Composition," *Cultural Critique* 12 (1989): 57–81; Peter Franklin, *The Idea of Music: Schoenberg and Others* (London: Palgrave Macmillan, 1985).

34. See Julian Johnson, *Who Needs Classical Music? Cultural Choice and Musical Value* (Oxford: Oxford University Press, 2002). For a critique, see Richard Taruskin, "The Musical Mystique: Defending Classical Music against Its Devotees," *New Republic*, October 22, 2007.

35. See James Hepokoski, *Sibelius, Symphony No. 5* (Cambridge: Cambridge University Press, 1993); Daniel Grimley, "Modernism and Closure: Nielsen's Fifth Symphony," *Musical Quarterly* 86, no. 1 (2002): 149–73; J. P. E. Harper-Scott, *Edward Elgar, Modernist* (Cambridge: Cambridge University Press, 2006); J. P. E. Harper-Scott, "'Our True North': Walton's First Symphony, Sibelianism, and the Nationalization of Modernism in England," *Music & Letters* 89, no. 4 (2008): 562–89.

36. See Byron Adams, ed., "British Modernism," special issue, *Musical Quarterly* 91 (2008); and Matthew Riley, ed., *British Music and Modernism, 1895–1960* (Aldershot: Ashgate, 2010).

37. Björn Heile has diagnosed a "modernism bashing" trend, using the introduction to *Western Music and Its Others* as an example. See Björn Heile, "Darmstadt as Other: British and American Responses to Musical Modernism," *Twentieth-Century Music* 1, no. 2 (2014); and Georgina Born and David Hesmondhalgh, "Introduction," in *Western Music and Its Others: Difference, Representation and Appropriation in Music* (Berkeley and Los Angeles: University of California Press, 2000).

38. Perhaps the most obvious example may be drawn from the backlash to Richard Taruskin's *Oxford History of Western Music,* perceived as anti-modernist in its definition, framing, and methodology. See J. P. E. Harper-Scott, *The Quilting Points of Musical Modernism: Revolution, Reaction and William Walton* (Cambridge: Cambridge University Press, 2012); and Franklin Cox, "Review: Richard Taruskin's The Oxford History of Western Music," www.searchnewmusic.org/cox_review.pdf; Rodney Lister, "Review," *Tempo* 60 (2006): 50–61.

39. For an introduction, see Douglas Mao and Rebecca L. Walkowitz, "The New Modernist Studies," *PMLA* 123, no. 3 (2008): 737–48.

40. See Bernard Gendron, "Jammin at Le Boeuf: Jazz and the Paris Avant-Garde," *Discourse* 12, no. 1 (1989): 3–27; Alyson Tischler, "A Rose Is a Pose: Steinian Modernism and Mass Culture," *Journal of Modern Literature* 26, nos. 3/4 (2003): 12–27; Karen Leick, *Gertrude Stein and the Making of American Celebrity* (New York: Routledge, 2009).

41. David Chinitz, "T. S. Eliot and the Cultural Divide," *PMLA* 110, no. 2 (1995): 236–47.

42. Huyssen, "High/Low in an Expanded Field," *Modernism/Modernity* 9, no. 3 (2002): 366.

43. Kevin J. H. Dettmar and Stephen Watt, eds., *Marketing Modernism: Self-Promotion, Canonization, Rereading* (Ann Arbor: University of Michigan Press, 1996); Joyce Wexler, *Who Paid for Modernism? Art, Money and the Fiction of Conrad, Joyce and Lawrence* (Fayetteville: University of Arkansas Press, 1997); Aaron Jaffe, *Modernism and the Culture of Celebrity* (Cambridge: Cambridge University Press, 2005).

44. Miriam Hansen, "The Mass Production of the Senses: Classical Cinema as Vernacular Modernism," *Modernism/Modernity* 6, no. 2 (1999): 60.

45. Brigid Cohen, *Stefan Wolpe and the Avant-Garde Diaspora* (Cambridge: Cambridge University Press, 2012), 11.

46. Björn Heile offers a similar warning, albeit from an ideological rather than a historicist standpoint, in a recent review article: Heile, "Musical Modernism, Sanitized," *Modernism/Modernity* 18, no. 3 (2011): 631–37.

47. Cohen, *Stefan Wolpe and the Avant-Garde Diaspora,* 9.

48. Anon., "The Middlebrow," *Punch* 169 (1925): 673.

49. Russell Lynes, "Highbrow, Lowbrow, Middlebrow" (1949), reprinted in *Wilson Quarterly* 1, no. 1 (1976): 149.

50. Woolf, "Middlebrow," 116.

51. Margaret Widdemer, "Message and Middlebrow," *Saturday Review of Literature* 9, no. 31 (1933): 1.

52. Lynes, "Highbrow, Lowbrow, Middlebrow," 152–56.

53. Leavis, *Fiction and the Reading Public,* 19.

54. Woolf, "Middlebrow," 118.

55. John Reith, *Broadcast over Britain* (London: Hodder and Stoughton, 1924), 175–76.

56. Reith, 175.

57. Theodor Adorno, "On the Fetish-Character in Music and the Regression of Listening" (1938), in *The Culture Industry* (New York: Routledge, 1991), 35.

58. Adorno, 36.

59. Lambert, *Music Ho!,* 168–69.

60. Lambert, 169–70.

61. Lambert, 170.

62. Leavis, *Fiction and the Reading Public,* 26.

63. Lambert, Letter to Cecil Beaton, February 11, 1936, quoted in Cecil Beaton, *Ballet* (London: Wingate, 1951), 58–60.

64. Leavis, *Fiction and the Reading Public.*

65. Reith, *Broadcast over Britain,* 130.

66. J. B. Priestley, quoted in Richard Hoggart, *The Uses of Literacy* (London: Chatto & Windus, 1957), 154.

67. Lambert, *Music Ho!,* 170.

68. Dwight MacDonald, "Masscult and Midcult" (1960), in *Against the American Grain* (New York: Da Capo, 1962), 54.

69. Woolf, "Middlebrow," 118.

70. Adorno, "On the Fetish-Character in Music," 36.

71. Virgil Thomson, "Age without Honor," *New York Herald Tribune,* October 11, 1940.

72. Theodor W. Adorno, "Gloss on Sibelius," trans. Susan H. Gillespie, in *Sibelius and His World,* ed. Daniel Grimley (Princeton: Princeton University Press, 2011), 336.

73. Ernest Newman, "The Present State of Music, IV," *New Witness,* September 14, 1916.

74. Cecil Gray, *Predicaments: Or, Music and the Future* (Oxford: Oxford University Press, 1936), 278.

75. Gray, 279.

76. Lambert, *Music Ho!,* 197.

77. Lambert, 239–40.

78. Joan Shelley Rubin, *The Making of Middlebrow Culture* (Chapel Hill: University of North Carolina Press, 1992); Janice Radway, *A Feeling for Books: The Book-of-the-Month Club, Literary Taste, and Middlebrow Desire* (Chapel Hill: University of North Carolina Press, 1997).

79. Tom Perrin, *The Aesthetics of Middlebrow Fiction: Popular US Novels, Modernism, and Form, 1945–1975* (New York: Palgrave Macmillan, 2015).

80. Nicola Humble, *The Feminine Middlebrow Novel, 1920s to 1950s: Class, Domesticity, and Bohemianism* (Oxford: Oxford University Press, 2001), 11–12.

81. Woolf, "Middlebrow," 115.

82. Reith, *Broadcast over Britain,* 176. For an examination of BBC attempts to promote modernist music, see Jenny Doctor, *The BBC and Ultra-Modern Music, 1922–1936* (Cambridge: Cambridge University Press, 1999).

83. "Letter to the Editor," *Musical Times* (1931): 444–35.

84. Lambert, *Music Ho!,* 178.

85. See Daniel Tracy, "Investing in 'Modernism': Smart Magazines, Parody and Middlebrow Professional Judgment," *Journal of Modern Periodical Studies* 1, no. 1 (2010): 38–63; Victoria Kingham, "The Excluded Middle: Cultural Polemics and Magazines in America,

1915–1933," in *Middlebrow Literary Cultures,* ed. Erica Brown and Mary Grover (New York: Palgrave, 2012).

86. See Michael Murphy, "One Hundred Percent Bohemia: Pop Decadence and the Aestheticization of the Commodity in the Rise of the Slicks," in Dettmar and Watt, *Marketing Modernisms,* 68–69.

87. J. B. Priestley, "High, Low, Broad," *Open House: A Book of Essays* (London, 1926), 166.

88. Priestly, 166–67.

89. Clement Greenberg, "Avant-Garde and Kitsch" (1939), in *Art and Culture: Critical Essays* (Boston: Beacon, 1961), 11.

90. Lambert, *Music Ho!,* 178.

91. Greenberg, "Avant-Garde and Kitsch," 15.

92. Greenberg, "Review of the Water-Color, Drawing, and Sculpture Sections of the Witney Annual," *Nation,* February 23, 1946; reprinted in *Arrogant Purpose, 1945–1949,* ed. John O'Brian (Chicago: University of Chicago Press, 1986), 57.

93. Kurt List, "The State of American Music," *Partisan Review* 15, no. 1 (1948): 85–90.

94. Adorno, *Philosophy of Modern Music,* 6.

95. Adorno, 11.

96. MacDonald, "Masscult and Midcult," 51.

97. Greenberg, "Review," 58.

98. Pierre Bourdieu, *Distinction: A Social Critique of the Judgment of Taste,* trans. Richard Nice (Cambridge, MA: Harvard University Press, 1984), 323.

99. See Humphrey Carpenter, *Benjamin Britten* (New York: Scribner's, 1992), 4–5; and Neil Powell, *Benjamin Britten: A Life for Music* (New York: Henry Holt, 2013), 7.

100. Admittedly, Britten's father did refuse to have a gramophone or wireless in the house, but Benjamin often spent evenings at neighbors' houses, enjoying recordings or broadcasts. By the time he was at Gresham's School or the Royal College of Music, he had daily access to these media. Powell, *Benjamin Britten,* 7.

101. Britten, April 7, 1930, in *Journeying Boy: The Diaries of the Young Benjamin Britten, 1928–1938,* ed. John Evans (London: Faber and Faber, 2010), 36.

102. Britten, January 9, 1931, in *Journeying Boy,* 60.

103. Britten, April 14, 1930, in *Journeying Boy,* 37.

104. Britten, "Arnold Schoenberg" (1951), in *Britten on Music,* ed. Paul Kildea (New York: Oxford University Press, 2003), 114.

105. Paul Kildea, *Selling Britten: Music and the Market Place* (Oxford: Oxford University Press, 2002).

106. Edward Sackville-West, "Benjamin Britten," *Vogue* (UK), October 1, 1951; Anon., "Benjamin Britten: Composer to His Majesty, the Child," *Saturday Review of Literature,* November 29, 1947.

107. Anon., "Opera's New Face," *Time,* February 16, 1948.

108. Kildea, *Selling Britten,* 208.

109. Kildea, 71–72.

110. Lantern, "Britten the Too-Brilliant," *Lantern* (September 1947): 2–5.

111. Britten, "On Receiving the First Aspen Award" (1964), in Kildea, *Britten on Music,* 262.

112. Britten, 262.

113. Britten, 261.

114. Britten, "An English Composer Sees America," *Tempo* 1, no. 2 (1940): 1–3.

115. Britten, "Au Revoir to the U.S.A." (1942), in Kildea, *Britten on Music,* 36.

116. Britten, 37.

117. Britten, "Verdi—a Symposium" (1951), in Kildea, *Britten on Music,* 102.

118. Britten to Elizabeth Mayer, May 22, 1943, in Mitchell and Reed, *Letters from a Life,* 2:1152.

119. See Carpenter, *Benjamin Britten,* 533.

120. Feste [Harvey Grace], "Ad Libitum," *Musical Times* 77, no. 1124 (1936): 889.

121. Robin Holloway, "Benjamin Britten: Tributes and Memories," *Tempo* 120 (1977): 5–6.

122. Charles Stuart, "Britten 'The Eclectic,'" Music Survey 2, no. 4 (1950): 250; Massimo Mila, "Benjamin Britten Is Dead," *Stampa,* December 5, 1976.

123. Denis ApIvor, "Contemporary Music and the Post-War Scene," *Critic* 1, no. 1 (1947): 45–47.

124. Constant Lambert, "Britten's New Concerto," *Listener,* August 25, 1938.

125. William Glock, "Music," *Observer,* June 24, 1943.

126. Elizabeth Lutyens, cited in Mitchell and Reed, *Letters from a Life,* 1:264.

127. Richard Taruskin, "The Poietic Fallacy," *Musical Times* 145, no. 1886 (2004): 7–34.

128. See Katharine Ellis, *Music Criticism in Nineteenth-Century France: La Revue et Gazette Musicale de Paris, 1834–80* (Cambridge: Cambridge University Press, 1995); Alexandra Wilson, *The Puccini Problem: Opera, Nationalism and Modernity* (Cambridge: Cambridge University Press, 2007).

129. Anon., "Occasional Notes," *Musical Times* 53 (1912): 646–48.

130. Britten, "Variations on a Critical Theme (1952)," in Kildea, *Britten on Music,* 116.

131. Britten to Lennox Berkeley, December 14, 1951, in Mitchell and Reed, *Letters from a Life,* 3:699.

132. Britten, "Variations on a Critical Theme," 117.

133. The composer's attack on critics was originally published in *Opera* magazine and elicited defensive responses from the press. Britten, 144.

134. Britten, 116.

135. See Kildea, *Selling Britten,* 207.

136. Igor Stravinsky and Robert Craft, *Themes and Episodes* (New York: Knopf, 1966), 15.

137. Igor Stravinsky to Rufina Ampenoff, December 12, 1964, in *Stravinsky: Selected Correspondence III,* ed. Robert Kraft (New York: Knopf, 1985), 450–51.

138. Britten, "On Receiving the First Aspen Award," 258.

139. One notable exception is Heather Wiebe's *Britten's Unquiet Pasts,* which places cultural ambivalence—with particular respect to the past—at the center of her account. Her book is also notable for interpreting this ambivalence as a sign not of Britten's marginality but of the opposite: an explanation of his centrality to a deeply ambivalent cultural establishment in postwar Britain. See Heather Wiebe, *Britten's Unquiet Pasts: Sound and Memory in Postwar Reconstruction* (Cambridge: Cambridge University Press, 2012).

140. See Donald Mitchell, "The Musical Atmosphere," in *Benjamin Britten: A Commentary on His Works from a Group of Specialists,* ed. Donald Mitchell and Hans Keller (London: Rockcliff, 1952); Carpenter, *Benjamin Britten;* and Kildea, *Selling Britten.*

141. Peter Tranchell, "Britten and the Brittenites," *Music & Letters* 34, no. 2 (1953): 132.

142. Paul Kildea, "Benjamin Britten: Inventing English Expressionism," *University of Toronto Quarterly* 74, no. 2 (2005): 657–70.

143. See Mervyn Cooke, "Introduction," in *The Cambridge Companion to Benjamin Britten,* ed. Mervyn Cooke (Cambridge: Cambridge University Press, 1999), 1–8.

144. Philip Brett, "The Britten Era," in *Decomposition: Post-Disciplinary Performance,* ed. Sue-Ellen Case, Philip Brett, and Susan Leigh Foster (Bloomington and Indianapolis: Indiana University Press, 2000), 109. For comparable political readings, see Paul Kildea, "Britten, Auden and 'Otherness,'" in Cooke, *Cambridge Companion to Britten,* 53.

145. For a posthumous collection of Brett's essays, see Philip Brett, *Music and Sexuality in Britten: Selected Essays,* ed. George E. Haggerty (Berkeley: University of California Press, 2006).

146. The exception is Lloyd Whitesell, who deliberately set out to resist this coded, esoteric understanding of queer identity and excavate a more inclusive one. See Lloyd Whitesell, "Britten's Dubious Trysts," *Journal of the American Musicological Society* 56, no. 3 (2003): 637–94.

147. Hans Keller, "The Musical Character," in Mitchell and Keller, *Benjamin Britten: A Commentary,* 322.

148. Claire Seymour, *The Operas of Britten: Expression and Evasion* (Woodbridge: Boydell, 2007); Paul Kildea, "On Ambiguity in Britten," in *Rethinking Britten,* ed. Philip Rupprecht (Oxford: Oxford University Press, 2013); and Kildea, "Inventing English Expressionism," 667.

149. One important exception is the work of Philip Rupprecht, whose attention to more direct or rhetorical modes of Britten's operatic signification has served as an important inspiration for my own approach. Philip Rupprecht, *Britten's Musical Language* (Cambridge: Cambridge University Press, 2002).

150. Stephen Best and Sharon Marcus, "Surface Reading: An Introduction," *Representations* 108, no. 1 (2009): 1–21.

151. Pierre Boulez, "'Opera Houses?—Blow Them Up!' Pierre Boulez versus Rolf Liebermann," *Opera* 19 (1968): 448.

152. Boulez, 446–47.

153. See Theodor Adorno, "Opera and the Long-Playing Record," *October* 55 (1990): 64; originally published as "'Die Oper Ueberwintert auf der Langspielplatte': Theodor W. Adorno über die Revolution der Schallplatte," *Der Spiegel* 23 (1969): 169.

154. Theodor Adorno, "Bourgeois Opera" (1955), in *Sound Figures,* trans. Rodney Livingstone (Stanford: Stanford University Press, 1999), 15.

155. Adorno, 16.

156. Adorno, 16.

157. Adorno, 16.

158. See Kildea, *Selling Britten,* chaps. 3–4.

159. For a discussion of tensions inherent in Britten's "occasional" works, see Wiebe, *Britten's Unquiet Pasts;* Kate Guthrie, "Democratizing Art: Music Education in Postwar Britain," *Musical Quarterly* 97, no. 4 (2014): 575–615. For an exploration of the historical distinction between Britten's "major" and "minor" works, see Christopher Chowrimootoo, "'Britten Minor': Constructing the Modernist Canon," *Twentieth-Century Music* 13, no. 2 (2016): 285.

160. Carpenter, *Benjamin Britten,* 193.

161. It is perhaps this fundamental concern with duplicity and riven-ness that—as Tom Perrin has pointed out—marked allegory as something of a stock middlebrow mode. See Perrin, *The Aesthetics of Middlebrow Fiction,* 24–25.

162. See Michel Foucault, *The Archaeology of Knowledge* (New York: Routledge, 2002).

163. David Savran, *A Queer Sort of Materialism: Recontextualizing American Theater* (Ann Arbor: University of Michigan Press, 2003).

164. Greenberg, "The State of American Writing" (1948), in O'Brian, *Arrogant Purpose,* 257.

165. Tracy, "Investing in 'Modernism'"; Lise Jaillant, *Modernism, Middlebrow and the Literary Canon* (New York: Pickering & Chatto, 2016).

166. Greenberg, "The State of American Writing," 257–58.

167. See Woolf, *The Waves* (London: Hogarth, 1931); Woolf, *Flush: A Biography* (London: Hogarth, 1933); and Woolf, *The Years* (London: Hogarth, 1937).

168. Joseph H. Auner, "Schoenberg and His Public in 1930: The Six Pieces for Male Chorus, Op. 35," in *Schoenberg and His World,* ed. Walter Frisch (Princeton: Princeton University Press, 1990).

169. See Schoenberg, "Success—the End of Bohemianism" (1928) and "How One Becomes Lonely" (1937) in *Style and Idea.*

170. See Schoenberg, "About Music Criticism" (1909) and "Sleepwalker" (1912) and "The Music Critic" (1912) in *Style and Idea.*

171. Lambert, *Music Ho!,* 30.

172. Lambert, 31–32.

2 SENTIMENTALITY UNDER ERASURE IN *PETER GRIMES*

1. Philip Whitaker, "The Admiral Had to Stand," *Sunday Express,* February 1946.

2. Desmond Shawe-Taylor, "Peter Grimes—I," *New Statesman and Nation,* June 9, 1945.

3. Anon., "New Opera: Benjamin Britten's 'Peter Grimes' is England's First for More Than Ten Years," *News Review,* June 14, 1945.

4. For celebrations of London's cultural victory over other major capitals, see also Anon., "British Opera—by Britten," *Express,* June 8, 1945. For the Lady Britannia reference, see Tyrone Guthrie, *Opera in English* (London: John Lane, The Bodley Head, 1945), 10.

5. Beverley Baxter, "One Man against the Mob," *Evening Standard,* June 9, 1945.

6. Edmund Wilson, "London in Midsummer" (1945), in *Europe without Baedeker: Sketches among the Ruins of Italy, Greece, & England* (New York: Doubleday, 1947).

7. The company's wartime activities featured prominently in several reviews. See Anon., "Britten's Opera, 'Peter Grimes,' Reopens Sadler's Wells Theatre: Fashionable Audience Attends Premiere of Young Composer's Work—Playhouse Shows Few Effects of the 'Blitz,'" *New York Times,* June 8, 1945; and, Anon., "Our Time: An All-British Opera," [source unidentified], June 1945.

8. Whitaker, "The Admiral Had to Stand."

9. Anon., "Peter Grimes," *New Statesman and Nation,* June 1945.

10. The reopening of the Royal Ballet was spun in a similar way. For more detail, see Kate Guthrie, "Awakening 'Sleeping Beauty': The Creation of National Ballet in Britain," *Music & Letters* 96, no. 3 (2015): 438.

11. Harold Sear, "Opera for Tomorrow," *Our Time* 4, no. 12 (July 1945); Scott Goddard, "Sadler's Wells Drew Its Old Crowds," *News Chronicle*, June 8, 1945.

12. Whitaker, "The Admiral Had to Stand."

13. Kildea, "Inventing English Expressionism?," 658; Arthur Oldham, "*Peter Grimes:* The Music; the Story Not Excluded," in Mitchell and Keller, *Benjamin Britten: A Commentary*, 110.

14. Donald Mitchell, "'Peter Grimes': Fifty Years On," in *The Making of Peter Grimes: Essays and Studies*, ed. Paul Banks (Woodbridge: Boydell & Brewer, 1996), 125.

15. I. A. Richards, *Practical Criticism: A Study of Judgment* (London: Routledge & Kegan Paul, 1929).

16. Richards, 258.

17. Richards, 258–59.

18. Richards, 260–63.

19. The Victorian or Georgian writers cast as sentimental in *Practical Criticism* include Phillip Bailey, Alfred Noyes, Thomas Hardy, and Wilfred Rowland Childe. Likewise, most of the examples of bad poetry given in Richards's *Principles of Literary Criticism* (1924) are Victorian. I. A. Richards, *Principles of Literary Criticism* (London: Routledge & Kegan Paul, 1924).

20. Richards, *Practical Criticism*, 245.

21. Leavis, *Fiction and the Reading Public*, 74–77.

22. Baxter, "One Man against the Mob."

23. Anon., "Our Time: An All-British Opera," [Source Unidentified], June 1945.

24. Whitaker, "The Admiral Had to Stand."

25. Frank Howes and Philip Hope-Wallace, *A Key to Opera* (London and Glasgow: Blackie, 1934), 187.

26. Mosco Carner, *Puccini: A Critical Biography* (New York: Alfred A. Knopf, 1959), 230.

27. Ferruccio Bonavia, "'Peter Grimes' at Sadler's Wells," *New York Times*, June 1945; Sear, "Opera for Tomorrow."

28. F. R. Leavis, *The Great Tradition: George Eliot, Henry James, Joseph Conrad* (London: Chatto & Windus, 1948); Stephen Spender, *The New Realism: A Discussion* (London: Hogarth, 1939).

29. Edward Upward, "Sketch for a Marxist Interpretation of Literature," in *The Mind in Chains: Socialism and the Cultural Revolution*, ed. Cecil Day Lewis (London: Frederick Muller, 1937), 46.

30. Montagu Slater, "The Purpose of a Left Review," *Left Review* 1, no. 9 (June 1935): 365.

31. John Grierson, "The Course of Realism" (1937), in *Grierson on Documentary*, ed. Forsyth Hardy (London: Collins, 1946), 138–39.

32. The ultimate aim of mass observation, according to Tom Harrisson and Charles Madge, was "to give both ear and voice to what the multitudes are feeling and doing." See Tom Harrisson and Charles Madge, *Britain by Mass-Observation* (1939; London: Cresset Library, 1986), 9.

33. Barbara Nixon, "The Theatre," in Day Lewis, *The Mind in Chains*, 94; David Gascoyne, 24. Auden's industrial poem "I chose this lean country" (1928).

34. For more detail on Britten's involvement in these genres, see Donald Mitchell, *Britten and Auden in the Thirties: The Year 1936* (London and Boston: Faber, 1981); and Philip

Reed, "Britten in the Cinema: Coal Face," in Cooke, *Cambridge Companion to Benjamin Britten.*

35. Benjamin Britten, "Conversation with Benjamin Britten," *Tempo* 1, no. 6 (1944): 4.

36. E. M. Forster, "George Crabbe: The Poet and the Man," *Listener,* May 29, 1941.

37. Eric Crozier, "Concert-Introduction to Peter Grimes," (London: Boosey and Hawkes, 1945), reproduced in Banks, *The Making of Peter Grimes,* 51.

38. Shawe-Taylor, "Peter Grimes—I"; Sear, "Opera for Tomorrow."

39. Eric Crozier, "Staging First Productions—I," in Herbert, *The Operas of Benjamin Britten,* 26.

40. Such detailed and workaday scenery was apparently characteristic of Slater's Left Theatre plays. See Steve Nicholson, "Montagu Slater and the Theatre of the Thirties," in *Recharting the Thirties,* ed. Patrick J. Quinn (London: Associated University Press, 1996), 207.

41. This response is taken from Lionel Bradley's epistolary reports on the premiere housed in the Lionel Bradley Collection at the Royal College of Music's Special Collections.

42. Desmond Shawe-Taylor, "Peter Grimes—II," *New Statesman and Nation,* June 16, 1945.

43. Montagu Slater, "Peter Grimes: An Opera in Three Acts and a Prologue," in Herbert, *The Operas of Benjamin Britten,* 102.

44. Ernest Newman, "'Peter Grimes' and After—I," *Sunday Times,* March 24, 1946; Wilson, "London in Midsummer," 220.

45. Ernest Newman, "Peter Grimes—II," *Sunday Times,* June 17, 1945.

46. For a recent account of the Sadler's Wells project, see Susie Gilbert, *Opera for Everybody: The Story of English National Opera* (London: Faber and Faber, 2009).

47. See Edward J. Dent, *A Theatre for Everybody* (Herts: Staple, 1945), 121.

48. Nixon, "The Theatre," 84.

49. John Grierson, "The First Principles of Documentary," in Hardy, *Grierson on Documentary,* 83.

50. "Many of [the Borough's] population," Crozier observed, "lived in squalor and poverty. People and buildings were bleak and unlovely. This general wretchedness must be reflected in the stage settings and costumes." Crozier, "Notes on the Production of Peter Grimes" (1946), in Banks, *The Making of Peter Grimes,* 10.

51. Crozier, "Staging First Productions—I," 26; Benjamin Britten, "Peter Grimes" (1945), in Kildea, *Britten on Music,* 50.

52. Slater, "Peter Grimes," 99.

53. Anon., "Theatre," *Observer,* June 10, 1945.

54. See, for example, Bonavia, "'Peter Grimes' at Sadler's Wells."

55. Slater, "Peter Grimes," 99.

56. Slater, 105.

57. Elspeth Grant, "New Opera Is Savage and Cruel," *Daily Sketch,* June 8, 1945.

58. Goddard, "Sadler's Wells Drew Its Old Crowds."

59. Ben Singer, *Melodrama and Modernity: Early Sensational Cinema and Its Contexts* (New York: Columbia University Press, 2001).

60. "It is clear that Peter Grimes, although he has committed no crime, is as doomed as a character in a Kafka novel." Anon, "Music: Opera's New Face," *Time,* February 16, 1948. For a discussion of modernism's "tragic vision," see Murray Krieger, *The Tragic Vision: The Confrontation of Extremity* (Baltimore: Johns Hopkins University Press, 1960).

61. Eric Blom, "Peter Grimes," *Birmingham Post,* June 8, 1945.

62. Shawe-Taylor, "Peter Grimes—II"; Julian Herbage, BBC Internal Memorandum (June 8, 1945), reproduced in Mitchell and Reed, *Letters from a Life,* 2:654.

63. Darkened sets were apparently a common technique in Slater's Left Theatre plays. See Nicholson, "Montagu Slater and the Theatre of the Thirties," 209.

64. Anon., "Theatre," *Observer,* June 10, 1945.

65. For discussion of this conjunction between modernism and 1930s realism, see Laura Feigel, *Literature, Cinema, Politics, 1930–45: Reading between the Frames* (Edinburgh: Edinburgh University Press, 2010).

66. George Orwell, "Charles Dickens" (1940), in *A Collection of Essays* (Orlando: Harcourt, 1970), 66.

67. Virginia Woolf, "The Leaning Tower" (1940), in *The Death of the Moth;* George Orwell, "The Road to Wigan Pier" (1937), in *Orwell's England,* ed. Peter Davison (London: Penguin, 2001), 163.

68. "At a distance and through the medium of books," Orwell explained, "I could agonize over their sufferings but I still hated them and despised them . . . I seem to have spent half the time denouncing the capitalist system and other half in raging over the insolence of bus conductors . . . This is the inevitable fate of the sentimentalist. All his opinions change into their opposites at the first brush of reality." Orwell, "The Road to Wigan Pier," 152, 165.

69. Dent, *A Theatre for Everybody,* 120. For more discussion, see Susie Gilbert, *Opera for Everybody,* esp. chap. 2.

70. William McNaught, "New Music: 'Peter Grimes,'" *Musical Times,* 87, no. 1241 (1946): 211.

71. E. J. Dent, Letter to Bernard Stevens (June 12, 1950), reproduced in Mitchell and Reed, *Letters from a Life,* 2:1264.

72. See Slater, "Peter Grimes," in Herbert, *The Operas of Benjamin Britten,* 90.

73. Slater, 92.

74. Dent implored the librettist "to make the characters talk in their own character, and to avoid carefully the temptation to put the author's own private philosophy of life into their mouths." Dent, Letter to Bernard Stevens.

75. Slater, "Peter Grimes," 102.

76. Ernest Newman, "'Peter Grimes' and After—I," *Sunday Times,* 24 March 24, 1946.

77. Newman, "'Peter Grimes' and After—I"; Dent, Letter to Bernard Stevens.

78. Newman, "'Peter Grimes' and After—I."

79. Tyrone Guthrie, *A Life in the Theatre* (New York and London: McGraw Hill, 1959), 252.

80. For a retrospective account, see Nancy Evans and Eric Crozier, "After Long Pursuit: Memoirs," *Opera Quarterly* 10, no. 3 (1994): 13–16. For Brett's discussion of the revisions to the libretto that resulted from these tensions, see Philip Brett, "'Fiery Visions' (and Revisions): 'Peter Grimes' in Progress," in *Benjamin Britten: Peter Grimes,* ed. Philip Brett (Cambridge: Cambridge University Press, 1983), 60–61.

81. Woolf, "A Letter to a Young Poet" (1932), in *The Virginia Woolf Reader,* ed. Michael Leaska (London: Harcourt, 1984), 267; Virginia Woolf, "The Narrow Bridge of Art" (1927), in *Collected Essays,* vol. 2 (London: Hogarth, 1966), 223–24.

82. F. B., "Peter Grimes: Another Success for Composer," *Daily Telegraph and Morning Post,* June 8, 1945.

83. Anon., "British Opera—by Britten." Ralph Hill made a similar point: "*Peter Grimes* does *not* follow the romantic tradition in which love interest predominates." Ralph Hill, "Britten's 'Peter Grimes,'" *Radio Times,* July 13, 1945.

84. Bonavia, "'Peter Grimes' at Sadler's Wells."

85. Slater, "Peter Grimes," 92.

86. Slater, 100.

87. Defensive appeals to the tragic conclusion were unsettled not just by a more holistic approach to the narrative, but also by contemporary examples, such as John Baxter's popular adaptation in 1941 of Walter Greenwood's novel, *Love on the Dole* (1933). While this story is marked by a tragic conclusion, even the producer described his film as a "more or less sentimental stud[y] of the hardships of the poor." See Jack C. Ellis, *John Grierson: Life, Contributions, Influence* (Carbondale; Edwardsville: Southern Illinois University Press, 2000), 279.

88. Newman, "'Peter Grimes'—I."

89. Slater, "Peter Grimes," 101.

90. Joseph Kerman, "Grimes and Lucretia," *Hudson Review* 2 (1949): 278.

91. James Chandler, *The Archaeology of Sympathy: The Sentimental Mode in Literature and Cinema* (Chicago: University of Chicago Press, 2013), 17.

92. See Philip Hope-Wallace, "Peter Grimes," *Time and Tide,* June 14, 1945; Anon., "Peter Grime," *Times,* June 8, 1945.

93. This understanding of sympathy goes back at least as far as Adam Smith, whose writing is often regarded as the philosophical basis for the modern sentimental novel. See Adam Smith, *Theory of the Moral Sentiments,* ed. Ryan Patrick Hanley (1759; New York and London: Penguin, 2009). For a now-classic explication of this connection, see Fred Kaplan, *Sacred Tears: Sentimentality in Victorian Literature* (Princeton: Princeton University Press, 1987).

94. Slater, "Peter Grimes," 90.

95. William Glock, "Music," *Observer,* June 14, 1945.

96. Slater, "Peter Grimes," 90.

97. Shawe-Taylor, "'Peter Grimes'—I."

98. Beverley Baxter, "The Crotchets of Benjamin Britten," *Daily Mail,* July 21, 1945.

99. Shawe-Taylor, "'Peter Grimes'—I."

100. Glock, "Music"; The longer quotation is taken from one of Lionel Bradley's letters, dated June 15, 1945, in the Bradley Collection (Royal College of Music).

101. Robin Holloway, "Benjamin Britten: The Sentimental Sublime," *Cambridge Review,* May 30, 1964; reprinted in *On Music: Essays and Diversions* (Brinkworth: Claridge, 2003), 205.

102. See Anon., "Music: Opening Night," *Time,* June 1945.

103. Anon., "Britten's New Opera: 'Peter Grimes,'" *Scotsman,* June 8, 1945.

104. "I know," he hedged, "that operas are not ethical treatises . . . [b]ut is there not something shocking in the attempt to win our sympathies for a character simply because of he is an outlaw and an enemy of society." Shawe-Taylor, "Peter Grimes—I."

105. F. B., "Peter Grimes."

106. Hope-Wallace, "Peter Grimes." Some more recent commentators have gone even further, casting Grimes as a harbinger of John Osborne's Jimmy Porter and the so-called

"angry young men" of the 1950s—that is, of even more repugnant protagonists to come. See Mitchell, "Peter Grimes: Fifty Years On," and Allan Hepburn, "Peter Grimes and the Rumour of Homosexuality," *University of Toronto Quarterly* 74, no. 2 (2005): 650.

107. "The highbrow novelist who 'creates' characters at all," Q. D. Leavis noted, "is apt to produce personalities that do not obey the literary agent's rule ('The principal characters must be likeable . . .'), that do not lend themselves to fantasying but cause disturbing emotional repercussions in the reader's emotional make-up." Leavis, *Fiction and the Reading Public*, 60.

108. F. R. Leavis, "Diabolic Intellect and the Noble Hero: A Note on Othello," *Scrutiny*, December 1937, 259–83.

109. Bonavia, "Peter Grimes at Sadler's Wells."

110. Hope-Wallace, "Peter Grimes."

111. Blom, "Peter Grimes."

112. See Virginia Woolf, "Mr. Bennett and Mrs. Brown," in *The Virginia Woolf Reader*, ed. Mitchell A. Leaska (Orlando: Harcourt, 1984), 202; Woolf, "George Eliot," *Times Literary Supplement*, November 20, 1919, reprinted in Gordon S. Haight, ed., *A Century of George Eliot Criticism* (London: Methuen, 1966), 189; This modernist opposition to the black-and-white morality of Victorian sympathy is discussed in Monica Miller, "Sympathetic Constellations: Towards a Modernist Sympathy" (PhD diss., University of California, Berkeley, 2012), xx; and Suzanne Keen, *Empathy and the Novel* (New York and Oxford: Oxford University Press, 2007), 58.

113. Peter Pears, "Neither a Hero nor a Villain," *Radio Times*, March 8, 1946, in Brett, *Benjamin Britten: Peter Grimes*, 152.

114. Whitaker, "The Admiral Had to Stand"; Hans Keller, "Peter Grimes," in Mitchell and Keller, *Benjamin Britten: A Commentary*, 111. Keller's psychoanalytic reflections in this chapter were part of part of a much more detailed set of notes, originally written in 1946 but published posthumously. See Hans Keller, "Three Psychoanalytic Notes on 'Peter Grimes [1946],'" ed. Christopher Wintle (London: Institute for Advanced Musical Studies, 1985).

115. Hope-Wallace, "Peter Grimes."

116. Keller, "Peter Grimes," 111–12.

117. Keller, 112.

118. Pears, "Neither a Hero nor a Villain," 152.

119. Newman, "'Peter Grimes'—I."

120. Whitaker, "The Admiral Had to Stand."

121. Newman, "Peter Grimes—I."

122. Lionel Bradley, Bradley Collection at the Royal College of Music's Special Collections. See also Anon. ("our dramatic critic"), "Opera Revival: Sadler's Wells Artists in Original Roles," February 1946: "this contemporary British opera . . . has none of the easy hummed melodies which make for a popular success."

123. After insisting (following Mosco Carner) that "modern" opera's lack of success came down to the "refusal of composers to write good singable tunes," W. R. Anderson continued: "This can be urged (if it be a defect) against Britten's 'Peter Grimes.' I cannot remember anything that I could call a tune." W. R. Anderson, "Round about Radio," *Musical Times*, August 1945. Baxter, "One Man against the Mob."

124. Anon., "New Opera: Benjamin Britten's 'Peter Grimes' is England's First for More than Ten Years," *News Review,* June 14, 1945.

125. See Arman Schwartz, *Puccini's Soundscapes: Realism and Modernity in Italian Opera* (Firenze: Leo S. Olschki, 2016), 50.

126. Benjamin Britten, *Peter Grimes* (London: John Lane, The Bodley Head, 1945), 8.

127. "Arias or other set pieces often seemingly retard the story while actually revealing the internal drama." Erwin Stein, "Opera and 'Peter Grimes,'" *Tempo* 12 (1945): 2–6.

128. Anon., "British Opera—by Britten."

129. Baxter, "One Man against the Mob."

130. Newman, "'Peter Grimes'—II." William McNaught went even further in describing the "excess of instrumental over vocal inspiration." McNaught, "Peter Grimes."

131. Newman, "'Peter Grimes'—II."

132. Ernest Roth, "Peter Grimes: A New British Opera," *Picture Post,* June 30, 1945; Anon., "Entertainments: 'Peter Grimes': Second Thoughts," *Times,* June 15, 1945.

133. Britten, "Peter Grimes" (1945), 50. For a discussion of Britten's apprenticeship in documentary realism, see Philip Reed, "The Incidental Music of Benjamin Britten: A Study and Catalogue Raisonné of His Music for Film, Theatre and Radio" (PhD diss., University of East Anglia, 1987), esp. 33–47.

134. As Reed points out, many of Britten's models at the GPO Film Unit—Walter Leigh, in particular—drew their inspiration more from Satie's *Parade* (1917) and the Italian futurists than the symphonic poems of Liszt, Elgar, and Debussy. Reed, "The Incidental Music of Benjamin Britten," 39.

135. Anon., "Music: Opera's New Face."

136. Blom, "Peter Grimes."

137. See also Schwartz, *Puccini's Soundscapes,* 73. For another discussion of modernism as "aspiring to the condition of noise," see Josh Epstein, *Sublime Noise: Musical Culture and the Modernist Writer* (Baltimore: Johns Hopkins University Press, 2014).

138. W. H. Auden, "Cav & Pag," in *The Complete Works of W. H. Auden,* vol. 3, ed. Edward Mendelson (Princeton: Princeton University Press, 2008), 360.

139. W. H. Auden, "The World of Opera," in *Secondary Worlds* (London: Faber, 1968), 116.

140. Schwartz, *Puccini's Soundscapes,* 61.

141. Schwartz, 67.

142. Reed, "The Incidental Music of Benjamin Britten," 89.

143. Slater, "Peter Grimes," 99.

144. According to the stage directions, "Ellen and Balstrode have come in and stand watching." Slater, "Peter Grimes," 113.

145. As Grimes "sings in a tone almost like prolonged sobbing," the stage directions inform us: "The voices shouting 'Peter Grimes' can still be heard but more distantly and more sweetly."

146. Baxter, "One Man against the Mob."

147. Shawe-Taylor, "Peter Grimes—II."

148. As Carolyn Abbate and Roger Parker have pointed out, emotional restraint was written into stage directions too, with the adverbs "carefully" and "quietly" included in the printed (full) score, telling the performers "that no histrionics, nothing remotely attention-seeking, nothing operatic should take place." Carolyn Abbate and Roger Parker, *A History of Opera: The Last Four Hundred Years* (New York: Norton, 2012), 538.

149. McNaught, "Peter Grimes."

150. Abbate and Parker, *A History of Opera,* 537.

151. Anon., "Peter Grimes."

152. Shawe-Taylor, "Peter Grimes—II."

153. Anon., "Entertainments."

154. Slater, "Peter Grimes," 113.

155. Shawe-Taylor, "Peter Grimes—II."

156. Slater, "Peter Grimes," 113.

157. Glock, "Music."

158. Goddard, "Sadler's Wells Drew Its Old Crowds."

159. Baxter, "The Crotchets of Benjamin Britten."

160. Baxter, "One Man against the Mob."

161. For a study of "difficulty" as a key modernist trope, see Leonard Diepeveen, *The Difficulties of Modernism* (New York and London: Routledge 2003).

162. Orwell implies as much when he compares the "callow coarseness" and "inane, squalid facts of everyday life" of Henry Miller's *Tropic of Cancer* with Joyce's altogether more "artistic" rendering of the same subject. George Orwell, "Inside the Whale" (1940), in *Inside the Whale, and Other Essays* (London: Penguin, 1962), 15.

163. Clive Hart, "James Joyce's Sentimentality," *James Joyce Quarterly* 41 (1964): 27.

164. Robert Scholes, *Paradoxy of Modernism* (New Haven: Yale University Press, 2006), 139.

165. Orwell suggested as much when he boiled *Ulysses* down to a vision of failed redemption. Orwell, "Inside the Whale," 27. This reassessment of Joycean priorities is echoed in Scholes, *Paradoxy of Modernism,* 126–27.

166. Suzanne Clark, *Sentimental Modernism: Women Writers and the Revolution of the Word* (Indianapolis and Bloomington: Indiana University Press, 1991).

167. Erwin Stein, "Anton Webern," *Musical Times* 87 (1946): 14–15.

3   THE TIMELY TRADITIONS OF *ALBERT HERRING*

1. Virginia Woolf, *Between the Acts* (Oxford and New York: Oxford University Press, 1998), 20.

2. There is some debate among scholars about whether Albert's "rebellion" actually changes anything. See Philip Brett, "Character and Caricature in 'Albert Herring,'" *Musical Times* 127 (1986): 545–47; Clifford Hindley, "Not the Marrying Kind: Britten's *Albert Herring,*" *Cambridge Opera Journal* 6 (1994): 159–74; Eric Walter White, *Benjamin Britten: His Life and Operas* (Berkeley: University of California Press, 1983).

3. Michael Kennedy, *Britten* (New York and London: Oxford University Press, 1981), 172.

4. Paul Kildea, "Pruning an English Country Garden," in *Glyndebourne Festival Programme 2008* (Lewes, Sussex: Glyndebourne Arts Trust, 2008), 78.

5. Wyndham Lewis, "A Later Arm Than Barbarity," *Outlook* 33 (1914): 299; Ezra Pound, *Make It New* (London: Faber and Faber, 1934). For scholarly discussions of modernism's opposition to the past, see Christopher Butler, *Literature, Music & Painting, 1900–1916* (Oxford: Oxford University Press, 1994); Michael H. Levenson, A *Genealogy of Modernism: A Study of English Literary Doctrine, 1908–1922* (Cambridge: Cambridge University Press, 1984).

6. See Rosalind Krauss, *The Originality of the Avant-Garde and Other Modernist Myths* (Cambridge, MA: MIT Press, 1986); and Elizabeth Outka, *Consuming Traditions: Modernity, Modernism, and the Commodified Authentic* (Oxford: Oxford University Press, 2008).

7. See Virginia Woolf, "Modern Novels," *Times Literary Supplement,* April 10, 1919; Woolf, "Modern Fiction" (1925), in *Virginia Woolf: Selected Essays,* ed. David Bradshaw (Oxford and New York: Oxford University Press, 2008), 6–12; Woolf, "Mr Bennett & Mrs Brown" (1922), in Bradshaw, *Virginia Woolf,* 32–36.

8. Woolf, "Mr Bennett and & Mrs Brown," 38.

9. Virginia Woolf, "Three Guineas" (1938), in *A Room of One's Own and Three Guineas* (New York and Oxford: Oxford University Press, 2000), 249–54.

10. Jane de Gay, *Virginia Woolf's Novels and the Literary Past* (Edinburgh: Edinburgh University Press, 2006), 187.

11. Woolf, *Between the Acts,* 108–9.

12. Virginia Woolf, "The Artist and Politics" (1936), in *Virginia Woolf: Collected Essays,* vol. 2, ed. Leonard Woolf (London: Chatto & Windus, 1967), 230.

13. Kingsley Martin, "Kingsley Martin on Honest, Outspoken Topicality," *New Statesman and Nation,* November 19, 1938.

14. "War is not a life: it is a situation; One which may neither be ignored nor accepted . . . The enduring is not a substitute for the transient, neither one for the other." T. S. Eliot, "A Note on War Poetry" (1942), in *Collected Poems, 1909–1962* (London: Harcourt Brace, 1991), 215.

15. Virginia Woolf, "The Leaning Tower" (1940), in Woolf, *Collected Essays,* 2:164.

16. See her critique of Joyce's *Ulysses* in Woolf, "Mr Bennett and Mrs Brown," 51–52.

17. Woolf, 51.

18. Woolf, 52.

19. Woolf, "Three Guineas," 365.

20. For a discussion of Britten's work in this period, see Mitchell, *Britten and Auden in the Thirties.*

21. Wilson, "London in Midsummer," 222; Baxter, "The Crotchets of Benjamin Britten."

22. For Britten's interview with *Life* magazine (August 26, 1946), see Donald Mitchell, Philip Reed, and Mervyn Cooke, eds., *Letters from a Life: Selected Letters of Benjamin Britten,* vol. 3 (London: Faber, 2004), 211; James McKechnie, Benjamin Britten, Eric Crozier, and John Piper, "An Opera Is Planned," Broadcast on the BBC Third Programme, June 19, 1947 [BBC Sound Archive].

23. Anon., "Britten's Latest," *Liverpool Post,* June 14, 1947.

24. It was this opposition that John Klein attempted to negate when he wrote: "strangely enough, what crushed Grimes has exhilarated Herring, though fundamentally they remain curiously alike." John Klein, "'Albert Herring': Benjamin Britten's Opera," *Musical Opinion,* August 1947.

25. Anon., "Albert Herring," in *Glyndebourne Festival Programme* (1947).

26. Laura Mooneyham, "Comedy among the Modernists: P. G. Wodehouse and the Anachronism of Comic Form," *Twentieth-Century Literature* 40 (1994): 118.

27. Jonathan Greenberg, *Modernism, Satire and the Novel* (Cambridge: Cambridge University Press, 2011).

28. W. H. Auden, "Notes on the Comic" (1952), in *The Dyer's Hand, and Other Essays* (New York: Random House, 1962), 385.

29. See P. G. Wodehouse, *Summer Lightning* (London: Herbert Jenkins, 1929), vii.

30. Eric Crozier, "Albert Herring: A Comic Opera in Three Acts" (1947), in Herbert, *The Operas of Benjamin Britten,* 140.

31. Crozier, 140.

32. "The spirit of provincialism," according to Dr. Marambot, Maupassant's narrator, "is nothing but natural patriotism . . . I love my house, my town and my province because I discover in them the customs of my own village." Guy de Maupassant, "Madame Husson's 'Rosier,'" in *Guy de Maupassant: The Best Short Stories* (Hertfordshire: Wordsworth, 1997), 148.

33. Nancy Evans, "Fifty Years of the Aldeburgh Festival" (Broadcast on BBC Radio 4, 1994) [BBC Sound Archive].

34. Orwell, "Inside the Whale," 21.

35. Richard Capell, "The World of Music: Transplanting a French Rose-Tree," *Daily Telegraph,* June 28, 1947.

36. Desmond Shawe-Taylor, "Glyndebourne," *New Statesman and Nation,* June 18, 1947.

37. The radio interview with Lord Elton was broadcast on the B.B.C. National Programme on June 10, 1937. It was summarized and discussed in Anon., "Are Highbrow Novels True to Life?," *Listener,* July 7, 1937.

38. Leavis, *Fiction and the Reading Public,* 59. Woolf, "Mr Bennett and Mrs Brown," 43–49.

39. Eric Crozier, "Foreword to *Albert Herring,*" *Tempo* 4 (1997): 10.

40. Crozier, 13.

41. D. C. B., "Albert Herring," *Punch,* July 9, 1947, my italics.

42. A. S., "A Chance to Laugh at Ourselves," *Recorder,* August 9, 1947.

43. Woolf, *Between the Acts,* 144–46.

44. "BRITTEN: it is that is extremely exciting to set everyday language, to try and cope with the problem of setting things like 'Well, come and serve me. I'm in a hurry . . . '—trying to find a musical equivalent for it. . . . We haven't yet quite faced the problem of setting absolutely contemporary pieces, which I think we must do soon. Herring is 1900 and if you think of the famous modern operas—well! *Butterfly* is about middle-class people, but the words creak a bit! CROZIER: "'Round his seat a garland let us twin'—[*laughs sarcastically*] that's my favorite line from Butterfly!" McKechnie, Britten, Crozier, and Piper, "An Opera Is Planned."

45. Crozier, "Albert Herring," 139.

46. Crozier, 157.

47. Martin Cooper, "Albert Herring," *Spectator,* June 27, 1947, my italics.

48. Anon., "'Albert Herring': Benjamin Britten's New Comic Opera," *Times,* June 21, 1947; E. B., "Benjamin Britten's New Opera: First Performance of 'Albert Herring,'" *Birmingham Post,* June 21, 1947.

49. W. R. Anderson, "Round about Radio," *Musical Times* 88 (1947): 256.

50. Capell, "The World of Music."

51. Michael Seidel, *Satiric Inheritance: Rabelais to Sterne* (Princeton: Princeton University Press, 1979), 263.

52. Keller, "Glyndebourne Preface," *Sound,* June 1947.

53. Keller, "The Musical Character."

54. Keller.

55. Keller.

56. Charles Stuart, "Maupassant Reversed," *Observer,* June 22, 1947.

57. Anon., "Notes of the Day," *Monthly Musical Record,* September 1947.

58. Lockspeiser, "A New Spirit in English Opera," *Yorkshire Post,* July 1947.

59. Crozier, "Albert Herring," 161.

60. Stuart, "Maupassant Reversed"; Capell, "The World of Music."

61. D. C. B., "Albert Herring"; Klein, "Albert Herring."

62. Christopher Herbert, "Comedy: The World of Pleasure," *Genre* 17 (1984): 406.

63. Klein, "'Albert Herring.'"

64. Cooper, "Albert Herring."

65. Lockspeiser, "A New Spirit in English Opera"; Capell, "The World of Music"; Neville Cardus, "Albert Herring," *Manchester Guardian,* October 10, 1947.

66. Shawe-Taylor, "Glyndebourne."

67. Clifford Hindley, "Not the Marrying Kind: Britten's *Albert Herring,*" *Cambridge Opera Journal* 6 (1994): 172.

68. Kildea, "Pruning an English Country Garden."

69. As Kildea puts it, "in *Albert Herring,* amid such jolly merriment, the appearance of a 'mad scene' is startling. The carpet is whipped from under the audience's feet and we are forced to rethink the whole opera, looking for clues in the earlier behavior and interaction of this ensemble cast, as though Hercule Poirot at a country-house murder." Kildea, 78.

70. Adorno, *Philosophy of Modern Music,* 10; Lambert, *Music Ho!,* 208–20.

71. Lambert, *Music Ho!,* 11.

72. "He has escaped from an academic set of rules only to be shackled by his own set of rules, and this self-imposed tyranny is taken over *en bloc* by his pupils." Ibid., 208.

73. Gray, *Predicaments,* 141.

74. Keller, "Principles of Composition" (1960), in *Essays on Music,* ed. Christopher Wintle (Cambridge: Cambridge University Press, 1994), 228.

75. Hans Keller, "Resistances to Britten's Music: Their Psychology" (1950), in Wintle, *Essays on Music,* 16.

76. Stuart, "Britten 'The Eclectic,'" 247–48.

77. Keller, "Principles of Composition," 228.

78. According to Mitchell, opposition to the composer's "eclecticism" and "traditionalism" was caused by suspicions of his "lack of 'personal idiom' and too masterful grasp of everyone else's." Mitchell, "The Musical Atmosphere," 10.

79. For a more detailed account of the various stylistic voices present through *Albert Herring,* see Peter Evans, *The Music of Benjamin Britten* (London: J. M. Dent, 1979), 144–62.

80. William Glock, "At Glyndebourne," *Time & Tide,* June 28, 1947; Anon., "'Albert Herring': Britten's New Opera," *Scotsman,* June 21, 1947.

81. This is a defense to which, at least according to Charles Stuart, even the composer subscribed: "I do not see why I should lock myself inside a narrow personal idiom. I write in the manner best suited to the words, theme or dramatic situation which I happen to be handling." Stuart, "Britten 'The Eclectic,'" 247.

82. Anon., "New English Comic Opera Success: 'Albert Herring' at Glyndebourne," *Sussex Daily News,* June 21, 1947.

83. Desmond Shawe-Taylor, "Britten's Comic Opera," *Listener,* June 12, 1947.

84. Dyneley Hussey, "New Britten Opera in World Premiere: 'Albert Herring,'" *New York Times,* June 21, 1947.

85. Harold Sear, "Was It an Opera, or Was It a Skit?," *Daily Worker,* June 24, 1947; Anderson, "Round about Radio."

86. Hussey, "New Britten Opera in World Premiere."

87. Earl of Harewood, "Albert Herring," in *Second Aldeburgh Festival Programme* (1949).

88. Shawe-Taylor, "Britten's Comic Opera."

89. Phoebe Douglas, "Benjamin Britten: Another Purcell—the Work of this Young Composer Heralds the Rebirth of English Music," *Town & Country,* December 1947.

90. Douglas, "Benjamin Britten."

91. Cardus, "Albert Herring."

92. Anon., "'Albert Herring.'"

93. Klein, "'Albert Herring.'"

94. Lockspeiser, "A New Spirit": "[O]ne wonders whether [Albert] may not be a reflection of the youthful Britten himself. There is always a temptation for a composer of operas to see himself in his heroes. He can hardly avoid it. Let us hope, then, that Britten, too, may have learnt the lesson of Herring—a lesson, in his case, of artistic independence, which an artist must continually strive to achieve and maintain."

95. T. S. Eliot, "Tradition and the Individual Talent," in *Selected Prose of T. S. Eliot,* ed. Frank Kermode (London: Faber and Faber, 1975), 37.

96. Eliot, 38.

97. This dialectical reading of Eliot's "Tradition and the Individual Talent" is explored in Jewel Spears Brooker, "Writing the Self: Dialectic and Impersonality in T. S. Eliot," in *T. S. Eliot and the Concept of Tradition,* ed. Giovanni Cianci and Jason Harding (Cambridge: Cambridge University Press, 2007).

98. Lambert, *Music Ho!,* 59.

99. "Like most remarkable composers [Britten] was inimitable, possessed of a distinctive voice which renovated every aspect of the classical tonal tradition in which he worked, a voice and sound too dangerous to imitate," *Grove Music Online,* s.v "Britten, Benjamin," by Philip Brett, www.oxfordmusiconline.com/subscriber/article/grove/music.

100. Woolf, *Between the Acts,* 177.

101. Woolf, 192.

102. On the one hand, its fixation on the manners and traditions of country life left critics like F. R. Leavis lamenting its "extraordinary vacancy and pointlessness," challenging its naïvely provincial disinterest in the "world 'out there.'" On the other, its forays into the realms of psychology and war encouraged others to anxiously defend *Between the Acts* as the very model of a topical modern novel. See F. R. Leavis, "After 'To the Lighthouse'" (1942), in *A Selection from Scrutiny,* vol. 2 (Cambridge: Cambridge University Press, 1968), 97; Hudson Strode, "The Genius of Virginia Woolf," *New York Times,* October 5, 1941; and, Malcolm Cowley, *New Republic,* October 6, 1941.

103. Woolf, *Between the Acts,* 164.

104. See Woolf, "Modern Novels," and Woolf, "Modern Fiction."

105. In *Fiction and the Reading Public,* Q. D. Leavis, for example, compares best-selling fiction's dependence on "stock characters" with highbrow denial of character. Leavis, *Fiction and the Reading Public,* 238–43, 60.

106. Evans, *The Music of Benjamin Britten,* 145. "If we are amused by characters who naturally draw on one fund of cliché or another," Evans explained, "it *must* be because of the *distortion* that is the composer's own comment." Evans, 146, my italics.

107. Philip Brett, "Character and Caricature in 'Albert Herring,'" *Musical Times* 127 (1976): 546.

108. Brian Young, "The Performance of Pastoral Politics: Britten's *Albert Herring,*" *History Workshop Journal* 55 (2003): 199.

109. Donald Mitchell, "The Serious Comedy of *Albert Herring,*" in *Cradles of the New: Writings on Music, 1951–1991,* ed. Mervyn Cooke (London: Faber and Faber, 1995), 358.

110. Occasionally, this tension came out in even more obvious ways than mere defensiveness: while Keller observed that "just as you fear (*or hope*) that she will go on forever shouting the same thing, the scene concludes," Stuart joked: "the Vicar sings so angelically about virtue in the first act that *one forgets to smile* at William Parson's bland characterization." Hans Keller, *The Rape of Lucretia: Albert Herring* (London and New York: Boosey & Hawkes, 1947), 24; Stuart, "Maupassant Reversed."

111. Douglas, "Benjamin Britten."

4   *THE TURN OF THE SCREW,* OR: THE GOTHIC MELODRAMA OF
MODERNISM

1. Elizabeth Bowen, *The Demon Lover, and Other Stories* (London: Jonathan Cape, 1945), 87.

2. Bowen, 82.

3. A. L., "Review: The Demon Lover and Other Stories. By Elizabeth Bowen," *Irish Monthly* 74 (1946): 88–89; and Hugh Bradenham, "The Demon Lover," *Life and Letters and the London Mercury and Bookman* 47 (1945): 216–18.

4. See, for example, Anon., "Shadows and Substance: The Demon Lover and Other Stories," *Times Literary Supplement,* November 3, 1945.

5. "Far from being a supernatural story, 'The Demon Lover' is a masterful dramatization of acute psychological delusion, of the culmination of paranoia in a time of war." Douglas Hughes, "Cracks in the Psyche: Elizabeth Bowen's 'The Demon Lover,'" *Studies in Short Fiction* 10 (1973): 413.

6. Sarah Dillon, "Elizabeth Bowen: 'The Demon Lover' and 'Mysterious Kor,'" in *A Companion to the British and Irish Short Story,* ed. Cheryl Alexander Malcolm and David Malcolm (Oxford: Blackwell, 2008), 236.

7. "James's *conte* is highly ambiguous and has been subjected to a variety of interpretations. Forty years ago it was accounted for in then fashionably Freudian terms, and one has to admit that only on this basis do the facts make sense." Wilfrid Mellers, "Turning the Screw," in *The Britten Companion,* ed. Christopher Palmer (London: Faber, 1985), 144–46.

8. Philip Brett, "Britten's Bad Boys: Male Relations in *The Turn of the Screw,*" *Repercussions* 1 (1992): 5–25.

9. Charles Poore, "Books of the Times," *New York Times,* March 19, 1953.

10. Dorothy Scarborough, *The Supernatural in Modern English Fiction* (New York and London: G. P. Putnam's Sons, 1917), 53.

11. Edith Birkhead, *The Tale of Terror: A Study for the Gothic Romance* (London: Constable, 1921); Montagu Summers, *The Gothic Quest: A History of the Gothic Novel* (London:

Fortune, 1938); Devendra Varma, *The Gothic Flame: Being a History of the Gothic Novel in England* (London: Arthur Barker, 1957).

12. Julian Petley, "'A Crude Sort of Entertainment for a Crude Sort of Audience': The British Critics and Horror Cinema," in *British Horror Cinema,* ed. Steve Chibnall and Julian Petley (London: Routledge, 2002).

13. Virginia Woolf, "Gothic Romance," *Times Literary Supplement,* May 5, 1921.

14. Woolf.

15. This is an idea advanced most forcefully by David Punter. See David Punter, "Introduction: The Ghost of a History," in *A Companion to the Gothic,* ed. David Punter (Oxford and Victoria: Blackwell, 2000), ix.

16. Virginia Woolf, "Henry James's Ghost Stories," *Times Literary Supplement,* December 22, 1921. Charles Poore made a similar observation more than thirty years later. Poore, "Books of the Times."

17. Jacques Barzun, "Henry James, Melodramatist" (1943), in *The Question of Henry James: A Collection of Critical Essays,* ed. F. W. Dupee (New York: Henry Holt, 1945).

18. For contempt for "melodrama," see discussions of Charles Dickens by George Orwell, Edmund Wilson, and F. R. Leavis: Orwell, "Charles Dickens"; Edmund Wilson, "The Two Scrooges," *New Republic,* March 4, 1940; Leavis, *The Great Tradition.*

19. Woolf, "Gothic Romance." Birkhead, *The Tale of Terror,* 223.

20. Woolf, "Gothic Romance"; Anon., "The Gothic Novel: Escape Literature of the 18th Century," *Times,* January 27, 1939.

21. Woolf, "Gothic Romance," 131.

22. Woolf, 133. For a more detailed account of the publication and distribution of gothic stories throughout the early years of the twentieth century, see "The Publishers and Circulating Libraries" (chap. 2) in Montague Summers, *The Gothic Quest: A History of the Gothic Novel* (New York: Russell & Russell, 1964).

23. Anon., "The Gothic Novel."

24. Edith Wharton, "Preface," in *Ghosts* (New York; London, 1937), ix.

25. Most of the plays were broadcast on the BBC Light Programme between 1943 and 1955. The series included a mixture of new plays written by John Dickson Carr and radio adaptations of classic gothic horror stories by Edgar Allan Poe, Robert Louis Stevens, W. W. Jacobs, and others. For a detailed discussion of gothic television, see Misha Kavka, "The Gothic on Screen," in *The Cambridge Companion to Gothic Fiction,* ed. Jerrold E. Hogle (Cambridge: Cambridge University Press, 2002).

26. British imitations of Universal-style horror films included those for which Boris Karloff (actually a British actor, named William Henry Pratt) or Bela Lugosi, the iconic Hollywood stars, were actually brought over to the United Kingdom: *The Ghoul* (T. Hayes Hunter, 1933), *The Mystery of the Marie Celeste* (Denison Clift, 1935), *The Dark Eyes of London* (Walter Summers, 1939). For a detailed summary, see Ian Conrich, "Horrific Films and 1930s British Cinema," in Chibnall and Petley, *British Horror Cinema.*

27. See Jeffrey Richards, "Tod Slaughter and the Cinema of Excess," in *The Unknown 1930s: An Alternative History of the British Cinema, 1929–1939,* ed. Jeffrey Richards (London and New York: I. B. Taurus, 1998).

28. Conrich, "Horrific Films and 1930s British Cinema."

29. Benjamin Britten, "Introduction," in *The Simple Symphony: String Orchestra (or String Quartet)* (Oxford: Oxford University Press, 1934); Britten, *A Journeying Boy.*

30. While a diary entry from October 1931 records enthusiasm for Dickens's *Barnaby Rudge*, another from August of the same year expresses "surprise" at enjoying *Wuthering Heights*. For further detail regarding these instances or other examples of Britten's enthusiasm for the literary supernatural, see Nicholas Clark, "'With Unextinguish'd Taper I Kept Watch': Britten and the Literary Supernatural," unpublished paper presented at "Literary Britten" Conference, Girton College, University of Cambridge, September 3, 2011.

31. Britten, *A Journeying Boy*, 113.

32. For Britten's full reaction to the A. J. Alan broadcasts, see Britten, *A Journeying Boy*, 133. Ackland's play, which Britten went to see on April 22, 1935, was a psychological drama entitled *The Old Ladies*. Britten, 258.

33. For references to these films in Britten's diary, see Britten, 326, 248.

34. A dramatized version of James's novel, adapted and produced by E. J. King Bull, with incidental music by Gerald Williams, conducted by Leslie Woodgate. Broadcast on Wednesday, June 1, 1932.

35. Diary Entry, June 1, 1932, in Mitchell and Reed, *Letters from a Life*, 1:255.

36. A recollection of W. H. Auden's reading of James's *Turn of the Screw* in the company of Britten and others at Amityville can be found in a letter to Britten from Elizabeth Mayer from 1953. Britten to Elizabeth Mayer, November 9, 1953, in Mitchell and Reed, *Letters from a Life*, 4:192.

37. Myfanwy Piper, in an interview with Humphrey Carpenter. See Humphrey Carpenter, *Benjamin Britten: A Biography* (London: Faber and Faber, 1992), 183.

38. For a detailed account of the commission, see Mitchell and Reed, *Letters from a Life*, 4:139.

39. Erwin Stein, "The Turn of the Screw," *Listener*, September 9, 1954.

40. "In questa assurda lotta fra gli spiriti, i fanciulli e una persona disperatamente cosciente della peccaminosita di quella situazione . . . non vè salvezza finale." Luigi Pestalozza, "Britten insegna con *Giro di vite* che il teatro musicale non e morto," *Avanti*, September 16, 1954.

41. Anon., "Britten's New Opera: 'The Turn of the Screw,'" *Times*, September 16, 1954. While this objection was not limited to Italians, it was often framed as such. While one critic observed that "Italians seemed a little worried by [Britten's] preoccupation with 'Morbidezza,'" another elaborated: "for a Latin race, *The Turn of the Screw* represents an attitude of mind as completely foreign to them as Puritanism . . . The idea that Evil has a concrete, positive existence is almost inconceivable for a Latin people." Felix Aprahamian, "Britten in Venice," *Sunday Times*, September 19, 1954; Massimo Mila, "The Turn of the Screw," *Score and I. M. A. Magazine* 10 (1954): 73–76.

42. In his memoirs, Lord Harewood recalls Britten's extreme sensitivity to disparaging remarks made by William Plomer—about "James's gingerly northern hauntings"—after he was asked to comment upon the libretto. George Henry Hubert Lascelles Harewood, *The Tongs and the Bones: The Memoirs of Lord Harewood* (London: George Weidenfield & Nicholson, 1981), 139.

43. Anon., "Britten's New Opera"; See: Anon., "English Opera Group: 'The Turn of the Screw,'" *Times*, October 7, 1954.

44. Kavka, "The Gothic on Screen," 209.

45. Piper, "Writing for Britten," in Herbert, *The Operas of Benjamin Britten*, 8; Benjamin Britten, "Benjamin Britten: Three Letters to Anthony Gishford," *Tempo* 120 (1977): 8.

46. Piper, "The Turn of the Screw: An Opera in Two Acts," in Herbert, *The Operas of Benjamin Britten,* 232.

47. "The Spiral Staircase," dir. Robert Siodmak (USA, RKO Productions, 1945); "The Face at the Window," dir. George King (UK, 1939).

48. Virgil Thomson, "Music and Musicians: Novelties in Venice," *New York Herald Tribune,* September 26, 1954.

49. Aprahamian, "Britten in Venice"; Anon., "Britten's New Opera."

50. "As I see it, the merit of the tale . . . lies in its ambiguities, in what it does not say. . . . Let them appear, substantial, before all eyes, and let them speak—does not that destroy the whole fabric of the tale, which, as far as its factual material goes, is a melodramatic anecdote of little significance?" Dyneley Hussey, "Britten and Mozart," *Listener,* 23 September 1954.

51. Myfanwy Piper, "Working for Britten," in Herbert, *The Operas of Benjamin Britten,* 8.

52. "That it is fatal to go for the bones without the wordy tissue was demonstrated by the stage play The Innocents . . . in losing the sense of time passing, the shifting of places, the gaps in the action, the long months when nothing and everything happened, by laying it on thick *and* fast, it lost the ambience and the drama as well." Piper, "Working for Britten."

53. Piper, "The Turn of the Screw," 233.

54. Martin Cooper, "Britten Opera at Venice," *Daily Telegraph,* September 15, 1954.

55. Mila, "The Turn of the Screw," 75.

56. Mila, 75. Colin Mason, "Britten's New Opera at Venice Festival," *Manchester Guardian Weekly,* September 23, 1954.

57. Cooper, "Britten's Opera at Venice"; Desmond Shawe-Taylor, "The Arts and Entertainment: The Turn of the Screw," *New Statesman and Nation,* October 1954.

58. Shawe-Taylor, "The Arts and Entertainment."

59. Piper, "The Turn of the Screw," 241.

60. Colin Mason, "Britten's New Opera at Venice."

61. Erwin Stein, "'The Turn of the Screw' and Its Musical Idiom," *Tempo* 34 (1954): 6–14; Shawe-Taylor, "The Arts and Entertainment."

62. Piper, "The Turn of the Screw," 242.

63. Mila, "The Turn of the Screw," 75.

64. Stein, "The Turn of the Screw." Anon., "Britten's New Opera."

65. Anon., "English Opera Group."

66. Anon., "Britten in Venice," *Time,* 27 September 1954. Elisabeth Mackenzie also supported this account, reporting: "at the end Mr. Britten, who conducted, was cheered again and again." Elisabeth Mackenzie, "Benjamin Britten's New Opera Triumphs," *News Chronicle,* September 15, 1954.

67. Mackenzie, "Benjamin Britten's New Opera Triumphs"; Anon., "Britten's New Opera."

68. Anon., "Britten in Venice."

69. Sheila Lynd, "This Britten Is Fascinating: But It's Not James' Story," [Source Unknown], October 7, 1954.

70. Shawe-Taylor, "The Arts and Entertainment."

71. Anon., "English Opera Group." Colin Mason also concurs, arguing that "the rest, with the exception of the finale of Act I, is wholly convincing." Mason, "Britten's New Opera."

72. Thomson, "Novelties in Venice."

73. See, for example, Ernest Newman, "Some Don't for Librettists," *Sunday Times,* October 10, 1954; Stein, "The Turn of the Screw."

74. Mason, "Britten's New Opera."

75. Shawe-Taylor, "The Arts and Entertainment."

76. At the time of his death in 1916, James was already being canonized by a number of modernist writers. While Ezra Pound described James's "opposition to tyranny" as considerably ahead of its time, T. S. Eliot praised the difficulty and intellectualism of his novels. By the 1940s, this characterization of James as a subtle cerebralist was solidified into a full-blown orthodoxy, particularly in the criticism of the Leavises. See: Ezra Pound, "Henry James," first published in *Little Review* (August 1918), collected in *Literary Essays of Ezra Pound*, ed. T. S. Eliot (London: Faber and Faber, 1954), 297; T. S. Eliot, "In Memory of Henry James," *Egoist* 1 (1918): 1–2; Q. D. Leavis, "Henry James: The Stories" (1947), in *A Selection from Scrutiny*, 100–106; Leavis, "The Institution of Henry James," in *A Selection from Scrutiny*, 107–13; F. R. Leavis, "The Appreciation of Henry James," in *A Selection from Scrutiny*, 114–23; F. R. Leavis, "James's 'What Maisie Knew': A Disagreement," *Scrutiny* 17 (1950): 115–27.

77. Echoing Edmund Wilson, Leavis insists that "the element of irony in Henry James is often underestimated," before concluding: "Henry James's triumph comes from doing without Balzac's sentimentality and in creating a subtler situation than Barzun credits him with." Leavis, "The Institution of Henry James"(1947), 112–13. In fact, even Barzun admitted that James's melodrama was often tempered or disguised by his attention to realistic detail.

78. Stein, "The Turn of the Screw."

79. Pestalozza, "Britten insegna con 'Giro di vite.'"

80. Franco Abbiati, "'Il Giro di Vite' di Britten presentato dall' English Opera Group," *Corriere della Sera*, September 15, 1954; Mason, "Britten's New Opera."

81. For a particularly well-known example of such a positive assessment, see: William Empson, *Seven Types of Ambiguity* (London: Chatto & Windus, 1930).

82. Mason, "Britten's New Opera.

83. Edmund Wilson, "The Ambiguity of Henry James" (1938), in Dupee, *The Question of Henry James*, 166.

84. Even after insisting that "almost everything, from beginning to end can be read equally in either of two senses," he concludes: "the story, on any other hypothesis [except for the psychological reading], would be, so far as I remember, the only thing James wrote that did not have some more or less serious point." Wilson, 165, 167.

85. Thomson, "Novelties in Venice." This idea of the "Governess as Ghost" was later used as the basis for Alejandro Amenábar's film adaptation of the novella in 2001, *The Others* (starring Nicole Kidman and Christopher Eccleston).

86. Henry James, *The Turn of the Screw, and The Aspern Papers* (Hertfordshire: Wordsworth, 1993), 20.

87. James, 50.

88. Piper, "The Turn of the Screw," 234.

89. Piper, 242.

90. Piper, 233.

91. Piper, 246.

92. Piper, 247.

93. Mellers, "Turning the Screw," 144.

94. "Incorporating the fact that she was overcome by his charm, the only thing we really have to get across with a little prologue proper seems more natural." Myfanwy Piper to Britten, in Mitchell and Reed, *Letters from a Life*, 4:264.

95. Piper, "The Turn of the Screw," 234–39.

96. For a discussion of the proto-psychoanalytical elements in early gothic novels, see Terry Castle, *The Female Thermometer: Eighteenth-Century Culture and the Invention of the Uncanny* (New York and Oxford: Oxford University Press, 1995).

97. Newman, "Some Don't for Librettists."

98. Stein, "The Turn of the Screw and Its Musical Idiom," 7.

99. Aprahamian, "Britten in Venice."

100. Aprahamian. This connection between symmetrical structure and musical unity is echoed by Colin Mason: "Technically, [Britten's music] carries this unification still further in the even more pronounced symmetry of structure." Mason, "Britten's New Opera."

101. Mason, "The Turn of the Screw."

102. Stein, "The Turn of the Screw and Its Musical Idiom," 6.

103. Stein, "The Turn of the Screw."

104. Thomson, "Novelties in Venice."

105. Eric Blom, "Music: Britten," *Observer*, October 10, 1954.

106. Shawe-Taylor, "The Arts and Entertainment," my italics.

107. Anon., "Britten's New Opera."

108. Philip Rupprecht, "'Something Slightly Indecent': British Composers, the European Avant-Garde, and National Stereotypes in the 1950s," *Musical Quarterly* 91 (2009): 275–326.

109. "Even so," Rupprecht continues, "the Screw remains a disturbing force, if only because we assume that any theme with so much control of the musical surface must have a discoverable function." Rupprecht, *Britten's Musical Language*, 144.

110. See, for example, Shawe-Taylor, "The Arts and Entertainment." For a recent discussion of the "two ways" of musical melodrama, and the interrelationship between melodrama as genre and melodrama as mode, see Dan Wang, "Melodrama, Two Ways," *19th-Century Music* 36 (2012): 122–35.

111. The term "mimomaniac" was first used as an insult against *Parsifal* by Friedrich Nietzsche. More recently, Mary Ann Smart has revived the term as a way of highlighting various aspects of synchronicity between music and stage movement in nineteenth-century opera, tracing such small-scale coordination back to influence of stage melodrama of the same period. See Nietzsche, "Nietzsche Contra Wagner" (1888), in *The Portable Nietzsche*, trans. and ed. Walter Kauffmann (Harmondsworth, UK: Penguin, 1968), 665; Mary Ann Smart, *Mimomania: Music and Gesture in Nineteenth-Century Opera* (Berkeley and Los Angeles: University of California Press, 2004).

112. According to one critic, the crude obviousness of the drama's conclusion was perfectly matched by the literalism of the music: "in the last scene, too, where the true nature of the drama is made plain—for it is the story of an exorcism—the music is equal to its task." Mila, "The Turn of the Screw," 75.

113. Louis Barcata, *Hamburger Fremdenblatt*, September 18, 1954.

114. Eric Blom, "Music: Britten"; Anon., "Britten in Venice," *Time*, September 27, 1954.

115. "The Turn of the Screw, by Benjamin Britten," Associated-Rediffusion publicity brochure.

116. Riccardo Malipiero, "Caloroso successo della nuova opera di Britten," *Il Popolo,* September 15, 1954.

117. Mila, "The Turn of the Screw," 75.

118. Blom, "Britten."

119. Abbiati, "Il Giro di Vite."

120. In a retrospective account of her collaboration with Britten on the opera, Piper notes: "Britten was determined that they should sing—and sing words (no nice anonymous, *supernatural humming or groaning*)." Piper, "Writing for Britten," 9, my italics.

121. Michel Chion, *Audio-Vision: Sound on Screen,* trans. Claudia Gorbman (New York: Columbia University Press, 1994), 129.

122. Abbiati, "Il Giro di Vite"; Mila, "The Turn of the Screw," 75.

123. Anon., "Britten's New Opera."

124. For a discussion of the role of sound in the gothic novel, see Frits Noske, "Sound and Sentiment: The Function of Music in the Gothic Novel," *Music & Letters,* 26, no. 2 (1981): 162–75; Isabella van Elferen, *Gothic Music: Sounds of the Uncanny* (Cardiff: University of Wales Press, 2012).

125. For a detailed discussion of Waxman's score for Rebecca, see David Neumeyer and Nathan Platte, *Franz Waxman's Rebecca: A Film Score Guide* (Maryland and Toronto: Scarecrow, 2012). For discussion of the tracks to Hammer Horror movies and their relation with musical modernism, see David Huckvale, *Hammer Film Scores and the Musical Avant-Garde* (North Carolina: McFarland, 2008).

126. Birkhead, *The Tale of Terror,* 227–28.

127. Elizabeth Bowen, "Introduction," in *The Second Ghost Book,* ed. Cynthia Asquith, 3rd ed. (1952; London: Pan Books, 1956), vii.

128. Woolf, "Henry James's Ghost Stories."

129. Woolf, "Gothic Romance."

130. Woolf.

131. In recent years, a handful of literary scholars have sought to explore connections between these two formerly opposed aesthetic traditions. For the most part, however, they have been content to focus on the ways in which Gothic writing prefigured some of the aims and aesthetics of literary modernism rather than on more unsettling aspects of the relationship: the extent to which modernism thrived on the putatively superficial conventions and thrills of gothic melodrama. See John Paul Riquelme, ed., *Gothic and Modernism: Essaying Dark Literary Modernity* (Baltimore: Johns Hopkins University Press, 2008); and Andrew Smith and Jeff Wallace, eds., *Gothic Modernisms* (Hampshire: Palgrave Macmillan, 2001).

132. Theodor W. Adorno and Hans Eisler, *Composing for the Films* (1947; London and New York: Continuum, 2007), 24–25.

5   *THE BURNING FIERY FURNACE* AND THE REDEMPTION OF RELIGIOUS KITSCH

1. Colin Stephenson, *Merrily on High* (New York: Morehouse-Barlow, 1973), 28.

2. Stephenson, 66.

3. Stephenson, 30.

4. Throughout the Old Testament Book of Daniel, on which the parable is based, the Babylonian king's decadent surroundings and luxurious objects are associated with false idols; the Israelites, representatives of authentic and unwavering faith, not only refuse to worship his golden statue, but they also abstain from the decadent food and gifts on offer at the Babylonian court (Daniel 1:8–17).

5. Stephenson, *Merrily on High*, 25.

6. For many, this was precisely the point. For an account of Anglo-Catholicism as a self-consciously antagonistic or countercultural movement, see John Shelton Reed, *Glorious Battle: The Cultural Politics of Victorian Anglo-Catholicism* (Nashville: Vanderbilt University Press, 1996).

7. John Maiden, "Fundamentalism and Anti-Catholicism in Inter-War English Evangelicalism," in *Evangelicalism and Fundamentalism in the United Kingdom during the Twentieth-Century*, ed. David Bebbington and David Ceri Jones (Oxford: Oxford University Press, 2013), 161.

8. For a fuller discussion of this tradition, see Richard Griffiths, *The Pen and the Cross: Catholicism and English Literature, 1850–2000* (London and New York: Continuum, 2010).

9. Anthony Burgess, "The Comedy of Ultimate Truths," in *Urgent Copy: Literary Studies* (New York: W. W. Norton, 1968), 28.

10. As Malcolm Spencer explained in an essay from 1924, "The Puritan Objection to Art": "To the puritan the danger of artistic misrepresentation outweighs the possible value of the power of art to suggest the good and the true." Malcolm Spencer, "The Puritan Objection to Art," in *The Necessity of Art*, ed. Percy Dearmer (London: Student Christian Movement, 1924), 106.

11. "The ultimate aim of the Anglo-Catholics," the commentator continued, "is to inflict upon the country a religious system resembling that of the Church of Rome, and it is difficult for those who value the freedom of the Gospel to unite with those whose aims are so completely diverse from their own." "Notes and Comments," *Churchman* 49 (January 1935): 3. See John Maiden, "Evangelical and Anglo-Catholic Relations, 1928–1983," in *Evangelicalism and the Church of England in the Twentieth Century: Reform, Resistance and Renewal* (Woodbridge: Boydell, 2014), 136–61.

12. For a detailed discussion of Eliot's theology, see Barry Spurr, *"Anglo-Catholic in Religion": T. S. Eliot and Christianity* (Cambridge: Lutterworth, 2010), 30–31.

13. See T. S. Eliot, "The Idea of a Christian Society" (1939), in *Christianity and Culture* (New York: Harcourt & Brace, 1949), 1–78.

14. See Callum G. Brown, *Religion and Society in Twentieth-Century Britain* (Harlow: Pearson, 2006), 291–96.

15. See Colin Campbell, *The Easternization of the West: A Thematic Account of Cultural Change in the Modern Era* (Boulder: Paradigm, 2007); and Paul Heelas and Linda Woodhead, *The Spiritual Revolution: Why Religion Is Giving Way to Spirituality* (Oxford: Blackwell, 2005). As Suzanne Newcombe points out, in more specific reference to Yoga in late-twentieth-century Britain, "the religiosity of yoga practitioners exemplified a personalization of spiritual ideas as well as a rejection of ecclesiastical-led authority." Suzanne Newcombe, "A Social History of Yoga and Ayurveda in Britain, 1950–1995" (PhD diss., University of Cambridge, 2008), 215.

16. For the place of religious liberalism in the broader context of social and political trends in the 1960s, see Hugh McLeod, *The Religious Crisis of the 1960s* (Oxford: Oxford University Press, 2007); and Brown, *Religion and Society in Twentieth-Century Britain.*

17. John A. T. Robinson, *Liturgy Coming to Life* (London: A. R. Mowbray, 1960), 26. Britten's affinity for Bishop Robinson was declared in a BBC radio interview, broadcast in November 1963. See Carpenter, *Benjamin Britten,* 421.

18. Robinson, *Liturgy Coming to Life,* 38.

19. Eliot's "objective correlative" in "Hamlet and his Problems" (1919), his call for linguistic precision in poetry, was an oblique rebuttal of aestheticist writing, as was his celebration of Donne's "intellectual" poetry in "The Metaphysical Poets" (1927). See T. S. Eliot, *The Sacred Wood* (1920; London: Faber and Faber, 1997).

20. T. E. Hulme, "Romanticism and Classicism" (1911), in *Selected Writings,* ed. Patrick McGuinness (New York: Routledge, 2003), 75–76.

21. Hulme, 71. As David Chinitz explains, "Eliot's religious conviction only reinforces his stand against aestheticism. Once an artistic obstacle, the 'religion of art' now becomes a secular heresy." David Chinitz, *T. S. Eliot and the Cultural Divide* (Chicago: University or Chicago Press, 2003), 173.

22. Hermann Broch, "Notes on the Problem of Kitsch," in *Kitsch: The World of Bad Taste,* ed. Gillo Dorfles (New York: Bell, 1969), 58. Broch's diagnosis of artistic kitsch is strikingly similar to Hulme's aforementioned analysis of Romantic aestheticism: "You don't believe in Heaven, so you begin to believe in a heaven on earth." Hulme, "Romanticism and Classicism," 71.

23. Broch, 58.

24. Theodor Adorno, "Bourgeois Opera" (1955), in *Sound Figures,* trans. Rodney Livingstone (Stanford: Stanford University Press, 1999), 24.

25. Peter Brook, *The Empty Space* (London: Penguin, 2008), 71.

26. Brook, 54.

27. Brook, 68.

28. Brook, 52.

29. As Graham Elliot points out, Britten spent his childhood attending St. John's Lowestoft, a church with a "strong evangelical, low church tradition." Graham Elliot, *Benjamin Britten: The Spiritual Dimension* (Oxford: Oxford University Press, 2006), 8. As Peter Pears later put it, Britten "was low church, and therefore inclined to be puritanical." See Alan Blyth, *Remembering Britten* (London: Hutchinson, 1981), 22.

30. Mitchell and Reed, *Letters from a Life,* 1:93.

31. Mitchell and Reed, 181.

32. Beth Britten, *My Brother Benjamin* (Buckinghamshire: Kensall, 1986), 200.

33. Britten, November 16, 1930, © Courtesy of the Britten-Pears Foundation.

34. Britten, April 19, 1936, in *Journeying Boy,* 345.

35. Friedrich Nietzsche, "The Case of Wagner," in *The Birth of Tragedy and the Case of Wagner,* trans. Walter Kaufmann (New York: Random House, 1967), 172.

36. W. H. Auden, "Introduction," in *Slick but Not Streamlined,* by John Betjeman (New York: Doubleday, 1947), 10–11. This idea of hymns as retaining their wondrous power, even for those who turned away from church dogma and theology, was prefigured in D. H. Lawrence, "Hymns in a Man's Life" (1928), in *Phoenix II,* ed. Warren Roberts and Harry T. Moore (London: Heinemann, 1968).

37. Auden, "Introduction," 9.

38. See Wiebe, *Britten's Unquiet Pasts,* chap. 2.

39. Anon., "Modern Chamber Music: Macnaughten-Lemare Concerts," *Times,* December 19, 1934; Edward Sackville-West, "Emerging Picture," *New Statesman and Nation,* January 23, 1943.

40. As W. Anthony Sheppard observes, "British critics of *Noye's Fludde* repeatedly speak of a sense of nostalgia experienced during these moments of participation." "Hymn singing," Sheppard notes, "is one of the most coercive of musical genres, for it is virtually impossible not to respond to the call of the organ, to rise and at least hum the tune of the hymn." W. Anthony Sheppard, *Revealing Masks: Exotic Influences and Ritualized Performance in Modernist Music Theater* (Berkeley and Los Angeles: University of California Press, 2001), 121.

41. Wiebe, *Britten's Unquiet Pasts,* 201.

42. Holloway, "Benjamin Britten: The Sentimental Sublime," 207. Elsewhere Holloway lamented that "the 'public' manner of the *War Requiem* [seemed] a betrayal of the authentic voice of the Serenade, the Nocturne, the Winter Words." Holloway, "Benjamin Britten: Tributes and Memories," 5–6.

43. Stravinsky's comparison of the *War Requiem* with Messiaen's *Turangalila-Symphonie* is particularly instructive, for Messiaen's work is often cited as one of the prime musical examples of religious kitsch. Stravinsky and Craft, *Themes and Episodes,* 14–15.

44. Stravinsky and Craft, 14–25.

45. Peter Evans, "Britten since the 'War Requiem,'" *Listener,* May 28, 1964.

46. Colin Mason, "Asceticism of Britten Song-Cycle," *Daily Telegraph,* December 7, 1965.

47. Jeremy Noble, "Britten's Babylon," *New Statesman,* June 17, 1966.

48. Colin Graham, "Production Notes and Remarks on the Style of Performing Curlew River," in *Benjamin Britten, Curlew River: A Parable for Church Performance* (London: Faber Music, 1964), 3–4.

49. Sheppard, *Revealing Masks.*

50. See Heather Wiebe, "Curlew River and the Cultural Encounter," in Rupprecht, *Rethinking Britten.*

51. See Newcombe, "A Social History of Yoga and Ayurveda."

52. A. R. "Britten: Curlew River" [recording], *Gramophone,* January 1966. Almost two decades later, Robin Holloway interpreted *Curlew River's* asceticism in a similar way: "a yearning to be cool and still and quiet; to escape the orgiastic debasement of excess and the excruciating exposure to feeling; . . . to recover primeval simplicity and freshness." Robin Holloway, "The Church Parables (II): Limits and Renewals," in *The Britten Companion,* ed. Christopher Palmer (London: Faber, 1984), 215, 220.

53. Holloway, "The Church Parables," 222.

54. William Plomer, "The Burning Fiery Furnace: Second Parable for Church Performance," in Herbert, *The Operas of Benjamin Britten,* 303–4.

55. Plomer.

56. Colin Graham, "Production Notes," in *Benjamin Britten, The Burning Fiery Furnace: A Parable for Church Performance* (London: Faber Music, 1966).

57. According to John Morrill, Orford Parish Church was one of the churches whose "popish" icons and images were defaced by the puritan William Dowsing during the seventeenth century. John Morrill, "A Liberation Theology: Aspects of Puritanism in the English

Revolution," in *Puritanism and Its Discontents*, ed. Laura Knoppers (Newark: University of Delaware Press, 2003), 39.

58. Anthony Lewis, "Britten 'Parable' Staged in Church: 'Fiery Furnace' Premiere Heard at British Festival," *New York Times*, June 11, 1966.

59. Edward Greenfield, "Britten's 'The Burning Fiery Furnace' at Aldeburgh," *Guardian*, 10 June 1966.

60. Goodwin, "Britten in Babylon," *Music and Musicians*, June 1966.

61. In review of "The Poet's Echo," Britten's song cycle from 1966, Desmond Shawe-Taylor included *The Burning Fiery Furnace* in a list of works that made up Britten's "austere period." Desmond Shawe-Taylor, "Two Aspects of Britten," *Sunday Times*, July 24, 1966. Shawe-Taylor, "Britten's Burning Fiery Furnace," *Sunday Times*, June 12, 1966.

62. It was clearly this aspect that another critic had in mind when comparing Britten's music to the "new idiom" of its predecessor, citing moments with similarly forbidding melodies, harmonies, and timbres as the furnace scene. Our Music Critic, "Britten's Parable of Nebuchadnezzar," *Times*, June 10, 1966.

63. Peter Stadlen, "Promenade Concert: Spellbinding Style of Britten Parable," *Daily Telegraph*, July 25, 1967.

64. Holloway, "The Church Parables," 223.

65. Lewis, "Britten 'Parable' Staged in Church."

66. Goodwin, "Britten in Babylon."

67. Lewis, "Britten 'Parable' Staged in Church." Goodwin echoed this point: "At first [the Babylonian hymn] sounds as if it might be the musical apex of the parable—until, from within the fiery furnace[,] . . . the words of the Benedicite are heard rising in ever-expanding strains built from initial plainchant." Goodwin, "Britten in Babylon."

68. Andrew Porter, "Aldeburgh Festival: The Burning Fiery Furnace," *Financial Times*, June 11, 1966.

69. Stadlen, "Promenade Concert."

70. "Once more Benjamin Britten has shown that music can stir the hearts and minds of men with an inward power and radiant imagination." Noel Goodwin, "The Up-to-Date IMPACT of a Medieval Mystery," *Daily Express*, June 10, 1966.

71. Graham, "Production Notes," in *The Burning Fiery Furnace*.

72. Plomer, "The Burning Fiery Furnace," 305.

73. Noble, "Britten's Babylon."

74. This is an association that Peter Evans made as early as 1979: "Fluctuations between textures in which there is considerable freedom of timing and those in which all strands are exactly aligned are more frequent than in *Curlew River*, for in this parable we pass often between individual thought and corporate faith or concerted, even regimented action. Indeed, the parable turns not on the particular question of racial toleration . . . [but] on the still broader question[,] one of the private conscience in conflict with the dictates of authority." Peter Evans, *The Music of Benjamin Britten* (London: J. M. Dent, 1979), 480.

75. Jeremy Noble, "Aldeburgh Festival," *Musical Times*, August 1966, 698.

76. Goodwin, "The Up-to-Date IMPACT of a Medieval Mystery."

77. Cited in Anon., "Britten's Parables Compared," *Times*, July 15, 1966.

78. "In 'The Burning Fiery Furnace,' we have one might say Britten's 'Meistersinger' after the 'Tristan' of 'Curlew River.'" Stadlen, "Promenade Concert."

79. This was a point made by several critics. Goodwin, for example, wrote: "where the first parable concentrated attention on a single human tragedy, the second . . . engages wider sympathies with the plight of three Jews in a foreign land who set up a resistance movement to Nebuchadnezzar." Goodwin, "Britten in Babylon." 49.

80. Stadlen, "Promenade Concert"; Noble, "Aldeburgh Festival." These assessments were later echoed by the director Colin Graham, as he reflected: "If *Curlew River* had been introvert in the Zen sense, *The Burning Fiery Furnace* was outgoing, fantastic and colorful." Colin Graham, "Staging First Productions 3," in Herbert, *The Operas of Benjamin Britten,* 49.

81. As Graham noted, they were inspired by a trip to Chartres Cathedral: "On the way to the Jours de Fete at Tours, a visit to Chartres Cathedral impressed us all with the magnificent colours and vivid imagery of the stained-glass windows. Here too, but in a sculpture, were Nebuchadnezzar and the Fiery Furnace, and here the second Church Parable was born." Graham, "Staging First Productions 3," 49.

82. Graham, "Production Notes," in *The Burning Fiery Furnace.*

83. Lewis, "Britten 'Parable' Staged in Church."

84. Our Music Critic, "Britten's Parable of Nebuchadnezzar."

85. Noble, "Aldeburgh Festival."

86. Porter, "Aldeburgh Festival."

87. Peter Evans, "Britten's New Church Opera: Peter Evans Introduces 'The Burning Fiery Furnace,'" *Listener,* June 16, 1966; John Warrack, "First Performances: Britten's *The Burning Fiery Furnace,*" *Tempo* 78 (1966): 23.

88. Warrack, "First Performances."

89. "At the moment when the Jewish youths are told they must accept Babylonian names, and first uneasily realize that they are outsiders, the instruments provide tense, ominous shudders with trills and tremolos. The music to which the Babylonians worship their god and beg him to humble their enemies has a sinister, horribly debased quality, with its vocal *portamenti* above heavy repeated notes and figures." Evans, "Britten's New Church Opera."

90. Plomer, "The Burning Fiery Furnace."

91. Greenfield, "Britten's 'The Burning Fiery Furnace' at Aldeburgh."

92. Plomer, "The Burning Fiery Furnace," 303.

93. In the words of Jeremy Noble: "on top of a mixture of medieval liturgical drama and Japanese No-play, the language of the prep school is too much to swallow." Noble, "Britten's Babylon."

94. Shawe-Taylor, "Two Aspects of Britten"; Porter, "Aldeburgh Festival."

95. Noble, "Britten's Babylon"; Evans, "Britten's New Church Opera."

96. Peter Stadlen, "Britten Uses System Entirely His Own," *Daily Telegraph,* June 10, 1966.

97. Shawe-Taylor, "Two Aspects of Britten"; Noble, "Britten's Babylon."

98. Lewis, "Britten's 'Parable' Staged in Church."

99. The biblical precedent was pointed out by a number of early critics. See, example, Porter, "Aldeburgh Festival," and Shawe-Taylor, "Britten's Burning Fiery Furnace."

100. Anon., *Faber Music News* (1966).

101. Shawe-Taylor, "Britten's Burning Fiery Furnace."

102. Evans, "Britten's New Church Opera"; Goodwin, "Britten in Babylon."

103. Shawe-Taylor, "Britten's Burning Fiery Furnace"; Noble, "Britten's Babylon."

104. Noble, "Aldeburgh Festival."

105. Noble, "Britten's Babylon." Noble's assessment was later echoed by Robin Holloway: "The orgy of abasement before 'Merodak' is ice-cold, horrible, and completely stunning. But its complement, the miracle in the furnace, badly hangs fire." Holloway, "The Church Parables (II): Limits and Renewals," 221.

106. "The youths," the critic explained, "sing the *Benedicite,* echoed in slower notes by the angel (sung by a boy) guarding them. The upward semitones starting each phrase, and especially the inverted major triad ending each, sound too easily comforting." Anon., "Britten's Parables Compared."

107. Anon., Faber Music News (1966).

108. Warrack, "Babylon Comes to Church," *Sunday Telegraph,* June 12, 1966. The dramatic happenings at the tomb of the Madwoman's son and her faith's reward of peace and sanity are here paralleled by the raising of the Image of Gold and the appearance of the Angel in the Furnace."

109. Our Music Critic, "Technical Innovations in Britten's Recent Works," *Times,* July 2, 1965.

110. Warrack, "Babylon Comes to Church."

111. Our Music Critic," "Britten's Parable of Nebuchadnezzar."

112. Peter Evans drew a similar conclusion about the Benedicite, contrasting it with the individualistic heterophony of the earlier trio: "only in the homophonic refrain of their prayer is all individuality finally submerged." Evans, *The Music of Benjamin Britten,* 481.

113. See Evans, 482–83.

114. AF Programme Book, Faber Music News (1966).

115. Greenfield, "Britten's 'The Burning Fiery Furnace' at Aldeburgh."

6   *DEATH IN VENICE* AND THE AESTHETICS OF SUBLIMATION

1. Iris Murdoch, *The Black Prince* (1973; London: Vintage, 2006), 257.

2. "Julian said, 'Bradley, if I asked you, would you come to Covent Garden with?' 'Yes, of course.' I would go to hell with her, and even to Covent Garden." Murdoch, 243.

3. The concept of "sublimation," as theorized by Sigmund Freud, entails the redirection of the body's animalistic drives and desires into more socially acceptable or useful channels, such as artistic creation or intellectual reflection. My looser use of the term seeks similarly to capture the process through which art's more visceral pleasures are translated into abstract intellectual reflection. For Freud's concept, see Sigmund Freud, *Five Lectures on Psycho-Analysis,* trans. James Strachey (New York and London: W. W. Norton, 1961), 56–60.

4. Some critics even championed the philosophical levels of Murdoch's novels with the explicit purpose of excusing or even erasing the more melodramatic details of her story lines. See, for example, Paul Levy, "Dame Iris Murdoch," *Independent,* February 10, 1999.

5. John Robert-Blunn, "Death in Venice," *Manchester Evening News,* September 5, 1973.

6. Robert-Blunn.

7. John Amis, cited in *Talking about Music 163: Benjamin Britten and Death in Venice,* BBC radio Broadcast from 1973 (BBC Sound Archives, British Library, 1973).

8. "It is, rather, about creativity, inspiration and, in immediate terms, about the way in which social conventions can inspire alarming guilt in an individual who begins to realize something in himself that he perceives as anti-social." Roger Baker, "Britten's *Death in Venice* His Masterpiece," *Advocate,* September 1973.

9. Martin Cooper, "New Britten Opera Has Sense of Atmosphere," *Daily Telegraph,* June 18, 1973.

10. For another example, see William Mann, "Something Old, Something New from Britten: *Death in Venice,*" *Times,* June 18, 1973.

11. Philip Brett, "Musicality, Essentialism and the Closet," in *Queering the Pitch: The New Gay and Lesbian Musicology,* ed. Philip Brett, Elizabeth Wood, and Gary C. Thomas (New York: Routledge, 1994), 19–21.

12. Theodor Adorno, "Opera and the Long-Playing Record," *October* 55 (1990): 64; originally published as "'Die Oper Ueberwintert auf der Langspielplatte': Theodor W. Adorno über die Revolution der Schallplatte," *Der Spiegel* 23 (1969): 169.

13. Herbert Lindenberger, "Anti-Theatricality in Twentieth-Century Opera," in *Against Theatre: Creative Destructions on the Modernist Stage,* ed. Alan Ackerman and Martin Puchner (New York: Palgrave Macmillan, 2007); Daniel Albright, "The New Music Theater," in *Modernism and Music: An Anthology of Sources* (Chicago: University of Chicago Press, 2004); Eric Salzman, "Some Notes on the Origins of New Music-Theater," *Theater* 30 (2000): 9–22.

14. "Grand Opera, of course, is the Deadly Theatre carried to absurdity . . . [E]verything in opera must change, but in opera change is blocked." Brook, *The Empty Space,* 20; Boulez, "'Opera Houses?—Blow Them Up!'"

15. Lord Harewood and Pierre Boulez, "Whither Opera?: Part I," *Opera* 20, no. 11 (1969): 922–30; Harewood and Boulez, "Whither Opera?: Part 2," *Opera* 20, no. 12 (1969): 1026–31.

16. Harewood and Boulez, "Whither Opera?," 922.

17. See Robert Adlington, "Music Theatre since the 1960s," in *The Cambridge Companion to Twentieth-Century Opera,* ed. Mervyn Cooke (Cambridge: Cambridge University Press, 2005), 228–29; Jonathan Cross, *The Stravinsky Legacy* (Cambridge: Cambridge University Press, 1998).

18. Arthur Jacobs and Stanley Sadie, *Opera: A Modern Guide* (1969; Newton Abbot: David & Charles, 1971), 487.

19. Jacobs, "An Operatic Halfway House?," *Musical Times* 110 (1969): 1127.

20. Jacobs, 1128.

21. Adorno, "Die Oper Ueberwintert auf der Langspielplatte."

22. Adorno, "Opera and the Long-Playing Record," 64.

23. Adorno, 64.

24. Martin Puchner, *The Drama of Ideas: Platonic Provocations in Theater and Philosophy* (Oxford: Oxford University Press, 2010).

25. The most prominent artistic responses to anti-operatic discourse came from the so-called Manchester School, in the music theater of Harrison Birtwistle, Alexander Goehr, and Peter Maxwell Davies. See Adlington, "Music Theatre since the 1960s."

26. Britten, "Conversation with Benjamin Britten," 4.

27. Britten, "An Interview with Benjamin Britten" (1967), in Kildea, *Britten on Music,* 308.

28. This wave of ritualistic works forms the subject of part two ("The Mysteries of British Theater; or, Dressing up for Church") of Sheppard, *Revealing Masks*.

29. Colin Graham, *Production Notes and Remarks on the Style of Performing Curlew River, by Benjamin Britten and William Plomer* (London: Faber, 1965).

30. Jacobs and Sadie, *Opera,* 483.

31. In reviewing *Death in Venice* for the *Guardian,* Edward Greenfield wrote: "With the central character encountering the same singer . . . at every turn, you could regard *Death in Venice* as the longest and greatest of the Church Parables, the story of a pilgrim and his tempter." Edward Greenfield, "Death in Venice," *Guardian,* June 18, 1973. This perspective has been echoed by more recent scholars. See Eric Roseberry, "Tonal Ambiguity in *Death in Venice:* A Symphonic View," in *Benjamin Britten: Death in Venice,* ed. Donald Mitchell (Cambridge, 1987), 97; and Sheppard, *Revealing Masks,* 138.

32. Myfanwy Piper, Letter to Benjamin Britten, August 31, 1971. © Courtesy of the Britten-Pears Foundation.

33. Colin Graham, "Music Weekly" (Broadcast on BBC Radio 3, June 12, 1973) [BBC Sound Archive].

34. Mann, "Something Old, Something New"; Greenfield, "Death in Venice."

35. Cooper, "New Britten Opera"; John Falding, "Death in Venice," *Birmingham Post,* June 18, 1973.

36. Bob Crimeen, "Death in Venice," *Sunday Herald Sun,* June 1973.

37. Edward Greenfield, "Ascent of Mann," *Guardian Weekly,* July 7, 1973.

38. Cooper, "New Britten Opera."

39. This kind of symbolic separation through different expressive media was recently used in Harrison Birtwistle's *Down by the Greenwood Side* (1969), a remaking of a Christmas Mummers's play in which Mrs. Green's singing provides stark contrast with the declamatory acting of the others.

40. Ned Rorem, "Britten's Venice," *New Republic,* February 8, 1975.

41. Kenneth Loveland, "Ultimate Refinement of Britten's Powers," *Luton Evening Post,* June 28, 1973.

42. Stephen Walsh, "Last Week's Broadcast Music by Stephen Walsh," *Listener,* June 28, 1973; Jeremy Noble, "Britten's "Death in Venice,'" *Listener,* June 21, 1973.

43. Bayan Northcott, "Venice Preserved," *New Statesman,* June 22, 1973.

44. Robert-Blunn, "Death in Venice."

45. Albright, *Modernism and Music,* 104.

46. "The subject of Britten's 'Death in Venice' . . . is the artist's nature and, in a profounder sense than Strauss's 'Capriccio,' the nature of art itself." Cooper, "New Britten Opera."

47. Conrad Wilson, "Britten's New Work a Sure Success," *Scotsman,* June 18, 1973.

48. Andrew Porter, "Death in Venice," *Financial Times,* June 20, 1973.

49. Patrick Carnegy, "Decadent Intoxications," *Times Educational Supplement,* June 29, 1973.

50. Alan Blyth, "Death in Venice," *Opera* 24 (1973): 689.

51. Baker, "Britten's *Death in Venice*"; Peter Heyworth, "Road to the Abyss: Peter Heyworth on Britten's 'Death in Venice,'" *Observer,* June 24, 1973.

52. Baker, "Britten's *Death in Venice*"; Cooper, "New Britten Opera."

53. These two spectacular set pieces respectively symbolized Aschenbach's ideal appreciation of Tadzio on the one hand, and a more material desire for the boy on the other.

54. Blyth, "Death in Venice," 689; Greenfield, "Death in Venice."

55. Myfanwy Piper, Notebook on *Death in Venice* © Courtesy of the Britten-Pears Foundation.

56. Benjamin Britten, Letter to Myfanwy Piper, May 12, 1971, my italics. © Courtesy of the Britten-Pears Foundation.

57. Rodney Milnes, "Mann and Boy," *Spectator,* June 30, 1973. Milnes's sentiments were echoed by Ned Rorem, in a review of the English Opera Group's production at the Metropolitan Opera House in 1974: "To make flesh of the ineffable is always a miscalculation. The success of parables like *Parsifal* or *Suddenly Last Summer* . . . lies in the invisible ideal. Tadzio inhabits our fantasy no less than Aschenbach's. To find him now in person, a dancer, is to find a perfectionist intent on selling his craft. Observed as a ballet sans text . . . *Death in Venice* becomes the saga of a flirty boy who lusts for an old man but whose mother interferes so he drowns himself." Rorem, "Britten's Venice."

58. Piper, Letter to Britten, February 28, 1972. © Courtesy of the Britten-Pears Foundation.

59. Britten, Letter to Piper, February 6, 1972. © Courtesy of the Britten-Pears Foundation.

60. André Lepecki, "Presence and Body in Dance and Performance Theory," in *Of the Presence of the Body: Essays in Dance and Performance Theory,* ed. André Lepecki (Middletown, CT: Wesleyan University Press, 2004), 2.

61. Daniel Albright, "Golden Calves: The Role of Dance in Opera," *Opera Quarterly* 22 (2006): 27.

62. Britten, Letter to Piper, May 12, 1971. © Courtesy of the Britten-Pears Foundation.

63. Northcott, "Venice Preserved."

64. Malcolm Rayment, "Edinburgh Festival: Britten's New Opera Disappoints," *Glasgow Herald,* September 6, 1973; Porter, "Death in Venice."

65. Porter's point about symbolism was echoed by Kenneth Loveland, who wrote that "some of the dancing goes on too long, and the symbolic points about Socratic Greece and the worship of Dionysus could be made in half the time." Loveland, "Ultimate Refinement."

66. Heyworth, "Road to the Abyss."

67. These visual connections are reinforced by musical ones: both passages rely on heavy and abrasive percussion and brass, extreme use of sequence and repetition, and a dense collection of musical climaxes. Insofar as both are based on Tadzio's musical theme, they even feature significant motivic overlap.

68. Thomas Mann, "Death in Venice," in *Stories of Three Decades,* trans. H. T. Lowe-Porter (1936; New York: Alfred A. Knopf, 1951), 434–35.

69. Murdoch, *The Black Prince,* 257.

70. Eric Bentley, *The Playwright as Thinker,* 4th ed. (1946; Minnesota: University of Minnesota Press, 2010), 87.

71. Joseph Kerman, *Opera as Drama* (1956; Berkeley and Los Angeles: University of California Press, 1988), 10.

72. His account of the cathartic moment from *Salome,* for example, combines culinary and sexual metaphors: "John the Baptist's severed head might as well be made of marzipan.

And it is for this sugary orgasm that all the fantastically involved aphrodisiac machinery has been required." Kerman, 209.

73. Kerman, 14.

74. Boulez, "Whither Opera? Part I," 925. As Eric Salzman has explained, the view of opera as "above all obsessed with voce, voce, voce" was the target of anti-operatic discourse in the 1950s and 1960s. Salzman, "Some Notes," 10.

75. Kerman, *Opera as Drama*, 207.

76. Kerman, 14.

77. Adorno, "Bourgeois Opera," 20.

78. Adorno, "On the Fetish-Character in Music," 298.

79. In a response to Boulez's criticisms, included within the same issue of *Opera* magazine, Rolf Liebermann describes the hidden subtext in Boulez's diatribe as "'My unwritten opera is the best.' An unintentionally comic remark!" Rolf Liebermann, "'Opera Houses?,'" *Opera* 19 (1968): 21.

80. Kerman, *Opera as Drama*, 16.

81. Kerman, 204.

82. This was the comparison made by Britten himself. Britten, "Verdi—a Symposium," 102.

83. Kerman, *Opera as Drama*, 10–11.

84. Kerman, 59.

85. Kerman, 227.

86. In *Contemplating Music*, Joseph Kerman points out that the lines between populist scholarship and didactic criticism were particularly thin in postwar Britain, before going on to champion the work of Donald Mitchell, Hans Keller, and Erwin Stein as models for the musicology of the future—a musicology in which the link between criticism and scholarship should be revived; Joseph Kerman, *Contemplating Music: Challenges to Musicology* (Cambridge, MA: Harvard University Press, 1985), 27–28.

87. Peter Evans, "Britten's 'Death in Venice,'" *Opera* 24 (1973): 490–96.

88. Noble, "Britten's 'Death in Venice.'"

89. Noble.

90. Carnegy, "Decadent Intoxications."

91. Porter, "Death in Venice."

92. Greenfield, "Death in Venice." In his later review for the *Guardian Weekly,* Greenfield was even more adamant that "the precise pointing of one passage against another helps to control the overall structure, to give what is fundamentally an emotional experience a tautness of form." Greenfield, "Ascent of Mann."

93. Gillian Widdicombe, "Death in Venice," *Financial Times,* September 6, 1973.

94. Rupprecht, *Britten's Musical Language,* 247.

95. Evans, "Britten's 'Death in Venice,'" 492.

96. Porter, "Death in Venice."

97. John Evans, "Twelve-Note Structures and Tonal Polarity," in Mitchell, *Benjamin Britten: Death in Venice,* 99.

98. Peter Maxwell Davies, "The Young British Composer," *Score* 15 (1956): 85. Maxwell Davies's critique is discussed and contextualized in Rupprecht, "'Something Slightly Indecent.'"

99. David Patrick Stearns, "Met's Ethereal 'Death in Venice,'" *Final Edition,* February 11, 1974.

100. Daniel Albright, *Musicking Shakespeare* (Rochester: University of Rochester Press, 2007), 296, my italics.

101. Wilson, "Britten's New Work."

102. Evans, "Britten's 'Death in Venice,'" 103.

103. Seymour, *The Operas of Benjamin Britten,* 313.

104. Ruth Sara Longobardi, "Reading between the Lines: An Approach to the Musical and Sexual Ambiguities of Death in Venice," *Journal of Musicology* 22, no. 3 (2005): 332–35.

105. Adorno, "Bourgeois Opera," 26.

106. Richard Taruskin, *Music in the Late Twentieth Century,* vol. 5, *The Oxford History of Western Music* (2005; New York and Oxford: Oxford University Press, 2010), 221–59.

107. Taruskin, 221–22.

108. For the most recent examples, see Herbert Lindenberger, *Situating Opera: Period, Genre, Reception* (Cambridge: Cambridge University Press, 2010), 68–69; and Richard Begam and Matthew Wilson Smith, eds., *Modernism and Opera* (Baltimore: Johns Hopkins University Press, 2016), 10.

109. Taruskin, *Music in the Late Twentieth Century,* 224.

110. Theodor Adorno, *Introduction to the Sociology of Music* (New York: Continuum, 1976), 80.

111. Adorno, 82–83.

112. Adorno, "Bourgeois Opera," 16.

113. Adorno, 15.

114. Boulez, "Whither Opera? Part I," 926.

115. Boulez, 27.

116. Begam and Smith, *Modernism and Opera,* 2.

117. Boulez, "'Opera Houses?—Blow Them Up!'" 440.

118. Heather Wiebe, "Confronting Opera in the 1960s: Birtwistle's *Punch and Judy,*" *Journal of the Royal Musical Association* 142, no. 1 (2017): 174.

119. Adlington, "Music Theatre since the 1960s," 226.

120. Rodney Milnes, "Towards Music Theatre," *Opera* 23, no. 12 (1972): 1067.

121. Boulez, "Whither Opera? Part I," 930.

122. Karel Goeyvaerts, "Paris—Darmstadt 1947–1956: Excerpt from the Autobiographical Portrait," *Revue belge de musicologie* 48 (1994): 46.

123. See Adorno, "Vers une musique informelle" (1960), in *Quasi una Fantasia: Essays on Modern Music,* trans. Rodney Livingston (London and New York: Verso, 1998), 269–322.

124. Adorno, *Alban Berg: Master of the Smallest Link,* trans. Juliane Brand and Christopher Hailey (Cambridge: Cambridge University Press, 1991), 86.

125. In describing his new building, to be built on the ruins of the bombed-out old opera house, Boulez writes: "That is what I mean by Centre; not only a house where one performs, but a house where people meet each other . . . You can invite [the audience] to discuss, to hear tapes of performances, to see some rehearsals." Boulez, "Whither Opera?," 929.

BIBLIOGRAPHY

Adorno, Theodor. *The Culture Industry: Selected Essays on Mass Culture.* Edited by J. M. Bernstein. New York: Routledge, 1991.

———. *Philosophy of Modern Music.* Translated by Anne G. Mitchell. New York: Seabury Press, 1973.

———. *Sound Figures.* Translated by Rodney Livingstone. Stanford: Stanford University Press, 1999.

Albright, Daniel, ed. *Modernism and Music: An Anthology of Sources.* Chicago: University of Chicago Press, 2003.

———. *Musicking Shakespeare: A Conflict of Theatres.* Rochester: University of Rochester Press, 2007.

Alexander, Peter F. "A Study of the Origins of Britten's Curlew River." *Music & Letters* 69 (1988): 229–43.

Auden, Wystan Hugh. *The Dyer's Hand, and Other Essays.* New York: Random House, 1962.

———. *Secondary Worlds.* London: Faber, 1968.

Banks, Paul, ed. *The Making of Peter Grimes: Essays and Studies.* Woodbridge: Boydell & Brewer, 1996.

Best, Stephen, and Sharon Marcus, "Surface Reading: An Introduction." *Representations* 108, no. 1 (2009): 1–21.

Birkhead, Edith. *The Tale of Terror: A Study for the Gothic Romance.* London: Constable, 1921.

Boulez, Pierre. "'Opera Houses?—Blow Them Up!' Pierre Boulez versus Rolf Liebermann." *Opera* 19 (1968): 446–47.

Bourdieu, Pierre. *Distinction: A Social Critique of the Judgment of Taste.* Translated by Richard Nice. Cambridge, MA: Harvard University Press, 1984.

Brett, Philip, ed. *Benjamin Britten: Peter Grimes.* Cambridge: Cambridge University Press, 1983.

———. "Character and Caricature in 'Albert Herring.'" *Musical Times* 127 (1986): 545–47.

———. *Music and Sexuality in Britten: Selected Essays*. Edited by George E. Haggerty. Berkeley: University of California Press, 2006.

Britten, Benjamin. *Britten on Music*. Edited by Paul Kildea. Oxford: Oxford University Press, 2008.

Brooks, Van Wyck. *America's Coming-of-Age*. New York: W. B. Huebsch, 1915.

Brown, Callum G. *Religion and Society in Twentieth-Century Britain*. Harlow: Pearson, 2006.

Brown, Erica, and Mary Grover, eds. *Middlebrow Literary Cultures: The Battle of the Brows, 1920–1960*. New York: Palgrave Macmillan, 2012.

Carpenter, Humphrey. *Benjamin Britten*. London: Faber and Faber, 1992.

Chandler, James. *The Archaeology of Sympathy: The Sentimental Mode in Literature and Cinema*. Chicago: University of Chicago Press, 2013.

Clark, Suzanne. *Sentimental Modernism: Women Writers and the Revolution of the Word*. Indianapolis and Bloomington: Indiana University Press, 1991.

Cohen, Brigid. *Stefan Wolpe and the Avant-Garde Diaspora*. Cambridge: Cambridge University Press, 2012.

Cooke, Mervyn, ed. *The Cambridge Companion to Benjamin Britten*. Cambridge: Cambridge University Press, 1999.

Cuddy-Keane, Melba. *Virginia Woolf, the Intellectual, and the Public Sphere*. Cambridge: Cambridge University Press, 2003.

Diepeveen, Leonard. *The Difficulties of Modernism*. New York, London: Routledge 2003.

Doctor, Jenny. *The BBC and Ultra-Modern Music, 1922–1936*. Cambridge: Cambridge University Press, 1999.

Dupee, Frederick Wilcox, ed. *The Question of Henry James: A Collection of Critical Essays*. New York: Henry Holt, 1945.

Eliot, Thomas Sternes. *Selected Prose of T. S. Eliot*. Edited Frank Kermode. London: Faber and Faber, 1975.

Evans, John, ed. *Journeying Boy: The Diaries of the Young Benjamin Britten, 1928–1938*. London: Faber and Faber, 2010.

Evans, Peter. *The Music of Benjamin Britten*. London: J. M. Dent, 1979.

Feigel, Laura. *Literature, Cinema, Politics, 1930–45: Reading between the Frames*. Edinburgh: Edinburgh University Press, 2010.

Franklin, Peter. *The Idea of Music: Schoenberg and Others*. London: Palgrave Macmillan, 1985.

Gilbert, Susie. *Opera for Everybody: The Story of English National Opera*. London: Faber and Faber, 2009.

Gray, Cecil. *Predicaments: Or, Music and the Future*. Oxford: Oxford University Press, 1936.

Greenberg, Clement. *Art and Culture: Critical Essays*. Boston: Beacon, 1961.

Greenberg, Jonathan. *Modernism, Satire and the Novel*. Cambridge: Cambridge University Press, 2011.

Guthrie, Kate. "Awakening 'Sleeping Beauty': The Creation of National Ballet in Britain." *Music & Letters* 96, no. 3 (2015): 418–48.

———. "Democratizing Art: Music Education in Postwar Britain." *Musical Quarterly* 97, no. 4 (2014): 575–615.

Hansen, Miriam. "The Mass Production of the Senses: Classical Cinema as Vernacular Modernism." *Modernism/Modernity* 6, no. 2 (1999): 59–77.

Harker, Jamie. *America the Middlebrow: Women's Novels, Progressivism, and Middlebrow Authorship between the Wars.* Amherst and Boston: University of Massachusetts Press, 2007.

Harper-Scott, J. P. E. *Edward Elgar, Modernist.* Cambridge: Cambridge University Press, 2006.

——. "'Our True North': Walton's First Symphony, Sibelianism, and the Nationalization of Modernism in England." *Music & Letters* 89, no. 4 (2008): 562–89.

——. *The Quilting Points of Musical Modernism: Revolution, Reaction, and William Walton.* Cambridge: Cambridge University Press, 2012.

Hart, Clive. "James Joyce's Sentimentality." *James Joyce Quarterly* 41 (1964): 25–36.

Heile, Björn. "Darmstadt as Other: British and American Responses to Musical Modernism." *Twentieth-Century Music* 1, no. 2 (2014): 161–78.

Hepokoski, James. *Sibelius, Symphony No. 5.* Cambridge: Cambridge University Press, 1993.

Herbert, David, ed. *The Operas of Benjamin Britten.* London: Herbert, 1979.

Hindley, Clifford. "Not the Marrying Kind: Britten's *Albert Herring.*" *Cambridge Opera Journal* 6, no. 2 (1994): 159–74.

Humble, Nicola. *The Feminine Middlebrow Novel, 1920s to 1950s: Class, Domesticity, and Bohemianism.* Oxford: Oxford University Press, 2001.

Huyssen, Andreas. *After the Great Divide: Modernism, Mass Culture, Postmodernism.* Bloomington: Indiana University Press, 1986.

Jaillant, Lise. *Modernism, Middlebrow and the Literary Canon.* New York: Pickering & Chatto, 2016.

Johnson, Julian. *Who Needs Classical Music? Cultural Choice and Musical Value.* Oxford: Oxford University Press, 2002.

Kaplan, Fred. *Sacred Tears: Sentimentality in Victorian Literature.* Princeton: Princeton University Press, 1987.

Keller, Hans. *Essays on Music.* Edited by Christopher Wintle. Cambridge: Cambridge University Press, 1994.

Kildea, Paul. *Benjamin Britten: A Life in the Twentieth-Century.* New York: Penguin, 2013.

——. "Benjamin Britten: Inventing English Expressionism." *University of Toronto Quarterly* 74, no. 2 (2005): 657–70.

——. "Pruning an English Country Garden." In *Glyndebourne Festival Programme 2008.* Glyndebourne, UK: Glyndebourne Arts Trust, 2008.

——. *Selling Britten: Music and the Market Place.* Oxford: Oxford University Press, 2002.

Lambert, Constant. *Music Ho! A Study of Music in Decline.* London: Penguin. 1948.

Leavis, F. R. *Mass Civilisation and Minority Culture.* Cambridge: Minority, 1930.

Leavis, Q. D. *Fiction and the Reading Public.* London: Chatto & Windus, 1932.

List, Kurt. "The State of American Music." *Partisan Review* 15, no. 1 (1948): 85–90.

Macdonald, Dwight. *Against the American Grain.* New York: Da Capo, 1962.

——. "A Theory of Mass Culture." *Diogenes* 3 (1953): 1–17.

McClary, Susan. "Terminal Prestige: The Case of Avant-Garde Musical Composition." *Cultural Critique* 12 (1989): 57–81.

Miller, Tyrus. *Late Modernism: Politics, Fiction, and the Arts between the World Wars.* Berkeley: University of California Press, 1999.

Mitchell, Donald, and Hans Keller, eds. *Benjamin Britten: A Commentary on His Works from a Group of Specialists.* London: Rockliff, 1952.

Orwell, George. *George Orwell: Inside the Whale, and Other Essays.* Middlesex and Victoria: Penguin, 1957.

Perrin, Tom. *The Aesthetics of Middlebrow Fiction: Popular US Novels, Modernism, and Form, 1945–1975.* New York: Palgrave Macmillan, 2015.

Powell, Neil. *Benjamin Britten: A Life for Music.* New York: Henry Holt, 2013.

Radway, Janice. *A Feeling for Books: The Book-of-the-Month Club, Literary Taste, and Middlebrow Desire.* Chapel Hill: University of North Carolina Press, 1997.

Reed, John Shelton. *Glorious Battle: The Cultural Politics of Victorian Anglo-Catholicism.* Nashville: Vanderbilt University Press, 1996.

Reed, Philip. "The Incidental Music of Benjamin Britten: A Study and Catalogue Raisonné of His Music for Film, Theatre and Radio." PhD diss., University of East Anglia, 1987.

Reith, John. *Broadcast over Britain.* London: Hodder and Stoughton, 1924.

Riquelme, John Paul, ed. *Gothic and Modernism: Essaying Dark Literary Modernity.* Baltimore: Johns Hopkins University Press, 2008.

Rubin, Joan Shelley. *The Making of Middlebrow Culture.* Chapel Hill: University of North Carolina Press, 1992.

Rupprecht, Philip. *Britten's Musical Language.* Cambridge: Cambridge University Press, 2002.

———, ed. *Rethinking Britten.* New York: Oxford University Press, 2003.

———. "'Something Slightly Indecent': British Composers, the European Avant-Garde, and National Stereotypes in the 1950s." *Musical Quarterly* 91 (2009): 275–326.

Savran, David. *A Queer Sort of Materialism: Recontextualizing American Theater.* Ann Arbor: University of Michigan Press, 2003.

Schoenberg, Arnold. *Style and Idea.* Translated by Leo Black. Edited by Leonard Stein. Berkeley: University of California Press, 1984.

Scholes, Robert. *Paradoxy of Modernism.* New Haven: Yale University Press, 2006.

Schwartz, Arman. *Puccini's Soundscapes: Realism and Modernity in Italian Opera.* Firenze: Leo S. Olschki, 2016.

Seidel, Michael. *Satiric Inheritance: Rabelais to Sterne.* Princeton: Princeton University Press, 1979.

Seymour, Claire. *The Operas of Britten: Expression and Evasion.* Woodbridge: Boydell, 2007.

Smart, Mary Ann. *Mimomania: Music and Gesture in Nineteenth-Century Opera.* Berkeley and Los Angeles: University of California Press, 2004.

Smith, Andrew, and Jeff Wallace, eds. *Gothic Modernisms.* Hampshire: Palgrave Macmillan, 2001.

Summers, Montagu. *The Gothic Quest: A History of the Gothic Novel.* London: Fortune, 1938.

Taruskin, Richard. "The Poietic Fallacy." *Musical Times* 145, no. 1886 (2004): 7–34.

———. *Music in the Early Twentieth Century.* Vol. 4, *The Oxford History of Western Music.* 2005; New York and Oxford: Oxford University Press, 2010.

———. *Music in the Late Twentieth Century.* Vol. 5, *The Oxford History of Western Music.* 2005; New York and Oxford: Oxford University Press, 2010.

Tracy, Daniel. "Investing in 'Modernism': Smart Magazines, Parody and Middlebrow Professional Judgment." *Journal of Modern Periodical Studies* 1, no. 1 (2010): 38–63.

Tranchell, Peter. "Britten and the Brittenites." *Music & Letters* 34, no. 2 (1953): 124–32.

Tratner, Michael. *Modernism and Mass Politics: Joyce, Woolf, Eliot, Yates.* Stanford: Stanford University Press, 1995.

Varma, Devendra. *The Gothic Flame: Being a History of the Gothic Novel in England.* London: Arthur Barker, 1957.

Ward-Griffin, Danielle. "Theme Park Britten: Staging the English Village at the Aldeburgh Festival." *Cambridge Opera Journal* 27, no. 1 (2015): 63–95.

Wellens, Ian. *Music on the Frontline: Nicolas Nabokov's Struggle against Communism and Middlebrow Culture.* Aldershot: Asghate, 2002.

Wiebe, Heather. *Britten's Unquiet Pasts: Sound and Memory in Postwar Reconstruction.* Cambridge: Cambridge University Press, 2012.

Woolf, Virginia. *The Death of the Moth, and Other Essays.* London: Hogarth, 1947.

Young, Brian. "The Performance of Pastoral Politics: Britten's *Albert Herring.*" *History Workshop Journal* 55, no. 1 (2003): 197–212.

INDEX

Abbate, Carolyn: on emotional restraint written into stage directions, 190n148; on the similar sentimental effects of the collapse into silence and speech, 59

abstraction: intellectual, 175; in Slater's libretto for *Peter Grimes*, 42; staging (in *Death in Venice*), 157, 161

Ackland, Rodney, 92

acousmêtre, 112

Adlington, Robert: on avant-garde composition and musical theater, 174

Adorno, Theodor, 153: on duplicity and ambivalence in Britten, 27; on familiarity vs. quality, 12; on the great divide as necessary, 6; on light music, 10; on LPs, 151; on *Lulu* (Berg), 116; on opera, 24, 120, 150–51, 162, 171–75; on postwar eclectics, 15; on Schoenberg, 28–29, 77; on Sibelius's music, 12; on uncompromising modernism, 5

aestheticism: religious, 26, 117–19; 121–24, 145; theological opposition to, 119

Alan, A. J., 92

Albert Herring, 25, 63–87; borrowed musical voices in, 78–85; poignancy in, 82

Albright, Daniel: on ballet in opera, 158; "body music," 167–68; on the philosophical opera, 155

ambiguity: 20, 23, 89, 94, 103–4

Amis, John: on *Death in Venice,* 149

Anderson, W. R.: on the lack of a meaningful story line in *Albert Herring,* 73

anti-heroism: in mid-century criticism, 48–49; in *Peter Grimes,* 49–50

antiques: fetishization of, 11–12

ApIvor, Denis: on Britten's eclecticism, 19

Archibald, William: *Innocents,* 94–95

asceticism: in bourgeois operatic music (Adorno), 173–74; in Britten's music, 121–33; of "holy theatre," 121

astrology: in *Peter Grimes,* 42

atonality: as shibboleth, 5; and tradition (Lambert), 85

Auden, W. H., 1–4, 41; on the hymn, 122; "outspoken topicality" of, 65–66; realism in opera (as a contradiction in terms), 57; realism in poetry, 34; on satire, 67

audience: "audience opera," 155; and composer (Lambert), 6; persuading vs. persuaded by, 5–6, 14, 28, 162; suffering, 61; sympathy, 45, 50

Auner, Joseph: on Schoenberg's contradictions, 28

Baker, Roger: comparing Britten's *Death in Venice* with Visconti's film version, 156; on interpreting *Death in Venice,* 149

Barzun, Jacques, 200n77: "Henry James, Melodramatist," 103; on melodrama, 90

"battle of the brows," 4, 7, 9

Baxter, Beverly: on London's standing (in light of *Peter Grimes* premiere), 30; on *Peter Grimes,* 61

CPSIA information can be obtained
at www.ICGtesting.com
Printed in the USA
LVHW01s0429130918
589968LV00007B/8/P